Complete Wor
Vol

19:

紧跟毛主席在大风大浪中前进

Astrid Ronaldson

Mao Zedong Volume 2
Iconoclast Publishing
Transcription By Maoist Documentation Project
Documents Sourced From Marxists.org (Marxist Internet Archive)
Compiled and Formatted by Astrid Ronaldson

Table of Contents

4

A STATEMENT ON CHIANG KAI-SHEK'S STATEMENT

December 28, 1936

In Sian Chiang Kai-shek accepted the demand for resistance to Japan put forward by Generals Chang Hsueh-liang and Yang Hu-cheng and the people of the Northwest and, as an initial step, he has ordered his civil war troops to withdraw from the provinces of Shensi and Kansu. This marks the beginning of Chiang's reversal of his wrong policy in the past decade.[1] It is a blow to the intrigues conducted by the Japanese imperialists and the Chinese "punitive" group [2] to stage-manage a civil war, foment splits and get Chiang killed in the Sian Incident. Their disappointment is already apparent. The indication that Chiang Kai-shek is beginning to wake up may be considered a sign of the Kuomintang's willingness to end the wrong policy it has pursued for ten years.

On December 26 Chiang Kai-shek issued a statement in Loyang, the so-called "Admonition to Chang Hsueh-liang and Yang Hucheng", which is so ambiguous and evasive as to be an interesting specimen among China's political documents. If Chiang really wants to draw a serious lesson from the incident and try to revitalize the Kuomintang, and if he wants to end his consistently wrong policy of compromise in foreign affairs and of civil war and oppression at home, so that the Kuomintang will no longer stand opposed to the wishes of the people, then as a token of good faith he should have produced a better piece of writing, repenting his political past and setting a new course for the future. The statement of December 26 cannot meet the demands of the Chinese masses.

However, it does contain one praiseworthy passage, in which Chiang asserts that "promises must be kept and action must be resolute". This means that, although he did not sign the terms set forth by Chang and Yang in Sian, he is willing to accept such demands as are beneficial to the state and the nation and will not break his word on the grounds that he did not sign. We shall see whether, after he has withdrawn his troops, Chiang will act in good faith and carry out the terms he has accepted. The terms are:

(1) to reorganize the Kuomintang and the National Government, expel the pro-Japanese group and admit anti-Japanese elements;

(2) to release the patriotic leaders in Shanghai [3] and all other political

prisoners, and guarantee the freedoms and rights of the people;

(3) to end the policy of "suppressing the Communists" and enter into an alliance with the Red Army to resist Japan;

(4) to convene a national salvation conference, representing all parties, groups, sections of the population and armies, to decide on the policy of resisting Japan and saving the nation;

(5) to enter into co-operation with countries sympathetic to China's resistance to Japan; and

(6) to adopt other specific ways and means to save the nation.

The fulfilment of these terms requires above all good faith, and also some courage. We shall judge Chiang by his future actions.

But his statement contains the remark that the Sian Incident was brought about under the pressure of "reactionaries". It is a pity that he did not explain what kind of people he meant by "reactionaries", nor is it clear how the word "reactionary" is defined in Chiang's dictionary. However, what is certain is that the Sian Incident took place under the influence of the following forces:

(1) the mounting indignation against Japan among the troops of Generals Chang and Yang and among the revolutionary people of the Northwest;

(2) the mounting indignation against Japan among the people of the whole country;

(3) the growth of the Left forces in the Kuomintang;

(4) the demand by the groups in power in various provinces for resistance to Japan and for the salvation of the nation;

(5) the stand taken by the Communist Party for a national united front against Japan; and

(6) the development of the world peace front.

All these are indisputable facts. It is just these forces that Chiang calls "reactionary"; while other people call them revolutionary, Chiang calls them "reactionary"--that is all. Since he declared in Sian that he would fight Japan in earnest, presumably he will not resume violent attacks on the revolutionary forces immediately after leaving Sian; not only does his own political life and that of his group hang upon his good faith, but they now have confronting them and obstructing their political path a force which has expanded to their detriment-- the "punitive" group which tried to get him killed in the Sian Incident. We therefore advise Chiang Kai-shek to revise his political dictionary, changing the word "reactionary" to "revolutionary", for it is better to use terms corresponding to the facts.

Chiang should remember that he owes his safe departure from Sian to the mediation of the Communist Party, as well as to the efforts of Generals Chang and Yang, the leaders in the Sian Incident. Throughout the incident, the Communist Party stood for a peaceful settlement and made every effort to that end, acting solely in the interests of national survival. Had the civil war spread and had Chang and Yang kept Chiang Kai-shek in custody for long, the incident could only have developed in favour of the Japanese imperialists and the Chinese "punitive" group. It was in these circumstances that the Communist Party firmly exposed the intrigues of the Japanese imperialists and of Wang Ching-wei,[4] Ho Ying- chin [5] and other members of the Chinese "punitive" group, and firmly advocated a peaceful settlement, which happened to coincide with the views of Generals Chang Hsueh-liang and Yang Hu-cheng and such members of the Kuomintang as T.V. Soong.[6] This is exactly what the people throughout the country call for, because they bitterly detest the present civil war.

Chiang was set free upon his acceptance of the Sian terms. From now on the question is whether he will carry out to the letter his pledge that "promises must be kept and action must be resolute", and strictly fulfil all the terms for saving the nation. The nation will not permit any further hesitation on his part or allow him any discount in fulfilling the terms. If he wavers on the issue of resisting Japan or delays in fulfilling his pledge, then the nation-wide revolutionary tide will sweep him away. Chiang and his group should bear in mind the old saying: "If a man does not keep his word, what is he good for?"

If Chiang can clean up the dirt created by the Kuomintang's reactionary policy over the past ten years, thoroughly correct his fundamental errors of compromise in foreign affairs and of civil war and oppression at home, immediately join the anti-Japanese front uniting all parties and groups and really take the military and political measures that can save the nation, then of course the Communist Party will support him. As early as August 25, the Communist Party promised such support to Chiang and the Kuomintang in its letter to the Kuomintang.[7] The people throughout the country have known for fifteen years that the Communist Party observes the maxim, "Promises must be kept and action must be resolute." They undoubtedly have more confidence in the words and deeds of the Communist Party than in those of any other party or group in China.

NOTES

1. Under the influence of the Chinese Red Army and the people's anti-Japanese movement, the Kuomintang's Northeastern Army headed by Chang Hsueh-liang and the Kuomintang's 17th Route Army headed by Yang Hu-cheng agreed to the anti-Japanese national united front proposed by the Communist Party of China and demanded that Chiang Kai-shek should unite with the Communist Party to resist Japan. He refused, became still more active in his military preparations for the "suppression of the Communists" and massacred young people in Sian who were anti-Japanese. Chang Hsueh-liang and Yang Hu-cheng took joint action and arrested Chiang Kai-shek. This was the famous Sian Incident of December 12, 1936. He was forced to accept the terms of unity with the Communist Party and resistance to Japan, and was then set free to return to Nanking.

2. The Chinese "punitive" group consisted of the pro-Japanese cements in the Kuomintang government in Nanking who tried to wrest power from Chiang Kai-shek during the Sian Incident. With Wang Ching-wei and Ho Yiag-chin as their leaders, they advocated a "punitive expedition" against Chang Hsueh-liang and Yang Hu-cheng. Availing themselves of the incident, they prepared to start large-scale civil war in order to dear the way for the Japanese invaders and wrest political power from Chiang Kai-shek.

3. Seven leaders of the patriotic anti-Japanese movement in Shanghai had been arrested by Chiang Kai-shek's government in November 1936. They were Shen Chun-ju, Chang Nai-chi, Tsou Tao-fen, Li Kung-pu, Sha Chien-li, Shih Liang and Wang Tsao-shih. They were kept in prison till July 1937.

4. Wang Ching-wei was the head of the pro-Japanese group in the Kuomintang. He had stood for compromise with the Japanese imperialists ever since their invasion of the Northeast in 1931. In December 1938 he left Chungking, openly capitulated to the Japanese invaders, and set up a puppet government in Nanking.

5. Ho Ying-chin, a Kuomintang warlord, was another leader of the pro-Japanese group. During the Sian Incident he actively plotted civil war by deploying Kuomintang troops for an attack on Shensi along the Lunghai Railway. He planned to kill Chiang Kai-shek by bombing Sian, in order to take over Chiang's position.

9

6. T.V. Soong was a pro-American member of the Kuomintang. Championing U.S. interests he, too, favoured a peaceful settlement of the Sian Incident, because U.S. imperialism was at loggerheads with Japanese imperialism with which it was then contending for supremacy in the Far East.

7. This letter sternly criticized the Kuomintang's reactionary rule and the decisions of the Second Plenary Session of its Central Executive Committee. It also set out the Communist Party's policy of forming an anti-Japanese national united front and renewing its co-operation with the Kuomintang. The main part of the letter reads:

In talking about "centralization and unification", the Second Plenary Session of the Central Executive Committee of your party is really confusing cause and effect. It must be emphasized that the civil war and disunity of the last ten years have been entirely caused by the disastrous policy of dependence on imperialism pursued by your party and your party's government, and especially the policy of non-resistance to Japan persisted in ever since the Incident of September 18, 1931. Under the slogan of "Internal pacification before resistance to foreign invasion", your party and your party's government have been carrying on incessant civil war and launching numerous encirclement campaigns against the Red Army, and have spared no effort in suppressing the patriotic and democratic movements of the people throughout the country. Being blind to the fact that Japanese imperialism is China's deadliest enemy, you have had no qualms even in recent months about abandoning northeastern and northern China, you have used all your strength to fight the Red Army and wage factional struggles within your own party, you have blocked the Red Army on its way to fight the Japanese and harassed its rear, you have ignored the nationwide demand for resistance to Japan and have deprived the people of their freedoms and rights. Patriotism is penalized and innocent people are in jail everywhere; treason is rewarded and traitors are jubilant over their new appointments and honours. To seek centralization and unification by means of this wrong policy is like "climbing a tree to seek fish" and will produce exactly the opposite results. We wish to warn you gentlemen that if you do not make a fundamental change in your erroneous policy, and if you do not direct your hatred against the Japanese imperialists but continue to direct it against your own countrymen, you will find it impossible even to maintain the status quo and any talk about centralization, unification and a so-called "modern state" will remain idle chatter. What the whole nation demands is centralization and unification for fighting Japan and saving the nation, not for fawning on the foreigners and persecuting our own people. The people are now eagerly demanding a government that can really save their country and themselves, a really democratic republic. They demand a democratic republican government which will serve their interests. The programme of such a government must principally provide for: first, resistance to foreign aggression; second, democratic rights for the people; and third, development of the national economy and elimination, or at least alleviation, of the people's sufferings. If there is any sense in your talk about a "modern state", this is the only programme genuinely meeting the needs of colonial and semi-colonial China in the present era. With eager hopes and firm determination the people are struggling for the realization of these objectives. But your party and your party's government are pursuing a policy that runs counter to their hopes and you will never win their confidence. The Chinese Communist Party and the Chinese Red Army hereby solemnly declare: we stand for the resting up of a unified democratic republic for the whole country and the convening of a parliament elected by universal suffrage, and we support an anti-Japanese national salvation congress representative of all the people and all the anti-Japanese armed forces in the country, and a unified national defence government for the whole country. We hereby declare: as soon as a unified democratic republic is set up for the whole of China, the Red areas will become one of its component parts, the representatives of the people of the Red areas will attend the all-China parliament, and the same democratic system will be set up in the Red areas as in other parts of China. We hold that the national defence council, which the Second Plenary Session of the Central Executive Committee of your party has decided to organize, and the national assembly, which your party and your party's government are in process of convening, cannot achieve centralization and unification for resisting Japan and saving the nation. According to the regulations of the national defence council passed by the Second Plenary Session of the Central Executive Committee of your party, this council will be confined to a few officials who hold power in your party and your party's government, and its task is merely to serve as an advisory body to that government. It is only too dear that such a council cannot achieve anything or win any confidence among the people. The same applies to the national assembly which you gentlemen propose to convene; according to the "Draft Constitution of the Republic of China" and the "Organic Law and Election Law of the National Assembly" passed by your party's government, this assembly will be merely an organ manipulated by a few officials of your party and your party's government, it will be nothing but an appendage for them, or a piece of ornamentation. A national defence council and a national assembly of this kind have nothing at all in common with the all-China congress for resistance to

Japan and for national salvation--the national defence council--and the Chinese democratic republic and its parliament which our Party has proposed. We hold that a national defence council for resistance to Japan and national salvation must include representatives of all the political parties and groups, all walks of life and all the armed forces, and must constitute a real organ of authority to decide the major polices for resisting Japan and saving the nation, and that a unified national defence government must be formed from this council. The national assembly must be a parliament elected by universal suffrage and the supreme organ of authority of the democratic republic of China. Only such a national defence council and such an all-China parliament will win the approval, support and participation of the people of the whole country and place the great cause of saving the nation and the people on a firm, unshakable foundation. Mere fine words are useless and will not win the people's approval. The failure of the various conferences held by your party and your party's government is the best proof of this. The declaration of the Second Plenary Session of the Central Executive Committee of your party stated, "Dangers and obstacles are only to be expected; but we will never, because of the difficulties and troubles that beset the nation, relax in the fulfilment of our duty." And again, "As to the survival of the nation, naturally our party will work for it persistently, body and soul." True enough, being the ruling party in the largest part of China, your party must bear the political responsibility for all past deeds. In view of the fact that the Kuomintang government is a one-party dictatorship, your party can never escape this responsibility. In particular, you can never shift onto others your responsibility for the loss of almost half of China, resulting from the absolutely wrong policy which your party has pursued since the September 18th Incident against the wishes of all the people and the interests of the whole nation. As we and all the people see it, since half of China has been abandoned by your party, it certainly cannot evade its duty of recovering the territory and restoring China's sovereignty. At the same time, even within your party many men of conscience are now clearly awake to the horrors of national subjugation and the inviolability of the people's will, they are beginning to turn in a new direction and feel indignant and dissatisfied with those in their midst who have brought disaster both to their party and to the nation. The Chinese Communist Party has full sympathy with this new turn and warmly applauds the noble spirit and awakening of these patriotic and conscientious members of the Kuomintang, their readiness to make sacrifices in the struggle, and their courage to introduce reforms when the nation is on the brink of ruin. We know that the number of awakened and patriotic people is increasing daily in your party's central and provincial headquarters, in its central and provincial governments, in educational, scientific, artistic, journalistic and industrial circles, among the women and in religious and medical circles, within the police service, among all kinds of popular organizations, and in particular among the broad ranks of the army and among both old and new Kuomintang members as well as Kuomintang leaders at various levels; this is very heartening. The Chinese Communist Party is always ready to join hands with these members of the Kuomintang and form a solid national united front with them to fight the nation's deadliest enemy, Japanese imperialism. We hope that they will speedily grow into a dominant force in the Kuomintang and prevail over those wicked and shameless members who have ignored the interests of the nation and virtually become Japanese agents and collaborators--members who are a disgrace to Dr. Sun Yat-sen's memory--and we hope that they will thus be able to revive the spirit of Dr. Sun's revolutionary Three People's Principles, reaffirm his Three Great Policies of alliance with Russia, co-operation with the Communist Party and assistance to the peasants and workers, and "work persistently, body and soul" for the realization of the revolutionary Three People's Principles, of the Three Great Policies and of Dr. Sun's revolutionary Testament. We hope that, together with the patriotic leaders of all political parties and groups and of all walks of life and together with all patriotic people, they will resolutely shoulder the responsibility of continuing Dr. Sun's revolutionary cause and will throw themselves into the struggle to drive out the Japanese imperialists and save the Chinese nation from subjugation, to win democratic rights for the people, to develop China's national economy and free the vast majority of its people from their sufferings, and to bring into being the democratic republic of China with a democratic parliament and democratic government. The Chinese Communist Party hereby declares to all members of the Kuomintang: if you really do this, we shall resolutely support you and are ready to form with you a solid revolutionary united front like that of the great revolutionary period of 1924-27 against imperialist and feudal oppression, for this is the only correct way today to save the nation from subjugation and ensure its survival.

ON GUERRILLA WARFARE

1937

Source: Selected Works of Mao Tse-tung: Vol. IX

Transcription/Markup: Maoist Documentation Project/Brian Baggins

1. What Is Guerrilla Warfare?

In a war of revolutionary character, guerrilla operations are a necessary part. This is particularly true in war waged for the emancipation of a people who inhabit a vast nation. China is such a nation, a nation whose techniques are undeveloped and whose communications are poor. She finds herself confronted with a strong and victorious Japanese imperialism. Under these circumstances, the development of the type of guerrilla warfare characterized by the quality of mass is both necessary and natural. This warfare must be developed to an unprecedented degree and it must co-ordinate with the operations of our regular armies. If we fail to do this, we will find it difficult to defeat the enemy.

These guerrilla operations must not be considered as an independent form of warfare. They are but one step in the total war, one aspect of the revolutionary struggle. They are the inevitable result of the clash between oppressor and oppressed when the latter reach the limits of their endurance. In our case, these hostilities began at a time when the people were unable to endure any more from the Japanese imperialists. Lenin, in People and Revolution,[A] said: 'A people's insurrection and a people's revolution are not only natural but inevitable.' We consider guerrilla operations as but one aspect of our total or mass war because they, lacking the quality of independence, are of themselves incapable of providing a solution to the struggle.

Guerrilla warfare has qualities and objectives peculiar to itself. It is a weapon that a nation inferior in arms and military equipment may employ against a more powerful aggressor nation. When the invader pierces deep into the heart of the weaker country and occupies her territory in a cruel and oppressive manner, there is no doubt that conditions of terrain, climate, and society in general offer obstacles to his progress and may be used to advantage by those who oppose him. In guerrilla warfare we turn these advantages to the purpose of resisting and defeating the enemy.

During the progress of hostilities, guerrillas gradually develop into orthodox forces that operate in conjunction with other units of the regular army. Thus the regularly organized troops, those guerrillas who have attained that status, and those who have not reached that level of development combine to form the military power of a national revolutionary war. There can be no doubt that the ultimate result of this will be victory.

Both in its development and in its method of application, guerrilla warfare has certain distinctive characteristics. We first will discuss the relationship of guerrilla warfare to national policy. Because ours is the resistance of a semi colonial country against an imperialism, our hostilities must have a clearly defined political goal and firmly established political responsibilities. Our basic policy is the creation of a national united anti-Japanese front. This policy we pursue in order to gain our political goal, which is the complete emancipation of the Chinese people. There are certain fundamental steps necessary in the realization of this policy, to wit:

1. Arousing and organizing the people.
2. Achieving internal unification politically.
3. Establishing bases.
4. Equipping forces.
5. Recovering national strength.
6. Destroying enemy's national strength.
7. Regaining lost territories.

There is no reason to consider guerrilla warfare separately from national

15

policy. On the contrary, it must be organized and conducted in complete accord with national anti-Japanese policy. It is only who misinterpret guerrilla action who say, as does Jen Ch'i Shan, "The question of guerrilla hostilities is purely a military matter and not a political one." Those who maintain this simple point of view have lost sight of the political goal and the political effects of guerrilla action. Such a simple point of view will cause the people to lose confidence and will result in our defeat.

What is the relationship of guerrilla warfare to the people? Without a political goal, guerrilla warfare must fail, as it must, if its political objectives do not coincide with the aspirations of the people and their sympathy, co-operation, and assistance cannot be gained. The essence of guerrilla warfare is thus revolutionary in character. On the other hand, in a war of counter-revolutionary nature, there is no place for guerrilla hostilities. Because guerrilla warfare basically derives from the masses and is supported by them, it can neither exist nor flourish if it separates itself from their sympathies and co-operation. There are those who do not comprehend guerrilla action, and who therefore do not understand the distinguishing qualities of a people's guerrilla war, who say: 'Only regular troops can carry on guerrilla operations.' There are others who, because they do not believe in the ultimate success of guerilla action, mistakenly say: 'Guerrilla warfare is an insignificant and highly specialized type of operation in which there is no place for the masses of the people' (Jen Ch'i Shan). Then there are those who ridicule the masses and undermine resistance by wildly asserting that the people have no understanding of the war of resistance (Yeh Ch'ing, for one). The moment that this war of resistance dissociates itself from the masses of the people is the precise moment that it dissociates itself from hope of ultimate victory over the Japanese.

What is the organization for guerrilla warfare? Though all guerrilla bands that spring from the masses of the people suffer from lack of organization at the time of their formation, they all have in common a basic quality that makes organization possible. All guerrilla units must have political and military leadership. This is true regardless of the source or size of such units. Such units may originate locally, in the masses of the people; they may be formed from an admixture of regular troops with groups of the people, or they may consist of regular army units intact. And mere quantity does not affect this matter. Such units may consist of a squad of a few men, a battalion of several hundred men, or a regiment of several thousand men.

All these must have leaders who are unyielding in their policies—resolute,

16

loyal, sincere, and robust. These men must be well-educated in revolutionary technique, self confident, able to establish severe discipline, and able to cope with counter-propaganda. In short, these leaders must be models for the people. As the war progresses, such leaders lack of discipline which at first will gradually overcome the lack of discipline which at first prevails; they will establish discipline in their forces, strengthening them and increasing their combat efficiency. Thus eventual victory will be attained.

Unorganized guerrilla warfare cannot contribute to victory and those who attack the movement as a combination of banditry and anarchism do not understand the nature of guerrilla action. They say, 'This movement is a haven for disappointed militarists, vagabonds, and bandits' (Jen Ch'i Shan), hoping thus to bring the movement into disrepute. We do not deny that there are corrupt guerrillas, nor that there are people who under the guise of guerrillas indulge in unlawful activities. Neither do we deny that the movement has at the present time symptoms of a lack of organization, symptoms that might indeed be serious were we to judge guerrilla warfare solely by the corrupt and temporary phenomena we have mentioned. We should study the corrupt phenomena and attempt to eradicate them in order to encourage guerilla warfare, and to increase its military efficiency. 'This is hard work, there is no help for it, and the problem cannot be solved immediately. The whole people must try to reform themselves during the course of the war. We must educate them and reform them in the light of past experience. Evil does not exist in guerrilla warfare but only in the unorganized and undisciplined activities that are anarchism,' said Lenin, in On Guerrilla Warfare.[B]

What is basic guerrilla strategy? Guerrilla strategy must be based primarily on alertness, mobility, and attack. It must be adjusted to the enemy situation, the terrain, the existing lines of communication, the relative strengths, the weather and the situation of the people.

In guerrilla warfare, select the tactic of seeming to come from the east and attacking from the west; avoid the solid, attack the hollow; attack; withdraw; deliver a lightning blow, seek a lightning decision. When guerrillas engage a stronger enemy, they withdraw when he advances; harass him when he stops; strike him when he is weary; pursue him when he withdraws. In guerilla strategy, the enemy's rear, flanks, and other vulnerable spots are his vital points, and there he must be harassed, attacked, dispersed, exhausted and annihilated. Only in this way can guerrillas carry out their mission of independent guerrilla action and coordination with the effort of the regular armies. But, in spite of the most complete preparation, there can be no victory if mistakes are made in the matter of command. Guerilla warfare based on the principles we have mentioned and carried out over a vast extent of territory in which communications are inconvenient will contribute tremendously towards ultimate defeat of the Japanese and consequent emancipation of the Chinese people.

A careful distinction must be made between two types of guerrilla warfare. The fact that revolutionary guerrilla warfare is based on the masses of the people does not in itself mean that the organization of guerrilla units is impossible in a war of counter-revolutionary character. As examples of the former type we may cite Red guerilla hostilities during the Russian Revolution; those of the Reds China; of the Abyssinians against the Italians for the past three years; those of the last seven years in Manchuria, and the vast anti-Japanese guerrilla war that is carried on in China today. All these struggles have been carried on in the interest of the whole people or the greater part of them; all had a broad basis in the national manpower and all have been in accord with the laws of historical development. They have existed and will continue to exist, flourish, and develop as long as they are not contrary to national policy.

The second type of guerrilla warfare directly contradicts the law of historical development. Of this type, we may cite the examples furnished by the White Russian guerrilla units organized by Denikin and Kolchak; those organized by the Japanese; those organized by the Italians in Abyssinia; those supported by the puppet governments in Manchuria and Mongolia, and those that will be organized here by Chinese traitors. All such have oppressed the masses and have been contrary to the true interests of the people. They must be firmly opposed. They are easy to destroy because they lack a broad foundation in the people.

If we fail to differentiate between the two types of guerrilla hostilities mentioned, it is likely that we will exaggerate their effect when applied by an invader. We might arrive at the conclusion that 'the invader can organize guerrilla units from among the people'. Such a conclusion might well diminish our confidence in guerrilla warfare. As far as this matter is concerned, we have but to remember the historical experience of revolutionary struggles.

Further, we must distinguish general revolutionary wars from those of a purely 'class' type. In the former case, the whole people of a nation, without regard to class or party, carry on a guerrilla struggle that is an instrument of the national policy. Its basis is, therefore, much broader than is the basis of a struggle of class type. Of a general guerrilla war, it has been said: 'When a nation is invaded, the people become sympathetic to one another and all aid in organizing guerrilla units. In civil war, no matter to what extent guerrillas are developed, they do not produce the same results as when they are formed to resist an invasion by foreigners' (Civil War in Russia). The one strong feature of guerrilla warfare in a civil struggle is its quality of internal purity. One class may be easily united and perhaps fight with great effect, whereas in a national revolutionary war, guerrilla units are faced with the problem of internal unification of different class groups. This necessitates the use of propaganda. Both types of guerrilla war are, however, similar in that they both employ the same military methods.

National guerrilla warfare, though historically of the same consistency, has employed varying implements as times, peoples, and conditions differ. The guerrilla aspects of the Opium War, those of the fighting in Manchuria since the Mukden incident, and those employed in China today are all slightly different. The guerrilla warfare conducted by the Moroccans against the French and the Spanish was not exactly similar to that which we conduct today in China. These differences express the characteristics of different peoples in different periods. Although there is a general similarity in the quality of all these struggles, there are dissimilarities in form. This fact we must recognize. Clausewitz wrote, in On War: 'Wars in every period have independent forms and independent conditions, and, therefore, every period must have its independent theory of war.' Lenin, in On Guerrilla Warfare said: 'As regards the form of fighting, it is unconditionally requisite that history be investigated in order to discover the conditions of environment, the state of economic progress and the political ideas that obtained, the national characteristics, customs, and degree of civilization.' Again: 'It is necessary to be completely unsympathetic to abstract formulas and rules and to study with sympathy the conditions of the actual fighting, for these will change in accordance with the political and economic situations and the realization of the people's aspirations. These progressive changes in conditions create new methods.'

If, in today's struggle, we fail to apply the historical truths of revolutionary guerrilla war, we will fall into the error of believing with T'ou Hsi Sheng that under the impact of Japan's mechanized army, 'the guerrilla unit has lost its historical function'. Jen Ch'i Shan writes: 'In olden days guerrilla warfare was part of regular strategy but there is almost no chance that it can be applied today.' These opinions are harmful. If we do not make an estimate of the characteristics peculiar to our anti-Japanese guerrilla war, but insist on applying to it mechanical formulas derived from past history, we are making the mistake of placing our hostilities in the same category as all other national guerrilla struggles. If we hold this view, we will simply be beating our heads against a stone wall and we will be unable to profit from guerrilla hostilities.

To summarize: What is the guerrilla war of resistance against Japan? It is one aspect of the entire war, which, although alone incapable of producing the decision, attacks the enemy in every quarter, diminishes the extent of area under his control, increases our national strength, and assists our regular armies. It is one of the strategic instruments used to inflict defeat on our enemy. It is the one pure expression of anti-Japanese policy, that is to say, it is military strength organized by the active people and inseparable from them. It is a powerful special weapon with which we resist the Japanese and without which we cannot defeat them.

2. The Relation Of Guerrilla Hostilities to Regular Operations

The general features of orthodox hostilities, that is, the war of position and the war of movement, differ fundamentally from guerrilla warfare. There are other readily apparent differences such as those in organization, armament, equipment supply, tactics, command; in conception of the terms 'front' and 'rear'; in the matter of military responsibilities.

When considered from the point of view of total numbers, guerrilla units are many, as individual combat units, they may vary in size from the smallest, of several score or several hundred men, to the battalion or the regiment, of several thousand. This is not the case in regularly organized units. A primary feature of guerrilla operations is their dependence upon the people themselves to organize battalions and other units. As a result of this, organization depends largely upon local circumstances. In the case of guerrilla groups, the standard of equipment is of a low order and they must depend for their sustenance primarily upon what the locality affords.

The strategy of guerrilla warfare is manifestly unlike that employed in orthodox operations, as the basic tactic of the former is constant activity and movement. There is in guerrilla warfare no such thing as a decisive battle; there is nothing comparable to the fixed, passive defence that characterizes orthodox war. In guerrilla warfare, the transformation of a moving situation into a positional defensive situation never arises. The general features of reconnaissance, partial deployment, general deployment, and development of the attack that are usual in mobile warfare are not common in guerrilla war.

There are differences also in the matter of leadership and command. In guerrilla warfare, small units acting independently play the principal role and there must be no excessive interference with their activities. In orthodox warfare particularly in a moving situation, a certain degree of initiative is accorded subordinates, but in principle, command is centralized. This is done because all units and all supporting arms in all districts must co-ordinate to the highest degree. In the case of guerrilla warfare, this is not only undesirable but impossible. Only adjacent guerrilla units can coordinate their activities to any degree. Strategically, their activities can be roughly correlated with those of the regular forces, and tactically, they must co-operate with adjacent units of the regular army. But there are no strictures on the extent of guerrilla activity nor is it primarily characterized by the quality of co-operation of many units.

When we discuss the terms 'front' and 'rear' it must be remembered, that while guerrillas do have bases, their primary field of activity is in the enemy's rear areas. They themselves have no rear. Because an orthodox army has rear installations (except in some special cases as during the 10,000-mile Long march of the Red Army or as in the case of certain units operating in Shansi Province), it cannot operate as guerrillas can.

As to the matter of military responsibilities, those of the guerrillas are to exterminate small forces of the enemy; to harass and weaken large forces; to attack enemy lines of communications; to establish bases capable of supporting independent operations in the enemy's rear, to force the enemy to disperse his strength; and to co-ordinate all these activities with those of the regular armies on distant battle fronts.

From the foregoing summary of differences that exist between guerrilla warfare and orthodox warfare, it can be seen that it is improper to compare the two. Further distinction must be made in order to clarify this matter. While the Eighth Route Army is a regular army, its North China campaign is essentially guerrilla in nature, for it operates in enemy's rear. On occasion, however, Eighth Route Army commanders have concentrated powerful forces to strike an enemy in motion and the characteristics of orthodox mobile warfare were evident in the battle at P'ing Hsing Kuan and in other engagements.

On the other hand, after the fall of Feng Ling Tu, the operations of Central Shansi, and Suiyuan, troops were more guerrilla than orthodox in nature. In this connection the precise character of Generalissimo Chiang's instructions to the effect that independent brigades would carry out guerrilla operations should be recalled. In spite of such temporary activities these orthodox units retained their identity and after the fall of Feng Line Tu, they were not only able to fight along orthodox lines but often found it necessary to do so. This is an example of the fact that orthodox armies may, due to changes in the situation, temporarily function as guerrillas.

Likewise, guerrilla units formed from the people may gradually develop into regular units and, when operating as such, employ the tactics of orthodox mobile war. While these units function as guerrillas, they may be compared to innumerable gnats, which, by biting a giant both in front and in rear, ultimately exhaust him. They make themselves as unendurable as a group of cruel and hateful devils, and as they grow and attain gigantic proportions, they will find that their victim is not only exhausted but practically perishing. It is for this very reason that our guerrilla activities are a source of constant mental worry to Imperial Japan.

While it is improper to confuse orthodox with guerrilla operations, it is equally improper to consider that there is a chasm between the two. While differences do exist, similarities appear under certain conditions and this fact must be appreciated if we wish to establish clearly the relationship between the two. If we consider both types of warfare as a single subject, or if we confuse guerrilla warfare with the mobile operations of orthodox war, we fall into this error : We exaggerate the function of guerrillas and minimize that of the regular armies. If we agree with Chang Tso Hua, who says - 'Guerrilla warfare is the primary war strategy of a people seeking to emancipate itself,' or with Kao Kang, who believes that 'Guerrilla strategy is the only strategy possible for oppressed people', we are exaggerating the importance of guerrilla hostilities. What these zealous friends I have just quoted do not realize is this: If we do not fit guerrilla operations into their proper niche, we cannot promote them realistically. Then, not only would those who oppose take advantage of our varying opinions to turn them to the own uses to undermine us, but guerrillas would be led assume responsibilities they could not successfully discharge and that should properly be carried out by orthodox force. In the meantime, the important guerrilla function of co-ordinating activities with the regular forces would be neglected.

Furthermore, if the theory that guerrilla warfare is our only strategy were actually applied, the regular forces would be weakened, we would be divided in purpose, and guerrilla hostilities would decline. If we say, ' Let us transform the regular forces into guerrillas', and do not place our first reliance on a victory to be gained by the regular armies over the enemy, we may certainly expect to see as a result the failure of the anti-Japanese war of resistance. The concept that guerrilla warfare is an end in itself and that guerrilla activities can be divorced from those of the regular forces is incorrect. If we assume that guerrilla warfare does not progress from beginning to end beyond its elementary forms, we have failed to recognize the fact that guerrilla hostilities can, under specific conditions, develop and assume orthodox characteristics. An opinion that admits the existence of guerrilla war, but isolates it, is one that does not properly estimate the potentialities of such war.

Equally dangerous is the concept that condemns guerrilla war on the ground that war has no other aspects than the purely orthodox. This opinion is often expressed by those who have seen the corrupt phenomena of some guerrilla regimes, observed their lack of discipline, and have seen them used as a screen behind which certain persons have indulged in bribery and other corrupt practices. These people will not admit the fundamental necessity for guerrilla bands that spring from the armed people. They say, 'Only the regular forces are capable of conducting guerrilla operations.' This theory is a mistaken one and would lead to the abolition of the people's guerrilla war.

A proper conception of the relationship that exists between guerrilla effort and that of the regular forces is essential. We believe it can be stated this way: 'Guerrilla operations during the anti-Japanese war may for certain time and temporarily become its paramount feature, particularly insofar as the enemy's rear is concerned. However, if we view the war as a whole, there can be no doubt that our regular forces are of primary importance, because it is they who are alone capable of producing the decision. Guerrilla warfare assists them in producing this favourable decision. Orthodox forces may under certain conditions operate as guerrillas, and the latter may, under certain conditions, develop to the status of the former. However, both guerrilla forces and regular forces have their own respective development and their proper combinations.'

To clarify the relationship between the mobile aspect of orthodox war and guerrilla war, we may say that general agreement exists that the principal element of our strategy must be mobility. With the war of movement, we may at times combine the war of position. Both of these are assisted by general guerrilla hostilities. It is true that on the battlefield mobile war often becomes positional; it is true that this situation may be reversed; it is equally true that each form may combine with the other. The possibility of such combination will become more evident after the prevailing standards of equipment have been raised. For example, in a general strategical counter-attack to recapture key cities and lines of communication, it would be normal to use both mobile and positional methods. However, the point must again be made that our fundamental strategical form must be the war of movement. If we deny this, we cannot arrive at the victorious solution of the war. In sum, while we must promote guerrilla warfare as a necessary strategical auxiliary to orthodox operations, we must neither assign it the primary position in our war strategy nor substitute it for mobile and positional warfare as conducted by orthodox forces.

3. Guerrilla Warfare In History

Guerrilla warfare is neither a product of China nor peculiar to the present day. From the earliest historical days, it has been a feature of wars fought by every class of men against invaders and oppressors. Under suitable conditions, it has great possibilities. The many guerrilla wars in history have their points of difference, their peculiar characteristics, their varying processes and conclusions, and we must respect and profit by the experience of those whose blood was shed in them. What a pity it is that

24

the priceless experience gained during the several hundred wars waged by the peasants of China cannot be marshaled today to guide us. Our only experience in guerrilla hostilities has been that gained from the several conflicts that have been carried on against us by foreign imperialists. But that experience should help the fighting Chinese recognize the necessity for guerrilla warfare and should confirm them in confidence of ultimate victory.

In September 1812, Napoleon, in the course of swallowing all of Europe, invaded Russia at the head of a great army totaling several hundred thousand infantry, cavalry, and artillery. At that time, Russia was weak and her ill-prepared army was not concentrated. The most important phase of her strategy was the use made of Cossack cavalry and detachments of peasants to carry on guerrilla operations. After giving up Moscow, the Russians formed nine guerrilla divisions of about five hundred men each. These, and vast groups of organized peasants, carried on partisan warfare and continually harassed the French Army. When the French Army was withdrawing, cold and starving, Russian guerrillas blocked the way and, in combination with regular troops, carried out counterattacks on the French rear, pursuing and defeating them. The army of the heroic Napoleon was almost entirely annihilated, and the guerrillas captured many officers, men, cannon, and rifles. Though the victory was the result of various factors and depended largely on the activities of the regular army the function of the partisan groups was extremely important. The corrupt and poorly organized country that was Russia defeated and destroyed an army led by the most famous soldier of Europe and won the war in spite of the fact that her ability to organize guerrilla regimes was not fully developed. At times, guerrilla groups were hindered in their operations and the supply of equipment and arms was insufficient. If we use the Russian saying, it was a case of a battle between "the fist and the axe" [Ivanov].

From 1918 to 1920, the Russian Soviets, because of the opposition and intervention of foreign imperialists and the internal disturbances of White Russian groups, were forced to organize themselves in occupied territories and fight a real war. In Siberia and Alashan, in the rear of the army of the traitor Denikin and in the rear of the Poles, there were many Red Russian guerrillas. These not only disrupted and destroyed the communications in the enemy's rear but also frequently prevented his advance. On one occasion, the guerrillas completely destroyed a retreating White Army that had previously been defeated by regular Red forces. Kolchak, Denikin, the Japanese, and the Poles, owing to the necessity of staving off the attacks of guerrillas, were forced to withdraw regular troops from the front. 'Thus not only was the enemy's manpower impoverished but he found himself unable to cope with the ever-moving guerrilla' [The Nature of Guerrilla Action].

The development of guerrillas at that time had only reached the stage where there were detached groups of several thousands in strength, old, middle-aged, and young. The old men organized themselves into propaganda groups known as 'silver-haired units'; there was a suitable guerrilla activity for the middle-aged; the young men formed combat units, and there were even groups for the children. Among the leaders were determined Communists who carried on general political work among the people. These, although they opposed the doctrine of extreme guerrilla warfare, were quick to oppose those who condemned it. Experience tells us that 'Orthodox armies are the fundamental and principal power, guerrilla units are secondary to them and assist in the accomplishment of the mission assigned the regular forces [Gusev, Lessons of Civil War.]. Many of the guerrilla regimes in Russia gradually developed until in battle they were able to discharge functions of organized regulars. The army of the famous General Galen was entirely derived from guerrillas.

During seven months in 1935 and 1936, the Abyssinians lost their war against Italy. The cause of defeat — aside from the most important political reasons that there were dissentient political groups, no strong government party, and unstable policy—was the failure to adopt a positive policy of mobile warfare. There was never a combination of the war of movement with large-scale guerrilla operations. Ultimately, the Abyssinians adopted a purely passive defence, with the result that they were unable to defeat the Italians. In addition to this, the fact that Abyssinia is a relatively small and sparsely populated country was contributory. Even in spite of the fact that the Abyssinian Army and its equipment were not modern, she was able to withstand a mechanized Italian force of 400,000 for seven months. During that period, there were several occasions when a war of movement was combined with large-scale guerrilla operations to strike the Italians heavy blows. Moreover, several cities were retaken and casualties totaling 140,000 were inflicted. Had this policy been steadfastly continued, it would have been difficult to have named the ultimate winner. At the present time, guerrilla activities continue in Abyssinia, and if the internal political questions can be solved, an extension of such activities is probable.

In 1841 and 1842, when brave people from San Yuan Li fought the English; again from 1850 to 1864, during the Taiping War, and for a third time in 1899 in the Boxer Uprising, guerrilla tactics were employed to a remarkable degree. Particularly was this so during the Taiping War, when guerrilla operations were most extensive and the Ch'ing troops were often completely exhausted and forced to flee for their lives.

In these wars, there were no guiding principles of guerrilla action. Perhaps these guerrilla hostilities were not carried out in conjunction with regular operations, or perhaps there was a lack of co-ordination. But the fact that victory was not gained was not because of any lack in guerrilla activity but rather because of the interference of politics in military affairs. Experience shows that if precedence is not given to the question of conquering the enemy in both political and military affairs, and if regular hostilities are not conducted with tenacity, guerrilla operations alone cannot produce final victory.

From 1927 to 1936, the Chinese Red Army fought almost continually and employed guerrilla tactics contently. At the very beginning, a positive policy was adopted. Many bases were established, and from guerrilla bands, the Reds were able to develop into regular armies. As these armies fought, new guerrilla regimes were developed over a wide area. These regimes co-ordinated their efforts with those of the regular forces This policy accounted for the many victories gained by the guerrilla troops relatively few in number, who were armed with weapons inferior to those of their opponents. The leaders of that period properly combined guerrilla operations with a war of movement both strategically and tactically. They depended primarily upon alertness. They stressed the correct basis for both political affaires and military operations. They developed their guerrilla bands into trained units. They then determined upon a ten year period of resistance during which time they overcame innumerable difficulties and have only lately reached their goal of direct participation in the anti-Japanese war. There is no doubt that the internal unification of China is now a permanent and definite fact, and that the experience gained during our internal struggles has proved to be both necessary and advantageous to us in the struggle against Japanese imperialism. There are many valuable lessons we can learn from the experience of those years. Principle among them is the fact that guerrilla success largely depend upon powerful political leaders who work unceasingly to bring about internal unification. Such leaders must work with the people; they must have a correct conception of the policy to be adopted as regards both the people and the enemy.

After 18 September 1931, strong anti-Japanese guerrilla campaigns were opened in each of the three north-east provinces. Guerrilla activity persists there in spite of the cruelties and deceits practiced by the Japanese at the expense of the people, and in spite of the fact that her armies have occupied the land and oppressed the people for the last seven years. The struggle can be divided into two periods . During the first, which extended from 18 September 1931 to January 1933, anti-Japanese guerrilla activity exploded constantly in all three provinces. Ma Chan Shan and Su Ping Wei established an anti-Japanese regime in Heilungkiang. In Chi Lin. the National Salvation Army and the Self-Defence Army were led by Wang Te Lin and Li Tu respectively. In Feng T'ien, Chu Lu and others commanded guerrilla units The influence of these forces was great. They harassed the Japanese unceasingly, but because there was an indefinite political goal, improper leadership, failure to co ordinate military command and operations and to work with the people, and, finally, failure to delegate proper political functions to the army, the whole organization was feeble, and its strength was not unified. As a direct result of these conditions, the campaigns failed and the troops were finally defeated by our enemy.

During the second period, which has extended from January 1933 to the present time, the situation has greatly improved, This has come about because great numbers of people who have been oppressed by the enemy have decided to resist him, because of the participation of the Chinese Communists in the anti-Japanese warm and because of the fine work of the volunteer units. The guerrillas have finally educated the people to the meaning of guerrilla warfare, and in the north-east, it has again become an important and powerful influence. Already seven or eight guerrilla regiments and a number of independent platoons have been formed, and their activities make it necessary for the Japanese to send troops after them month after month. These units hamper the Japanese and undermine their control in the north-east, while, at the same time they inspire a Nationalist revolution in Korea. Such activities are not merely of transient and local importance but directly contribute to our ultimate victory.

However, there are still some weak points. For instance: National defence policy has not been sufficiently developed; participation of the people is not general; internal political organization is still in its primary stages, and the force used to attack the Japanese and the puppet governments is not yet sufficient. But if present policy is continued tenaciously, all these weaknesses will be overcome. Experience proves that guerrilla war will develop to even greater proportions and that, in spite of the cruelty o the Japanese and the many methods they have device to cheat the people, they cannot extinguish guerrilla activities extinguish guerrilla activities in the three north-eastern provinces.

The guerrilla experiences of China and of other countries that have been outlined; prove that in a war of revolutionary nature such hostilities are possible, natural and necessary. They prove that if the present anti-Japanese war for the emancipation of the masses of the Chinese people is to gain ultimate victory, such hostilities must expand tremendously.

Historical experience is written in iron and blood. We must point out that the guerrilla campaigns being waged in China today are a page in history that has no precedent. Their influence will not be confined solely to China in her present anti-Japanese war but will be world-wide.

4. Can Victory Be Attained By Guerrilla Operations?

Guerrilla hostilities are but one phase of the war of resistance against Japan and the answer to the question of whether or not they can produce ultimate victory can be given only after investigation and comparison of all elements of our own strength with those of the enemy. The particulars of such a comparison are several. First, the strong Japanese bandit nation is an absolute monarchy. During the course of her invasion of China, she had made comparative progress in the techniques of industrial production and in the development of excellence and skill in her army, navy, and airforce. But in spite of this industrial progress, she remains an absolute monarchy of inferior physical endowments. Her manpower, her raw materials, and her financial resources are all inadequate and insufficient to maintain her in protracted warfare or to meet the situation presented by a war prosecuted over a vast area. Added to this is the anti-war feeling now manifested by the Japanese people, a feeling that is shared by the junior officers and, more extensively, by the soldiers of the invading army. Furthermore, China is not Japan's only enemy. Japan is unable to employ her entire strength in the attack on China; she cannot, at most, spare more than a million men for this purpose, as she must hold any in excess of that number for use against other possible opponents. Because of these important primary considerations, the invading Japanese bandits can hope neither to be victorious in a protracted struggle nor to conquer a vast area. Their strategy must be one of lightning war and speedy decision. If we can hold out for three or more years, it will be most difficult for Japan to bear up under the strain.

In the war, the Japanese brigands must depend upon lines of communication linking the principal cities as routes for the transport of war materials. The most important considerations for her are that her rear be stable and peaceful and that her lines of communication be intact. It is not to her an advantage to wage war over a vast area with disrupted lines of communication. She cannot disperse her strength and fight in a number of places, and her greatest fears are these eruptions in her rear and disruption of her lines of communication. If she can maintain communications, she will be able at will to concentrate powerful forces speedily at strategic points to engage our organized units in decisive battle. Another important Japanese objective is to profit from the industries, finances, and manpower in captured areas and with them to augment her own insufficient strength. Certainly, it is not to her advantage to forgo these benefits, not to be forced to dissipate her energies in a type of warfare in which the gains will not compensate for the losses. It is for these reasons that guerrilla warfare conducted in each bit of conquered territory over a wide area will be a heavy blow struck at the Japanese bandits. Experience in the five northern provinces as well as in Kiangsu, Chekiang and Anhwei has absolutely established the truth of this assertion.

China is a country half colonial and half feudal; it is a country that is politically, militarily, and economically backward. This is an inescapable conclusion. It is a vast country with great resources and tremendous population, a country in which the terrain is complicated and the facilities for communication are poor. All theses factors favour a protracted war, they all favour the application of mobile warfare and guerilla operations. The establishment of innumerable anti-Japanese bases behind the enemy's lines will force him to fight unceasingly in many places at once, both to his front and his rear. He thus endlessly expends his resources.

We must unite the strength of the army with that of the people, we must strike the weak spots in the enemy's flanks, in his front, in his rear. We must make war everywhere and cause dispersal of his forces and dissipation of his strength. Thus the time will come when a gradual change will become evident in the relative position of ourselves and our enemy, and when that day comes, it will be the beginning of our ultimate victory over the Japanese.

Although China's population is great, it is unorganized. This is a weakness which must be then into account.

The Japanese bandits have merely to conquer territory but rapacious, and murderous policy of the extinction of the Chinese race. We must unite the nation without regard to parties and follow our policy of resistance to the end. China today is not the China of old. It is not like Abyssinia. China today is at the point of her greatest historical progress. The standards of literacy among the masses have been raised; the rapprochement of Communists and Nationalists has laid the foundation for an anti-Japanese war front that is constantly being strengthened and expanded; government, army and people are all working with great energy; the raw material resources and the economic strength of the nation are waiting to be used; the unorganized people are becoming an organized nation.

These energies must be directed toward the goal of protracted war so that should the Japanese occupy much of our territory or even most of it, we shall still gain final victory. Not only must those behind our lines organize for resistance but also those who live in Japanese-occupied territory in every part of the country. The traitors who accept the Japanese as fathers are few in number, and those who have taken oath that they would prefer death to abject slavery are many. If we resist with this spirit, what enemy can we not conquer and who can say that ultimate victory will not be ours?

The Japanese are waging a barbaric war along uncivilized lines. For that reason, Japanese of all classes oppose the policies of their government, as do vast international groups. On the other hand, because China's cause is righteous, our countrymen of all classes and parties are united to oppose the invader; we have sympathy in many foreign countries including even Japan itself. This is perhaps the most important reason why Japan will lose and China will win.

The progress of the war for the emancipation of the Chinese people will be in accord with these facts. The guerrilla war of resistance will be in accord with these facts, and that guerrilla operations correlated with those of our regular forces will produce victory is the conviction of the many patriots who devote their entire strength to guerrilla hostilities.

5. Organization For Guerilla Warfare

Four points must be considered under this subject. These are:

How are guerrilla bands formed?
How are guerrilla bands organized?
What are the methods of arming guerrilla bands?
What elements constitute a guerrilla band?

These are all questions pertaining to the organization armed guerrilla units; they are questions which those who had no experience in guerilla hostilities do not understand and on which they can arrive at no sound decisions; indeed, they would not know in what manner to begin.

How Guerrilla Units Are Originally Formed

The unit may originate in any one of the following ways:

a) From the masses of the people.
b) From regular army units temporarily detailed for the purpose.
c) From regular army units permanently detailed.
d) From the combination of a regular army unit and a unit recruited from the people.
e) From the local militia.
f) From deserters from the ranks of the enemy.
g) From former bandits and bandit groups.

In the present hostilities, no doubt, all these sources will be employed.

In the first case above, the guerrilla unit is formed from the people. This is the fundamental type. Upon the arrival of the enemy army to oppress and slaughter the people, their leaders call upon them to resist. They assemble the most valorous elements, arm them with old rifles or whatever firearms they can, and thus a guerrilla unit begins. Orders have already been issued throughout the nation that call upon the people to form guerrilla units both for local defense and for other combat. If the local governments approve and aid such movements, they cannot fail to prosper. In some places, where the local government is not determined or where its officers have all fled, the leaders among the masses (relying on the sympathy of the people and their sincere desire to resist Japan and succor the country) call upon the people to resist, and they respond. Thus, many guerrilla units are organized. In circumstances of this kind, the duties of leadership usually fall upon the shoulders of young students, teachers, professors, other educators, local soldiery, professional men, artisans, and those without a fixed profession, who are willing to exert themselves to the last drop of their blood. Recently, in Shansi, Hopeh, Chahar, Suiyuan, Shantung, Chekiang, Anhwei, Kiangsu, and other provinces, extensive guerrilla hostilities have broken out. All these are organized and led by patriots. The amount of such activity is the best proof of the foregoing statement. The more such bands there are, the better will the situation be. Each district, each county, should be able to organize a great number of guerrilla squads, which, when assembled, form a guerrilla company.

There are those who say: 'I am a farmer', or, 'I am a student'; 'I can discuss literature but not military arts.' This is incorrect. There is no profound difference between the farmer and the soldier. You must have courage. You simply leave your farms and become soldiers. That you are farmers is of no difference, and if you have education, that is so much the better.

When you take your arms in hand, you become soldiers; when you are organized, you become military units.

Guerrilla hostilities are the university of war, and after you have fought several times valiantly and aggressively, you may become a leader of troops and there will be many well-known regular soldiers who will not be your peers. Without question, the fountainhead of guerrilla warfare is in the masses of the people, who organize guerrilla units directly from themselves.

The second type of guerrilla unit is that which is organized from small units of the regular forces temporarily detached for the purpose. For example, since hostilities commenced, many groups have been temporarily detached from armies, divisions, and brigades and have been assigned guerrilla duties. A regiment of the regular army may, if circumstances warrant, be dispersed into groups for the purpose of carrying on guerrilla operations. As an example of this, there is the Eighth Route Army, in North China. Excluding the periods when it carries on mobile operations as an army, it is divided into its elements and these carry on guerrilla hostilities. This type of guerrilla unit is essential for two reasons. First, in mobile-warfare situations, the co-ordination of guerrilla activities with regular operations is necessary. Second, until guerrilla hostilities can be developed on a grand scale, there is no one to carry out guerrilla missions but regulars. Historical experience shows us that regular army units are not able to undergo the hardships of guerrilla campaigning over long periods. The leaders of regular units engaged in guerrilla operations must be extremely adaptable. They must study the methods of guerrilla war. They must understand that initiative, discipline, and the employment of stratagems are all of the utmost importance. As the guerrilla status of regular units is but temporary, their leaders must lend all possible support to the organization of guerrilla units from among the people. These units must be so disciplined that they hold together after the departure of the regulars.

The third type of unit consists of a detachment of regulars who are permanently assigned guerrilla duties. This type of small detachment does not have to be prepared to rejoin the regular forces. Its post is somewhere in the rear of the enemy, and there it becomes the backbone of guerrilla organization. As an example of this type of organization we may take the Wu Tat Shan district in the heart of the Hopeh-Chahar-Shansi area. Along the borders of these provinces, units from the Eighth Route Army have established a framework or guerrilla operations. Around these small cores, many detachments have been organized and the area of guerrilla activity greatly expanded. In areas in which there is a possibility of cutting the enemy's lines of supply, this system should be used. Severing enemy, supply routes destroys his lifeline; this is one feature that cannot be neglected. If, at the time the regular forces withdraw from a certain area, some units left behind, these should conduct guerrilla operations in the enemy's rear. As an example of this, we have the guerrilla bands now continuing their independent operations in the Shanghai- Woosung area in spite of the withdrawal of regular forces.

The fourth type of organization is the result of a merger between small regular detachments and local guerrilla units. The regular forces may dispatch a squad, a platoon, or a company, which is placed at the disposal of the local guerrilla commander. If a small group experienced in military and political affairs is sent, it becomes the core of the local guerrilla unit. These several methods are all excellent, and if properly applied, the intensity of guerilla warfare can be extended. In the Wu Tat Shan area, each of these methods has been used.

The fifth type mentioned above is from the local militia, from police and home guards. In every North China province, there are now many of these groups, and they should be formed in every locality. The government has issued mandate to the effect that the people are not to depart from war areas. The officer in command of the county, the commander of the peace-preservation unit, the chief of police are all required to obey this mandate. They cannot retreat with their forces but must remain at their stations and resist.

The sixth type of unit is that organized from troops that come over from the enemy—the Chinese 'traitor' troops employed by the Japanese. It is always possible to produce disaffection in their ranks, and we must increase our propaganda efforts and foment mutinies among such troops. Immediately after mutinying, they must be received into our ranks and organized. The concord of the leaders and the assent of the men must be gained, and the units rebuilt politically and reorganized militarily. Once this has been accomplished, they become successful guerrilla units. In regard to this type of unit, it may be said that political work among them is of utmost importance.

The seventh type of guerrilla organization is that formed from bands of bandits and brigands. This, although difficult, must be carried out with utmost vigour lest the enemy use such bands to his own advantages. Many bandit groups pose as anti-Japanese guerrillas, and it is only necessary to correct their political beliefs to convert them.

In spite of inescapable differences in the fundamental types of guerrilla bands, it is possible to unite them to form a vast sea of guerrillas. The ancients said, 'Tai Shan is a great mountain because it does not scorn the merest handful of dirt; the rivers and seas are deep because they absorb the waters of small streams.' Attention paid to the enlistment and organization of guerrillas of every type and from every source will increase the potentialities of guerrilla action in the anti-Japanese war. This is something that patriots will not neglect.

THE METHOD OF ORGANIZING GUERRILLA REGIMES

Many of those who decide to participate in guerrilla activities do not know the methods of organization. For such people, as well as for students who have no knowledge of military affairs, the matter of organization is a problem that requires solution. Even among those who have military knowledge, there are some who know nothing of guerrilla regimes use they are lacking in that particular type of experience. The subject of the organization of such regimes is not confined to the organization of specific units but includes all guerrilla activities within the area where the regime functions.

As an example of such organization, we may take a geographical area in the enemy's rear. This area may comprise many counties. It must be sub-divided and individual companies or battalions formed to accord with the sub-divisions. To this 'military area', a military commander and political commissioners are appointed. Under these, the necessary officers both military and political, are appointed. In the military headquarters, there will be the staff, the aides, the supply officers, and the medical personnel. These are controlled by the chief of staff, who acts in accordance with orders from the commander. In the political headquarters, there are bureaus of propaganda organization, people's mass movements, and miscellaneous affairs. Control of these is vested in the political chairman.

The military areas are sub-divided into smaller districts in accordance with local geography, the enemy situation locally, and the state of guerrilla development. Each of these smaller divisions within the area is a district, each of which may consist of from two to six counties. To each district, a military commander and several political commissioners are appointed. Under their direction, military and political headquarters are organized. Tasks are assigned in accordance with the number of guerrilla troops available. Although the names of the officers in the 'district' correspond to those in the larger 'area', the number of the functionaries assigned in the former case should be reduced to the least possible. In order to unify control, to handle guerrilla troops that come from different sources, and to harmonize military operations and local political affairs, a committee of from seven to nine members should be organized in each area and district. This committee, the members of which are selected by the troops and the local political officers, should function as a forum for the discussion of both military and political matters.

All the people in an area should arm themselves and be organized into two groups. One of these groups is a combat group, the other a self-defence unit with but limited military quality. Regular combatant guerrillas are organized into one of three general types of units. The first of these is the small unit, the platoon or company. In each county, three to six units may be organized. The second type is the battalion of from two to four companies. One such unit should be organized in each county. While the unit fundamentally belongs to the county in it was organized, it may operate in other counties. While in areas other than its own, it must operate in conjunction with local units in order to take advantage of their manpower, their knowledge of local terrain and local customs, and their information of the enemy.

The third type is the guerrilla regiment, which consists of from two to four of the above-mentioned battalion units. If sufficient manpower is available, a guerrilla a brigade of from two to four regiments may be formed.

Each of the units has its own peculiarities of organization. A squad, the smallest unit, has a strength of from nine to eleven men, including the leader and the assistant leader. Its arms may be from two to five Western-style rifles, with the remaining men armed with rifles of local manufacture, fowling-pieces, etc., spears, or big swords. Two to four such squads form a platoon. This too has a leader and an assistant leader, and when acting independently, it is assigned a political officer to carry on political propaganda work. The platoon may have about ten rifles, with the remainder of its four of such units from a company, which, like the platoon, has a leader, an assistant leader, and a political officer. All these units are under the direct supervision of the military commanders of the areas in which they operate.

The battalion unit must be more thoroughly organized and better equipped than the smaller units. Its discipline and its personnel should be superior. If a battalion is formed from company units, it should not deprive subordinate units entirely of their manpower and their arms. If in a small area, there is a peace-preservation corps, a branch of the militia, or police, regular guerrilla units should not be dispersed over it.

The guerrilla unit next in size to the battalion is the regiment. This must be under more severe discipline than the battalion. In an independent guerrilla regiment, there may be ten men per squad, three squad per platoon, three platoons per company, three companies per battalion, and three battalions to the regiment. Two of such regiments form a brigade. Each of these units has a commander, a vice-commander, and a political officer.

In North China, guerrilla cavalry units should be established. These may be regiments of from two to four companies, or battalions.

All these units from the lowest to the highest are combatant guerrilla units and receive their supplies from the central government. Details of their organization are shown in the tables.

All the people of both sexes from the ages of sixteen to forty-five must be organized into anti-Japanese self-defence units, the basis of which is voluntary service. As a first step, they must procure arms, then they must be given both military and political training. Their responsibilities are : local sentry duties, securing information of the enemy, arresting traitors, and preventing the dissemination of enemy propaganda. When the enemy launches a guerrilla-suppression drive, these units, armed with what weapons there are, are assigned to certain areas to deceive, hinder, and harass him. Thus, the defence units assist the combatant guerrillas. They have other functions. They furnish stretcher-bearers to transport the wounded , carriers to take food to the troops, and comfort missions to provide the troops with tea and rice. If a locality can organize such a self-defence unit as we have described, the traitors cannot hide nor can bandits and robbers disturb the peace of the people. Thus the people will continue to assist the guerrilla and supply manpower to our regular armies. 'The organization of self-defence units is a transitional step in the development of universal conscription. Such units are reservoirs of manpower for the orthodox forces.'

There have been such organizations for some time in Shansi, Shensi, Honan, and Suiyuan. The youth organizations in different provinces were formed for the purpose of educating the young. They have been of some help. However, they were not voluntary, and confidence of the people was thus not gained. These organizations were not widespread, and their effect was almost negligible. This system was, therefore, supplanted by the new-type organizations,. Which are organized on the principles of voluntary co-operation and non-separation of the members from their native localities. When the members of these organizations are in their native towns, they support themselves . Only in case of military necessity are they ordered to remote places, and when this is done, the government must support them. Each member of these groups must have a weapon even if the weapon is only a knife, a pistol, a lance, or a spear.

In all places where the enemy operates, these self-defence units should organize within themselves a small guerrilla group of perhaps from three to ten men armed with pistols or revolvers. This group is not required to leave its native locality.

The organization of these self-defence units is mentioned in this book because such units are useful for the purposes of inculcating the people with military and political knowledge, keeping order in the rear, and replenishing the ranks of the regulars. These groups should be organized not only in the active war zones but in every province in China. 'The people must be inspired to co-operate voluntarily. We must not force them, for if we do, it will be ineffectual.' This is extremely important.

In order to control anti-Japanese military organization as a whole, it is necessary to establish a system of military areas and districts along the lines we have indicated.

EQUIPMENT OF GUERRILLAS
In regard to the problem of guerrilla equipment, it must be understood that guerrillas are lightly-armed attack groups, which require simple equipment. The standard of equipment is based upon the nature of duties assigned; the equipment of low-class guerrilla units is not as good as that of higher-class units. For example, those who are assigned the task of destroying rail communications are better equipped than those who do not have that task. The equipment of guerrillas cannot be based on what the guerrillas want, to even what they need, but must be based on what is available for their use. Equipment cannot be furnished immediately but must be acquired gradually. These are points to be kept in mind .

The question of equipment includes the collection, supply, distribution, and replacement of weapons, ammunition, blankets, communication materials, transport, and facilities for propaganda work. The supply of weapons and ammunition is most difficult, particularly at the time the unit is established, but this problem can always be solved eventually. Guerrilla bands that originate in the people are furnished with revolvers, pistols, rifles, spears, big swords, and land mines and mortars of local manufacture. Other elementary weapons are added and as many new-type rifles as are available are distributed. After a period of resistance, it is possible to increase the supply of equipment by capturing it from the enemy. In this respect, the transport companies are the easiest to equip, for in any successful attack, we will capture the enemy's transport.

An armory should be established in each guerrilla district for the manufacture and repair of rifles and for the production of cartridge, hand grenades and bayonets. Guerrillas must not depend to much on an armory. The enemy is the principal source of their supply.

For destruction of railway tracks, bridges, and stations in enemy-controlled territory, it is necessary to gather together demolition materials. Troops must be trained in the preparation and use of demolitions, and a demolition unit must be organized in each regiment.

As for minimum clothing requirements, these are that each man shall have at least two summer-weight uniforms, one suit of winter clothing, two hats, a pair of wrap puttees, and blanket. Each man must have a pack or a bag for food. In the north, each man must have an overcoat. In acquiring this clothing, we cannot depend on captures made by the enemy, for it is forbidden for captors to take clothing from their prisoners. In order to maintain high morale in guerrilla forces, all the clothing and equipment mentioned should be furnished by the representatives of the government in each guerrilla district. These men may confiscate clothing from traitors or ask contributions from those best able to afford them. In subordinate groups, uniforms are unnecessary.

Telephone and radio equipment is not necessary in lower groups, but all units from regiment up are equipped with both. This material can be obtained by contributions from the regular forces and by capture from the enemy.

In the guerrilla army in general, and at bases in particular, there must be a high standard of medical equipment. Besides the services of the doctors, medicines must be procured. Although guerrillas can depend on the enemy for some portion of their medical supplies, they must, in general, depend upon contributions. If Western medicines are not available, local medicines must be made to suffice.

The problem of transport is more vital in North-China than in the south, for in the south all that are necessary are mules and horses. Small guerrilla units need no animals, but regiments and brigades will find them necessary. Commanders and staffs of units from companies up should be furnished a riding animal each. At times, two officers will have to share a horse. Officers whose duties are of minor nature do not have to be mounted.

Propaganda materials are very important. Every large guerrilla unit should have a printing press and a mimeograph stone. They must also have paper on which to print propaganda leaflets and notices. They must be supplied with large brushes. In guerrilla areas, there should be a printing press or a lead-type press.

For the purpose of printing training instructions, this material is of the greatest importance.

In addition to the equipment listed above, it is necessary to have field-glasses, compasses, and military maps. An accomplished guerrilla group will acquire these things.

Because of the proved importance of guerrilla hostilities in the anti-Japanese war, the headquarters of the Nationalist Government and the commanding officers of the various war zones should do their best to supply the guerrillas with what they actually need and are unable to get for themselves. However, it must be repeated that guerrilla equipment will in the main depend on the efforts of the guerrillas themselves. If they depend on higher officers too much, the psychological effect will be to weaken the guerrilla spirit of resistance.

ELEMENTS OF THE GUERRILLA ARMY
The term 'element' as used in the title to this section refers to the personnel, both officers and men, of the guerrilla army. Since each guerrilla group fights in a protracted war, its officers must be brave and positive men whose entire loyalty is dedicated to the cause of emancipation of the people. An officer should have the following qualities: great powers of endurance so that in spite of any hardship he sets an example to his men and be a model for them; he must be able to mix easily with the people; his spirit and that of the men must be one in strengthening the policy of resistance to the Japanese. If he wishes to gain victories, he must study tactics. A guerrilla group with officers of this calibre would be unbeatable. I do not mean that every guerrilla group can have, at its inception, officers of such qualities. The officers must be men naturally endowed with good qualities which can be developed during the course of campaigning. The most important natural quality is that of complete loyalty to the idea of people's emancipation. If this is present,

the others will develop; if it is not present, nothing can be done. When officers are first selected from a group, it is this quality that should receive particular attention. The officers in a group should be inhabitants of the locality in which the group is organized, as this will facilitate relations between them and the local civilians. In addition, officers so chosen would be familiar with conditions. If in any locality there are not enough men of sufficiently high qualifications to become officers, an effort must be made to train and educate the people so these qualities may be developed and the potential officer material increased. There can be no disagreements between officers native to one place and those from other localities.

A guerrilla group ought to operate on the principle that only volunteers are acceptable for service. It is a mistake to impress people into service. As long as a person is willing to fight, his social condition or position is no consideration, but only men who are courageous and determined can bear the hardships of guerrilla campaigning in a protracted war.

A soldier who habitually breaks regulations must be dismissed from the army. Vagabonds and vicious people must not be accepted for service. The opium habit must be forbidden, and a soldier who cannot break himself of the habit should be dismissed. Victory in guerrilla war is conditioned upon keeping the membership pure and clean.

It is a fact that during the war the enemy may take advantage of certain people who are lacking in conscience and patriotism and induce them to join the guerrillas for the purpose of betraying them. Officers must, therefore, continually educate the soldiers and inculcate patriotism in them. This will prevent the success of traitors. The traitors who are in the ranks must be discovered and expelled, and punishment and expulsion meted out to those who have been influenced by them. In all such cases, the officers should summon the soldiers and relate the facts to them, thus arousing their hatred and detestation for traitors. This procedure will serve as well as a warning to the other soldiers. If an officer is discovered to be a traitor, some prudence must be used in the punishment adjudged. However, the work of eliminating traitors in the army begins with their elimination from among the people.

Chinese soldiers who have served under puppet governments and bandits who have been converted should be welcomed as individuals or as groups. They should be well-treated and repatriated. But care should be used during their reorientation to distinguish those whose idea is to fight the Japanese from those who may be present for other reasons.

6. The Political Problems Of Guerrilla Warfare

In Chapter 1, I mentioned the fact that guerrilla troops should have a precise conception of the political goal of the struggle and the political organization to be used in attaining that goal. This means that both organization and discipline of guerrilla troops must be at a high level so that they can carry out the political activities that are the life of both the guerilla armies and of revolutionary warfare.

First of all, political activities depend upon the indoctrination of both military and political leaders with the idea of anti-Japanism. Through them, the idea is transmitted to the troops. One must not feel that he is anti-Japanese merely because he is a member of a guerrilla unit. The anti-Japanese idea must be an ever-present conviction, and if it is forgotten, we may succumb to the temptations of the enemy or be overcome with discouragement. In a war of long duration, those whose conviction that the people must be emancipated is not deep rooted are likely to become shaken in their faith or actually revolt. Without the general education that enables everyone to understand our goal of driving out Japanese imperialism and establishing a free and happy China, the soldiers fight without conviction and lose their determination.

The political goal must be clearly and precisely indicated to inhabitants of guerrilla zones and their national consciousness awakened. Hence, a concrete explanation of the political systems used is important not only to guerrilla troops but to all those who are concerned with the realization of our political goal. The Kuomintang has issued a pamphlet entitled System of National Organization for War, which should be widely distributed throughout guerrilla zones. If we lack national organization, we will lack the essential unity that should exist between the soldiers and the people.

A study and comprehension of the political objectives of this war and of the anti-Japanese front is particularly important for officers of guerrilla troops. There are some militarists who say: 'We are not interested in politics but only in the profession of arms.' It is vital that these simple-minded militarists be made to realize the relationship that exists between politics and military affairs. Military action is a method used to attain a political goal. While military affairs and political affairs are not identical, it is impossible to isolate one from the other.

It is to be hoped that the world is in the last era of strife. The vast majority of human beings have already prepared or are preparing to fight a war that will bring justice to the oppressed peopled of the world. No matter how long this war may last, there is no doubt that it will be followed by an unprecedented epoch of peace The war that we are fighting today for the freedom of all human beings, and the independent, happy, and liberal China that we are fighting to establish will be a part of that new world order. A conception like this is difficult for the simple-minded militarist to grasp and it must therefore be carefully explained to him.

There are three additional matters that must be considered under the broad question of political activities. These are political activities, first, as applied to the troops; second, as applied to the people; and, third, as applied to the enemy. The fundamental problems are: first, spiritual unification of officers and men within the army; second spiritual unification of the army and the people; of the army and the people; and, last, destruction of the unity of the enemy. The concrete methods for achieving these unities are discussed in detail in pamphlet Number 4 of this series, entitled Political Activities in Anti-Japanese Guerrilla Warfare.

A revolutionary army must have discipline that is established on a limited democratic basis. In all armies, obedience the subordinates to their superiors must be exacted. This is true in the case of guerrilla discipline, but the basis for guerrilla discipline must be the individual conscience. With guerrillas, a discipline of compulsion is ineffective. In any revolutionary army, there is unity of purpose as far as both officers and men are concerned, and, therefore, within such an army, discipline is self-imposed. Although discipline in guerrilla ranks is not as severe as in the ranks of orthodox forces, the necessity for discipline exists. This must be self-imposed, because only when it is, is the soldier able to understand completely, why he fights and why he must obey. This type of discipline becomes a tower of strength within the army, and it is the only type that can truly harmonize the relationship that exists between officers and soldiers.

In any system where discipline is externally imposed, the relationship that exists between officer and man is characterized by indifference of the one to the other. The idea that officers can physically beat or severely tongue-lash their men is a feudal one and is not in accord with the conception of self-imposed discipline. Discipline of the feudal type will destroy internal unity and fighting strength. A discipline self-imposed is the primary characteristic of a democratic system in the army .

A secondary characteristic is found in the degree of liberties accorded officers and soldiers. In a revolutionary army, all individuals enjoy political liberty and the question, for example, of the emancipation of the people must not only be tolerated but discussed, and propaganda must encouraged. Further, in such an army, the mode of living of the officers and the soldiers must not differ too much, and this is particularly true in the case of guerilla troops. Officers should live under the same conditions as their men, for that is the only way in which they can gain from their men the admiration and confidence so vital in war. It is incorrect to hold to a theory of equality in all things. But there must be equality of existence in accepting the hardships and dangers of war, thus we may attain to the unification of the officer and soldier groups a unity both horizontal within the group itself, and vertical, that is, from lower to higher echelons. It is only when such unity is present that units can be said to be powerful combat factors.

There is also a unity of spirit that should exist between troops and local inhabitants. The Eighth Route Army put into practice a code known as 'Three Rules and the Eight Remarks', which we list here:

Rules:

All actions are subject to command.
Do not steal from the people.
Be neither selfish nor unjust.

Remarks:

Replace the door when you leave the house.
Roll up the bedding on which you have slept.
Be courteous.
Be honest in your transactions.
Return what you borrow.
Replace what you break.
Do not bathe in the presence of women.
Do not without authority search those you arrest.

The Red Army adhered to this code for ten years and the Eighth Route Army and other units have since adopted it.

Many people think it impossible for guerrillas to exist for long in the enemy's rear. Such a belief reveals lack of comprehension of the relationship that should exist between the people and the troops. The former may be likened to water the latter to the fish who inhabit it. How may it be said that these two cannot exist together? It is only undisciplined troops who make the people their enemies and who, like the fish out of its native element cannot live.

44

We further our mission of destroying the enemy by propagandizing his troops, by treating his captured soldiers with consideration, and by caring for those of his wounded who fall into our hands. If we fail in these respects, we strengthen the solidarity of our enemy.

7. The Strategy Of Guerrilla Resistance Against Japan

It has been definitely decided that in the strategy of our war against Japan, guerrilla strategy must be auxiliary to fundamental orthodox methods. If this were a small country, guerrilla activities could be carried out close to the scene of operations of the regular army and directly complementary to them. In such a case, there would be no question of guerrilla strategy as such. Nor would the question arise if our country were as strong as Russia, for example, and able speedily to eject an invader. The question exists because China, a weak country of vast size, has today progressed to the point where it has become possible to adopt the policy of a protracted war characterized by guerrilla operations. Although these may at first glance seem to be abnormal or heterodox, such is not actually the case.

Because Japanese military power is inadequate, much of the territory her armies have overrun is without sufficient garrison troops. Under such circumstances the primary functions of guerrillas are three: first, to conduct a war on exterior lines, that is, in the rear of the enemy; second, to establish bases, and, last, to extend the war areas. Thus, guerrilla participation in the war is not merely a matter of purely local guerrilla tactics but involves strategical considerations.

Such war, with its vast time and space factors, establishes a new military process, the focal point of which is China today. The Japanese are apparently attempting to recall a past that saw the Yuan extinguish the Sung and the Ch'ing conquer the Ming; that witnessed the extension of the British Empire to North America and India; that saw the Latins overrun Central and South America. As far as China today is concerned, such dreams of conquest are fantastic and without reality. Today's China is better equipped than was the China of yesterday, and a new type of guerrilla hostilities is a part of that equipment. If our enemy fails to take these facts into consideration and makes too optimistic an estimate of the situation, he courts disaster.

Though the strategy of guerrillas is inseparable from war strategy as a whole, the actual conduct of these hostilities differs from the conduct of orthodox operations. Each type of warfare has methods peculiar to itself, and methods suitable to regular warfare cannot be applied with success to
45

the special situations that confront guerrillas.

Before we treat the practical aspects of guerrilla war, it might be well to recall the fundamental axiom of combat on which all military action is based. This can be stated: 'Conservation of one's own strength; destruction of enemy strength.' A military policy based on this axiom is consonant with a national policy directed towards the building of a free and prosperous Chinese state and the destruction of Japanese imperialism. It is in furtherance of this policy that government applies in military strength. Is the sacrifice demanded by war in conflict with the idea of self-preservation? Not at all. The sacrifices demanded are necessary both to destroy the enemy and to preserve ourselves; the sacrifice of a part of the people is necessary to preserve the whole. All the considerations of military action are derived from this axiom. Its application is as apparent in all tactical and strategical conceptions as it is in the simple case of the soldier who shoots at his enemy from a covered position.

All guerrilla units start from nothing and grow. What methods should we select to ensure the conservation and development of our own strength and the destruction of that of the enemy? The essential requirements are the six listed below:

Retention of the initiative; alertness; carefully planned tactical attacks in a war of strategical defence; tactical speed in a war strategically protracted, tactical operations on exterior lines in a war conducts strategically on interior lines.
Conduct of operations to complement those of the regular army.
The establishment of bases.
A clear understanding of the relationship that exits between the attack and the defence.
The development of mobile operations.
Correct command.

The enemy, though numerically weak, is strong in the quality of his troops and their equipment; we, on the other hand, are strong numerically but weak as to quality. These considerations have been taken into account in the development of the policy of tactical offence, tactical speed, and tactical operations on exterior lines in a war that, strategically speaking, is defensive in character, protracted in nature, and conducted along interior lines. Our strategy is based on these conceptions. They must be kept in mind in the conduct of all operations.

Although the element of surprise is not absent in orthodox warfare, there are fewer opportunities to apply it than there are during guerrilla hostilities. In the latter, speed is essential. The movements of guerrilla troops must be secret and of supernatural rapidity; the enemy must be taken unaware, and the action entered speedily. There can be no procrastination in the execution of plans; no assumption of a negative or passive defence; no great dispersion of forces in many local engagements. The basic method is the attack in a violent and deceptive form.

While there may be cases where the attack will extend over a period of several days (if that length of time in necessary to annihilate an enemy group), it is more profitable to launch and push an attack with maximum speed. The tactics of defence have no place in the realm of guerrilla warfare. If a delaying action is necessary, such places as defiles, river crossings, and villages offer the most suitable conditions, for it is in such places that the enemy's arrangements may be disrupted and he may be annihilated.

The enemy is much stronger than we are, and it is true that we can hinder, distract, disperse, and destroy him only if we disperse our own forces. Although guerrilla warfare is the warfare of such dispersed units, it is sometimes desirable to concentrate in order to destroy an enemy. Thus, the principle of concentration of force against a relatively weaker enemy is applicable to guerrilla warfare.

We can prolong this struggle and make of it a protracted war only by gaining positive and lightning-like tactical decisions; by employing our manpower in proper concentrations and dispersions; and by operation on exterior lines in order to surround and destroy our enemy. If we cannot surround whole armies, we can at least partially destroy them, if we cannot kill the Japanese, we can capture them. The total effect of many local successes will be to change the relative strengths of the opposing forces. The destruction of Japan's military power, combined with the international sympathy for China's cause and the revolutionary tendencies evident in Japan, will be sufficient to destroy Japanese imperialism.

We will next discuss initiative, alertness, and the matter of careful planning. What is meant by initiative in warfare? In all battles and wars, a struggle to gain and retain the initiative goes on between the opposing sides, for it is the side that holds the initiative that has liberty of action. When an army loses the initiative, it loses its liberty; its role becomes passive; it faces the danger of defeat and destruction.

It is more difficult to obtain the initiative when defending on interior lines than it is while attacking on exterior lines. This is what Japan is doing. There are, however, several weak points as far as Japan is concerned. One of these is lack of sufficient manpower for the task; another is her cruelty to the inhabitants of conquered areas; a third is the underestimation of Chinese strength, which has resulted in the differences between military cliques, which, in turn, have been productive of many mistakes in the direction of her military forces. For instance, she has been gradually compelled to increase her manpower in China while, at the same time. the many arguments over plans of operations and disposition of troops have resulted in the loss of good opportunities for improvement of her strategical position. This explains the fact that although the Japanese are frequently able to surround large bodies of Chinese troops, they have never yet been able to capture more than a few. The Japanese military machine is thus being weakened by insufficiency of manpower, inadequacy of resources, the barbarism of her troops, and the general stupidity that has characterized the conduct of operations. Her offensive continues unabated, but because of the weaknesses pointed out, her attack must be limited in extent. She can never conquer China. The day will come — indeed already has in some areas — when she will be forced into a passive role. When hostilities commenced, China was passive, but as we enter the second phase of the war we find ourselves pursuing a strategy of mobile warfare, with both guerrillas and regulars operating on exterior lines. Thus, with each passing day, we seize some degree of initiative from the Japanese.

The matter of initiative is especially serious for guerrilla forces, who must face critical situations unknown to regular troops. The superiority of the enemy and the lack of unity and experience within our own ranks may be cited. Guerrillas can, however, gain the initiative if they keep in mind the weak points of the enemy. Because of the enemy's insufficient manpower, guerrillas can operate over vast territories, because he is a foreigner and a barbarian, guerrillas can gain the confidence of millions of their countrymen; because of the stupidity of enemy commanders, guerrillas can make full use of their own cleverness. Both guerrillas and regulars must exploit these enemy weaknesses while, at the same time, our own are remedied. Some of our weaknesses are apparent only and are, in actuality, sources of strength. For example, the very fact that most guerrilla groups are small makes it desirable and advantageous for them to appear and disappear in the enemy's rear. With such activities, the enemy is simply unable to cope. A similar liberty of action can rarely be obtained by regular forces.

When the enemy attacks the guerrillas with more than one column, it is difficult for the latter to retain the initiative. Any error, no matter how slight, in the estimation of the situation is likely to result in forcing the guerrillas into a passive role. They will then find themselves unable to beat oft the attacks of the enemy.

It is apparent that we can gain and retain the initiative only by a correct estimation of the situation and a proper arrangement of all military and political factors. A too pessimistic estimate will operate to force us into a passive position, with consequent loss of initiative; an overly optimistic estimate, with its rash ordering of factors, will produce the same result.

No military leader is endowed by heaven with an ability to seize the initiative. It is the intelligent leader who does so after a careful study and estimate of the situation and arrangement of the military and political factors involved. When a guerrilla unit, through either a poor estimate on the part of its leader or pressure from the enemy, is forced into a passive position, its first duty is to extricate itself. No method can be prescribed for this, as the method to be employed will, in every case, depend on the situation. One can, if necessary, run away. But there are times when the situation seems hopeless and, in reality, is not so at all. It is at such times that the good leader recognizes and seizes the moment when he can regain the lost initiative.

Let us revert to alertness. To conduct one's troops with alertness is an essential of guerrilla command. Leaders must realize that to operate alertly is the most important factor in gaining the initiative and vital in its effect of the relative situation that exists between our forces and those of the enemy. Guerrilla commanders adjust their operations to the enemy situation, to the terrain, and to prevailing local conditions. Leaders must be alert to sense changes in these factors and make necessary modifications in troop dispositions to accord with them. The leader must be like a fisherman, who, with his nets, is able both to cast them and to pull them out in awareness of the depth of the water, the strength of the current or the presence of any obstructions that may foul them. As the fisherman controls his nets through the lead ropes, so the guerrilla leader maintains contact with control over his units. As the fisherman must change his position, so must the guerrilla commander. Dispersion, concentration, constant change of position—it is in these ways that guerrillas employ, their strength.

In general, guerrilla units disperse to operate:

When the enemy is in over-extended defence, and sufficient force cannot be concentrated against him, guerrillas must disperse, harass him, and demoralize him.

When encircled by the enemy, guerrillas disperse to withdraw.

When the nature of the ground limits action, guerrillas disperse.

When the availability of supplies limits action, they disperse.

Guerrillas disperse in order to promote mass movements over a wide area.

Regardless of the circumstances that prevail at the time of dispersal, caution must be exercised in certain matters:

A relatively large group should be retained as a central force. The remainder of the troops should not be divided into groups of absolutely equal size. In this way, the leader is in a position to deal with any circumstances that may arise.

Each dispersed unit should have clear and definite responsibilities. Orders should specify a place to which to proceed, the time of proceeding, and the place, time, and method of assembly.

Guerrillas concentrate when the enemy is advancing upon them, and there is opportunity to fall upon him and destroy him. Concentration may be desirable when the enemy is on the defensive and guerrillas wish to destroy isolated detachments in particular localities. By the term 'concentrate', we do not mean the assembly of all manpower but rather of only that necessary for the task. The remaining guerrillas are assigned missions of hindering and delaying the enemy, of destroys isolated groups, or of conducting mass propaganda.

In addition to the dispersion and concentration of forces, the leader must understand what is termed 'alert shifting'. When the enemy feels the danger of guerrillas, he will generally send troops out to attack them. The guerrillas must consider the situation and decide at what time and at what place they wish to fight. If they find that they cannot fight, they must immediately shift. Then the enemy may be destroyed piecemeal. For example; after a guerrilla group has destroyed an enemy detachment at one place, it may be shifted to another area to attack and destroy a second detachment. Sometimes, it will not be profitable for a unit to become engaged in a certain area, and in that case, it must move immediately.

When the situation is serious, the guerrilla must move with the fluidity of water and the ease of the blowing wind. Their tactics must deceive, tempt, and confuse the enemy. They must lead the enemy to believe that they will attack him from the east and north, and they must then strike him from the west and the south. They must strike, then rapidly disperse. They must move at night.

Guerrilla initiative is expressed in dispersion, concentration, and the alert shifting of forces. If guerrillas are stupid and obstinate, they will be led to passive positions and severely damaged. Skill in conducting guerrilla operations, however, lies not in merely understanding the things we have discussed but rather in their actual application on the field of battle. The quick intelligence that constantly watches the ever-changing situation and is able to seize on the right moment for decisive action is found only in keen and thoughtful observers.

Careful planning is necessary if victory is to be won in guerrilla war, and those who fight without method do not understand the nature of guerrilla action. A plan is necessary regardless of the size of the unit involved; a prudent plan is as necessary in the case of the squad as in the case of the regiment. The situation must be carefully studied, then an assignment of duties made. Plans must include both political and military instruction; the matter of supply and equipment, and the matter of co-operation with local civilians. Without study of these factors, it is impossible either to seize the initiative or to operate alertly. It is true that guerrillas can make only limited plans, but even so, the factors we have mentioned must be considered.

The initiative can be secured and retained only following a positive victory that results from attack. The attack must be made on guerrilla initiative; that is, guerrillas must not permit themselves to be maneuvered into a position where they are robbed of initiative and where the decision to attack is forced upon them. Any victory will result from careful planning and alert control. Even in defence, all our efforts must be directed toward a resumption of the attack, for it is only by attack that we can extinguish our enemies an preserve ourselves. A defence or a withdrawal is entirely useless as far as extinguishing our enemies is concerned and of only temporary value. as far as the conservation of our forces is concerned. This principle is valid both for guerrillas and regular troops. The differences are of degree only; that is to say, in the manner of execution.

The relationship that exists between guerrilla and the orthodox forces is important and must be appreciated. Generally speaking, there are types of co-operation between guerrillas and orthodox groups. These are:

Strategical co-operation.
Tactical co-operation.

Battle co-operation.

Guerrillas who harass the enemy's rear installations and hinder his transport are weakening him and encouraging the national spirit of resistance. They are co-operating strategically. For example, the guerrillas in Manchuria had no functions of strategical co-operation with orthodox forces until the war in China started. Since that time, their faction of strategical co-operation is evident, for if they can kill one enemy, make the enemy expend one round of ammunition, or hinder one enemy group in its advance southward, our powers of resistance here are proportionately increased. Such guerrilla action has a positive action on the enemy nation and on its troops, while, at the same time, it encourages our own countrymen. Another example of strategical co-operation is furnished by the guerrillas who operate along the P'ing-Sui, P'ing-Han, Chin-P'u, T'ung-Pu, and Cheng-T'ai railways. This co-operation began when the invader attacked, continued during the period when he held garrisoned cities in the areas, and was intensified when our regular forces counter-attacked, in an effort to restore the lost territories.

As an example of tactical co-operation, we may cite the operations at Hsing-K'ou, when guerrillas both north and south of Yeh Men destroyed the T'ung-P'u railway and the motor roads near P'ing Hosing Pass and Yang Fang K'ou. A number of small operating base were established, and organized guerrilla action in Shansi complemented the activities of the regular forces both there and in the defence of Honan. similarly, during the south Shantung campaign, guerrillas in the five northern provinces co-operated with the army's operation on the Hsuchow front.

Guerrilla commanders in rear areas and those in command of regiments assigned to operate with orthodox units must co-operate in accordance with the situation. It is their function to determine weak points in the enemy dispositions, harass them, to disrupt their transport, and to undermine their morale, If guerrilla action were independent, the results to be obtained from tactical co-operation would be lost and those that result from strategical co-operation greatly diminished. In order to accomplish their mission and improve the degree of co-operation, guerrilla units must be equipped with some means of rapid communication. For this purpose, two way radio sets are recommended.

Guerrilla forces in the immediate battle area are responsible for close co-operation with regular forces, Their principal functions are to hinder enemy transport to gather information, and to act as outposts and sentinels. Even without precise instructions from the commander of the regular forces, these missions, as well as any others that contribute to the general success, should be assumed.

The problem of establishment of bases is of particular importance. This is so because this war is a cruel and protracted struggle. The lost territories can be restored only by a strategical counter-attack and this we cannot carry out until the enemy is well into China. Consequently, some part of our country — or, indeed, most of it — may be captured by the enemy and become his rear area. It is our task to develop intensive guerrilla warfare over this vast area and convert the enemy's rear into an additional front. Thus the enemy will never be able to stop fighting. In order to subdue the occupied territory, the enemy will have to become increasingly severe and oppressive.

A guerrilla base may be defined as an area, strategically located, in which the guerrillas can carry out their duties of training, self-preservation and development. Ability to fight a war without a rear area is a fundamental characteristic of guerrilla action, but this does not mean that guerrilla can exist and function over a long period of time without the development of base areas. History shows us many example of peasant revolts that were unsuccessful, and it is fanciful to believe that such movements, characterized by banditry and brigandage, could succeed in this era of improved communications and military equipment. Some guerrilla leaders seem to think that those qualities are present in today's movement, and before such leaders can comprehend the importance of base areas in the long-term war, their mind must be disabused of this idea.

The subject of bases may be better understood if we consider:

The various categories of bases.
Guerrilla areas and base areas.
The establishment of bases.
The development of bases.

Guerrilla bases may be classified according to their location as: first, mountain bases; second, plains bases; and last, river, lake, and bay bases. The advantages of bases in mountainous areas are evident. Those which are now established are at Ch'ang P'o Chan, Wu Tai Shan, Taiheng Shan, Tai Shan, Yen Shan, and Mao Shan. These bases are strongly protected. Similar bases should be established in all enemy rear areas.

Plains country is generally not satisfactory for guerrilla operating bases,

53

but this does not mean that guerrilla warfare cannot flourish in such country or that bases cannot be established there. The extent of guerrilla development in Hopeh and west Shantung proves the opposite to be the case Whether we can count on the use of these bases over long periods of time is questionable. We can, however, establish small bases of a seasonal or temporary nature. This we can do because our barbaric enemy simply does not have the manpower to occupy all the areas he has overrun and because the population of China is so numerous that a base can established anywhere. Seasonal bases in plains country may be established in the winter when the rivers are frozen over, and in the summer when the crops are growing. Temporary bases may be established when the enemy is otherwise occupied. When the enemy advances, the guerrillas who have established bases in the plains area are the first to engage him. Upon their withdrawal into mountainous country, they should leave behind them guerrilla groups dispersed over the entire area. Guerrillas shift from base to base on the theory that they must be in one place one day and another place the next.

There are many historical examples of the establishment of bases in river, bay, and lake country, and this is one aspect of our activity that has so far received little attention. Red guerrillas held out for many years in the Hungtze Lake region. We should establish bases in the Hungtze and Tai areas and along rivers and watercourses in territory controlled by the enemy so as to deny him access to, and free use of, the water routes.

There is a difference between the terms base area and guerrilla area. An area completely surrounded by territory occupied by the enemy is a 'base area'. Wu Tai Shan, and Taiheng Shan are examples of base areas. On the other hand, the area east and north of Wu Tai Shan (the Shansi-Hopeh-Chahar border zone) is a guerrilla area. Such areas can be controlled by guerrillas only while they actually physically occupy them. Upon their departure, control reverts to a puppet pro-Japanese government. East Hopeh. for example, was at first a guerrilla area rather than a base area. A puppet government functioned there. Eventually, the people, organized and inspired by guerrillas from the Wu Tai mountains, assisted in the transformation of this guerrilla area into a real base area. Such a task is extremely difficult, for it is largely dependent upon the degree to which the people can be inspired. In certain garrisoned areas, such as the cities and zones contiguous to the railways, the guerrillas see unable to drive the Japanese and puppets out. These areas remain guerrilla areas. At other times, base areas might become guerrilla areas due either to our own mistakes or to the activities of the enemy.

Obviously, in any given area In the war zone, any one or three situations may develop: The area may remain in Chinese hands; it may be lost to the Japanese and puppets or it may be divided between the combatants. Guerrilla leaders should endeavour to see that either the first or the last of these situations is assured.

Another point essential in the establishment of bases is the co-operation that must exist between the armed guerrilla bands and the people. All our strength must be used to spread the doctrine of armed resistance to Japan, to arm the people, to organize self-defence units, and to train guerrilla bands. This doctrine must be spread among the people, who must be organized into anti-Japanese groups. Their political instincts must be sharpened and their martial ardour increased If the workers, the farmers, the lovers of liberty, the young men, the women, and the children are not organized, they will never realize their own anti-Japanese power. Only the united strength of the people can eliminate traitors, recover the measure of political power that has been lost, and conserve and improve what we still retain.

We have already touched on geographic factors in our discussion of bases, and we must also mention the economic aspects of the problem. What economic policy should be adopted? Any such policy must offer reasonable protection to commerce and business. We interpret 'reasonable protection' to mean the people must contribute money in proportion to the money they have. Farmers will be required to furnish a certain share of their crops to guerrilla troops. Confiscation, except in the case of business run by traitors, is prohibited .

Our activities must be extended over the entire periphery of the base area if we wish to attack the enemy's bases and thus strengthen and develop our own. This will afford us opportunity to organize, equip, and train the people, thus furthering guerrilla policy as well as the national policy of protected war. At times, we must emphasize the development and extension of base areas; at other times, the organization, training, or equipment of the people.

Each guerrilla base will have its own peculiar problems of attack and defence. In general, the enemy, in an endeavour to consolidate his gains, will attempt to extinguish guerrilla bases by dispatching numerous bodies of troops over a number of different routes. This must be anticipated and the encirclement broken by counter-attacks As such enemy columns are without reserves, we should plan on using our main forces to attack one of them by surprise and devote our secondary effort to continual hindrance and harassment. At the same time, other forces should isolate enemy garrison troops and operate on their lines of supply and communication. When one column has been disposed of, we may turn our attention to one of the others. In a base area as large as Wu Tat Shan, for example, there are four or five military sub-divisions. Guerrillas in these sub-divisions must co-operate to form a primary force to counterattack the enemy, or the area from which he came, while a secondary force harasses and hinders him.

After defeating the enemy in any area, we must take advantage of the period he requires for reorganization to press home our attacks. we must not attack an objective we are not certain of winning. We must confine our operations to relatively small areas and destroy the enemy and traitors in those places.

When the inhabitants have been inspired, new volunteers accepted trained, equipped, and organized, our operations may be extended to include cities and lines of communication not strongly held. We may hold these at least for temporary (if not for permanent) periods. All these are our duties in offensive strategy. Their object is to lengthen the period that the enemy must remain on the defensive. Then our military activities and our organization work among the masses of the people must be zealously expanded; and with equal zeal, the strength of the enemy attacked and diminished. It is of great importance that guerrilla units be rested and instructed. During such times as the enemy is on the defensive, the troops may get some rest and instruction may be carried out.

The development of mobile warfare is not only possible but essential. This is the case because our current war is a desperate and protracted struggle. If China were able to conquer the Japanese bandits speedily and to recover her lost territories, there would there would be no question of long-term war on a national scale. Hence there would no question of the relation of guerrilla hostilities into mobile warfare of an orthodox nature, both the quantity and quality of guerrilla must be improved. Primarily, more men must join the armies; then the quality of equipment and standards of training must be improved. Political training must be emphasized and our organization, the technique of handling our weapons, our tactics — all must be improved. Our internal discipline must be strengthened. The soldiers must be educated politically. There must be a gradual change from guerrilla formations to orthodox regimental organization. The necessary bureaus and staffs, both political and military, must be provided. At the same time, attention must be paid to the creation of suitable supply, medical, and hygiene units. The standards of equipment must be raised and types of weapons increased. Communication equipment must not be forgotten. Orthodox standards of discipline must be established.

Because guerrilla formations act independently and because they are the most elementary of armed formations, command cannot be too highly centralized. If it were, guerilla action would be too limited in scope. At the same time, guerrilla activities, to be most effective, must be co-ordinated, not only in so far as they themselves are concerned, but additionally with regular troops operating in the same areas. This co-ordination is a function of the war zone commander and his staff.

In guerrilla base areas, the command must be centralized for strategical purposes and decentralized for tactical purposes. Centralized strategical command takes care of the general management of all guerrilla units, their co-ordination within war zones, and the general policy regarding guerrilla base areas. Beyond this, centralization of command will result in interference with subordinate units, as, naturally, the tactics to apply to concrete situations can be determined only as these various situations arise. This is true in orthodox warfare when communications between lower and higher echelons break down. In a word, proper guerrilla policy will provide for unified strategy and independent activity.

Each guerrilla area is divided into districts and these in turn are divided into sub-districts. Each sub-division has its appointed commander, and while general plans are made by higher commanders, the nature of actions is determined by inferior commanders. The former may suggest the nature of the action to be taken but cannot define it. Thus inferior groups heave more or less complete local control.

TABLE — I

ORGANIZATION OF AN
INDEPENDENT GUERRILLA COMPANY

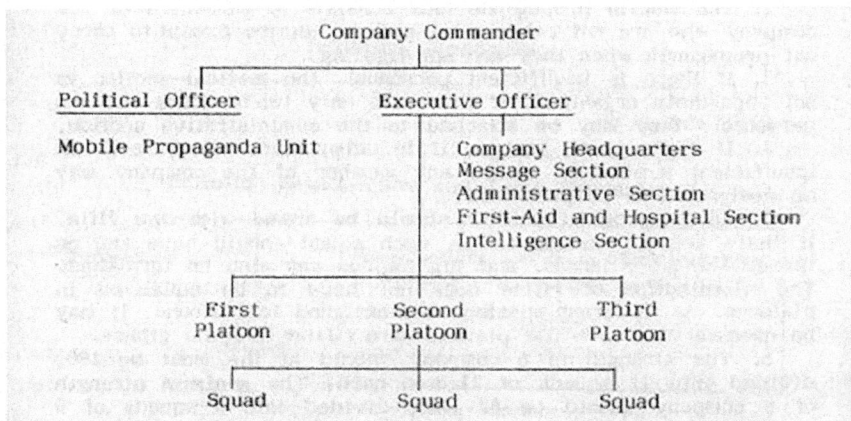

```
                        Company Commander
        ┌───────────────────────┴──────────────────────┐
   Political Officer                        Executive Officer

   Mobile Propaganda Unit                  Company Headquarters
                                           Message Section
                                           Administrative Section
                                           First-Aid and Hospital Section
                                           Intelligence Section
        ┌───────────────────────┼──────────────────────┐
      First                  Second                   Third
      Platoon                Platoon                  Platoon
        │                       │                       │
      Squad                   Squad                    Squad
```

TABLE OF ORGANIZATION,
GUERRILLA COMPANY

RANK	PERSONNEL	ARM
Company Leader	1	Pistol
Political Officer	1	Pistol
Executive Officer	1	Pistol
Company Headquarters		
Message Section Chief	1	
Signal	1	
Administrative Section Chief	1	Rifle
Public Relations	3	Rifle
Duty Personnel	2	
Barber	1	
Cooks	10	
Medical Section Chief	1	
Assistant	1	
First Aid and Nursing	4	
Intelligence Section Chief	1	Rifle
Intelligence	9	Rifle
Platoon Leaders	3	Rifle
Squad Leaders	9	Rifle
Nine Squads (8 each)	72	Rifle
TOTAL	122	3 Pistols 98 Rifles

NOTES

1. Each squad consists of from 9 to 11 men. In case men or arms are not sufficient, the third platoon may be dispensed with or one squad organized as company headquarters.

2. The mobile propaganda unit consists of members of the Company who are not relieved of primary duties except to carry out propaganda when they are not fighting.

3. If there is insufficient personnel, the medical section is not separately organized. If there are only two or three medical personnel, they may be attached to the administrative section.

4. If there is no barber, it is unimportant. If there is an insufficient number of cooks, any member of the company may be designated to prepare food.

5. Each combatant soldier should be armed with the rifle. If there are not enough rifles, each squad should have two or three. Shotguns, lances, and big swords can also be furnished. The distribution of rifles does not have to be equalized in platoons . As different missions are assigned to platoons, it may be necessary to give one platoon more riffles than the others.

6. The strength of a company should at the most be 180, divided into 12 squads of 11 men each. The minimum strength of a company should be 82 men, divided into 6 squads of 9 men each.

TABLE 2

**ORGANIZATION OF
AN INDEPENDENT GUERRILLA BATTALION**

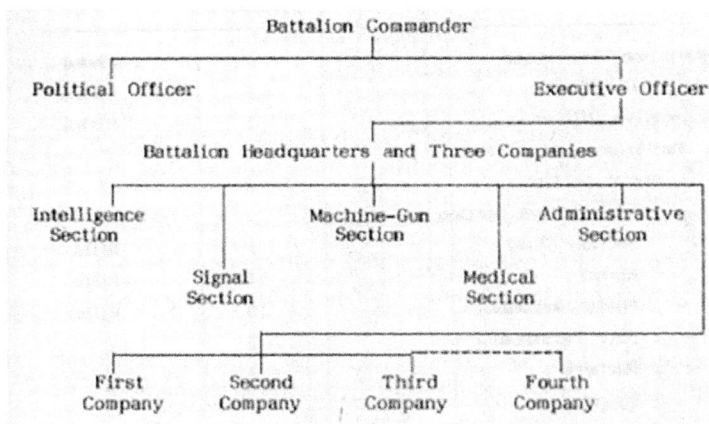

NOTES

1. Total headquarters of an independent guerrilla battalion may vary from a minimum of 46 to a maximum of 110.

2. When there are 4 companies to a battalion, regimental organization should be used.

3. Machine-gun squads may be heavy or light. A light machine-gun squad has from 5 to 7 men. A heavy machine-gun squad has from 7 to 9 men.

4. The intelligence section is organized in from 2 to 4 squads, at least one of which is made up of plain-clothed men. If horses are available, one squad should be mounted.

5. If no men are available for stretcher-bearers, omit them and use the cooks or ask aid from the people.

6. Each company must have at least 25 rifles. The remaining weapons may be fowling -pieces, etc., big swords, or locally made shotguns.

TABLE OF ORGANIZATION, GUERRILLA BATTALION (INDEPENDENT)

RANK	PERSONNEL	ARM
Battalion Commander	1	Pistol
Political Officer	1	Pistol
Executive Officer	1	Pistol
Battalion Headquarters		
Signal Section	2	
Administrative Section		
Section Chief	1	Rifle
Runner	1	Rifle
Public Relations	10	Rifle
Duty Personnel	2	
Barbers	3	
Supply	1	
Cooks	10	
Medical Section		
Medical Officer	1	
Stretcher-bearers	6	
Nursing	4	
Intelligence Section		
Section Chief	1	Pistol
Intelligence	30	Pistol
Machine-gun Section	As Available	As Available
Total, Headquarters	75	34 Pistols 12 Rifles
Three Companies (122 each)	366	9 Pistols 294 Rifles
TOTAL	441	43 Pistols 306 Rifles

TABLE 3

ORGANIZATION OF
AN INDEPENDENT GUERRILLA REGIMENT

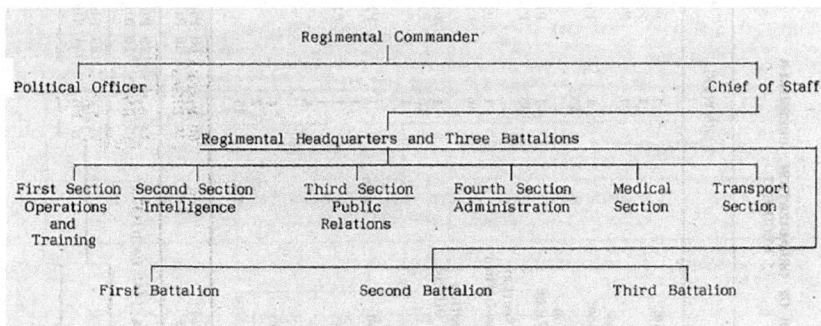

				Regimental Commander			
Political Officer							Chief of Staff
			Regimental Headquarters and Three Battalions				
First Section Operations and Training	Second Section Intelligence		Third Section Public Relations	Fourth Section Administration	Medical Section	Transport Section
	First Battalion			Second Battalion		Third Battalion	

NOTES

1. See Tables 1 and 2 for company and battalion organization.

2. Battalions and companies have no transport sections.

3. The hand weapon may be either revolver or pistol. Of these, each regiment should have more than 100.

TABLE OF ORGANIZATION,
GUERRILLA REGIMENT

RANK	PERSONNE	ARM
Regimental Commander	1	Pistol
Political Officer	1	Pistol
Chief of Stuff	1	Pistol
Operations Section		
Operations Officer	1	Pistol
Clerks	15	
Intelligence Section		
Intelligence Officer	1	Pistol
Personnel	36	Pistols
Public-Relations Section		
Public-Relations Officer	1	Pistol
Personnel	36	Rifles
Administrative Section		
Administrative Officer	1	Pistol
Clerks	15	Pistols
Runner	1	
Transport Section		
Chief of Section	1	Pistol
Finance	1	
Traffic Manager	1	Pistol
Supply	1	
Drivers	5	
Medical Section		
Chief of Section	1	
Doctors	2	
Nurses	15	
Total, Regimental Headquarters	137	60 Pistols 36 Rifles
Three Battalions (441 each)	1323	129 Pistols 918 Rifles
TOTAL	1460	189 Pistols 954 Rifles

Independent Guerrilla Brigade

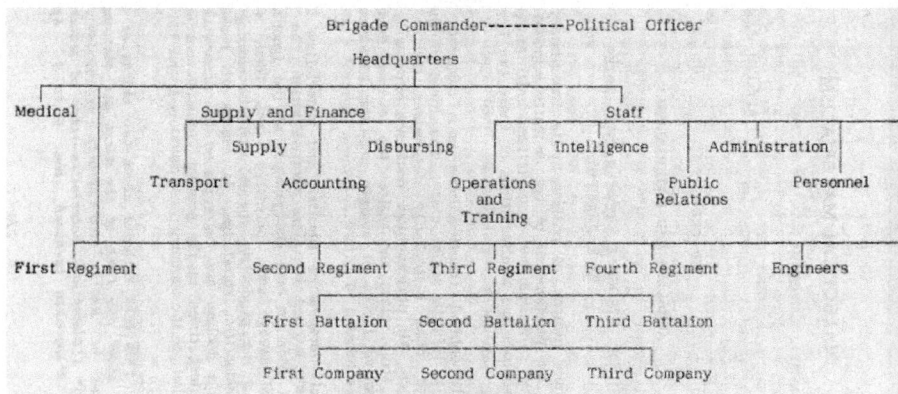

INDEPENDENT GUERRILLA BRIGADE
(OR DIVISION)

Brigade Commander---------Political Officer

Headquarters

Medical	Supply and Finance			Staff	
	Supply	Disbursing		Intelligence	Administration
Transport	Accounting		Operations and Training	Public Relations	Personnel

First Regiment	Second Regiment	Third Regiment	Fourth Regiment	Engineers
	First Battalion	Second Battalion	Third Battalion	
	First Company	Second Company	Third Company	

TO HSU TEH-LI

February 1937

[(1877-1968) went to Japan and joined Sun Yat-sen's Alliance Society (T'ung Meng Hui) in 1912. Hsu visited France, Germany and Belgium in 1920-3 as a student and a worker also Russia to study at the Sun Yat-sen University in Moscow in 1928-30. At the age of 57 he joined the Long March.]

Old Comrade Hsu,

You were my teacher twenty years ago; you are still my teacher; you will continue to be my teacher in future. When the revolution failed and many members left the party, even defecting to the enemy, you joined [the party] in the autumn of 1927 and adopted an extremely active attitude. From then until now you have shown through a long period of bitter struggle greater positiveness, less fear of difficulty and more humility in learning new things than many younger members of the party. 'Age', 'declining physical and mental abilities', and 'hardships and obstacles' have all surrendered to you, in spite of the fact that they have served as excuses for the timidity of many people. You know a great deal but always feel a deficiency in your knowledge, whereas many 'half-buckets of water' [people of superficial knowledge] make a lot of noise. What you think is what you say or what you do, whereas other people hide filthy things in a corner of their minds. You enjoy being with the masses all the time, whereas some others enjoy being without the masses. You are always a model of obedience to the party and its revolutionary discipline, whereas some others regard the discipline as restraint for others but not for themselves. For you, it is 'revolution first', 'work first', and 'other people first', whereas for some others it is 'limelight first', 'rest first', and 'oneself first'. You always pick the most difficult things to do, never avoiding your responsibilities, whereas some others choose easy work to do, always shunning responsibilities. In all these respects, I admire you and willing to continue to learn from you. I also hope that other party members will learn from you. I write this congratulatory letter to you on your sixtieth birthday with my wishes that you will enjoy good health and a long life and continue to be a model for all the members of our revolutionary party and all the people.

Revolutionary Salute !

THE TASKS OF THE CHINESE COMMUNIST PARTY IN THE PERIOD OF RESISTANCE TO JAPAN

May 3, 1937

[Comrade Mao Tse-tung delivered this report at the National Conference of the Communist Party of China, held in Yenan in May 1937.]

THE PRESENT STAGE OF DEVELOPMENT OF CHINA'S EXTERNAL AND INTERNAL CONTRADICTIONS

1. As the contradiction between China and Japan has become the principal one and China's internal contradictions have dropped into a secondary and subordinate place, changes have occurred in China's international relations and internal class relations, giving rise to a new stage of development in the current situation.

2. China has long been in the grip of two acute and basic contradictions, the contradiction between China and imperialism and the contradiction between feudalism and the masses of the people. In 1927 the bourgeoisie, represented by the Kuomintang, betrayed the revolution and sold China's

national interests to imperialism, thus creating a situation in which the state power of the workers and peasants stood in sharp antagonism to that of the Kuomintang, and, of necessity, the task of the national and democratic revolution devolved upon the Chinese Communist Party alone.

3. Since the Incident of September 18, 1931 and especially since the Northern China Incident of 1935, [1] the following changes have taken place in these contradictions:

(1) The contradiction between China and imperialism in general has given way to the particularly salient and sharp contradiction between China and Japanese imperialism. Japanese imperialism is carrying out a policy of total conquest of China. Consequently, the contradictions between China and certain other imperialist powers have been relegated to a secondary position, while the rift between these powers and Japan has been widened. Consequently also, the Chinese Communist Party and the Chinese people are faced with the task of linking China's anti-Japanese national united front with the world peace front. This means that China should not only unite with the Soviet Union, which has been the consistently good friend of the Chinese people, but as far as possible should work for joint opposition to Japanese imperialism with those imperialist countries which, at the present time, are willing to maintain peace and are against new wars of aggression. The aim of our united front must be resistance to Japan, and not simultaneous opposition to all the imperialist powers.

(2) The contradiction between China and Japan has changed internal class relations within China and has confronted the bourgeoisie and even the warlords with the question of survival, so that they and their political parties have been undergoing a gradual change in their political attitude. This has placed the task of establishing an anti-Japanese national united front before the Chinese Communist Party and the Chinese people. Our united front should include the bourgeoisie and all who agree to the defence of the motherland, it should represent national solidarity against the foreign foe. This task not only must, but can, be fulfilled.

(3) The contradiction between China and Japan has changed matters for the masses throughout the country (the proletariat, the peasantry and the urban petty bourgeoisie) and for the Communist Party, and it has changed the Party's policy. More and more people have risen to fight for national salvation. The policy proclaimed by the Communist Party after the September 18th Incident was to conclude agreements with those sections of the Kuomintang which were willing to co-operate with us for resistance,

subject to three conditions (stop attacking the revolutionary base areas, guarantee the freedoms and rights of the people, arm the people), and it has developed into a policy of establishing an anti-Japanese united front of the whole nation. This is the reason for the following steps taken by our Party: in 1935, the August declaration [2] and the December resolution; [3] in 1936, the abandonment of the "anti-Chiang Kai-shek" slogan in May, [4] the letter to the Kuomintang in August, [5] the resolution on the democratic republic in September, [6] and the insistence on a peaceful settlement of the Sian Incident in December; and in 1937, the February telegram to the Third Plenary Session of the Central Executive Committee of the Kuomintang. [7]

(4) Because of the contradiction between China and Japan, a change has also occurred in the Chinese warlord regimes and the civil wars among them, which are the product of the imperialist policy of spheres of influence and of China's semi-colonial economic conditions. Japanese imperialism fosters such separate regimes and civil wars for the purpose of facilitating exclusive Japanese domination of China. Certain other imperialist powers are temporarily in favour of unity and peace in China in their own interests. The Chinese Communist Party and the Chinese people on their part are exerting their utmost efforts against civil wars and splits and for peace and unity.

(5) In terms of relative political importance the development of the national contradiction between China and Japan has demoted the domestic contradictions between classes and between political groupings to a secondary and subordinate place. But they still exist and have by no means diminished or disappeared. The same is true of the contradictions between China and the imperialist powers other than Japan. Therefore, the Chinese Communist Party and the Chinese people are faced with the following task--to make the appropriate adjustments with regard to those internal and external contradictions which can and must be adjusted at present so as to fit in with the general task of unity against Japan. This is the reason for the Chinese Communist Party's policies of peace and unity, democracy, bettering the life of the people and negotiations with foreign countries that are opposed to Japan.

4. The first stage of the new period in the Chinese revolution began on December 9, 1935 and ended when the Kuomintang's Central Executive Committee held its Third Plenary Session in February 1937. The major events in this stage were the movements for national salvation among the students and cultural and press circles; the Red Army's entry into the Northwest; the Communist Party's work of propaganda and organization

for its anti-Japanese national united front policy; the anti-Japanese strikes in Shanghai and Tsingtao; [8] the relative stiffening of British policy towards Japan; [9] the Kwangtung-Kwangsi Incident ; [10] the resistance in Suiyuan and the movement in its support; [11] Nanking's somewhat firmer attitude in the Sino-Japanese negotiations; [12] the Sian Incident; and finally, the Third Plenary Session of the Central Executive Committee of the Kuomintang in Nanking. [13] These events all centred on the basic contradiction, which is the antagonism between China and Japan; they all centred directly on the historical need for an anti-Japanese national united front.

The basic task of the revolution at this stage was to struggle for internal peace and stop the internal armed conflicts, so that there could be unity against Japan. During this stage the Communist Party issued its call, "Stop the civil war and unite against Japan", a call which in the main has been put into effect, and thereby created the primary prerequisite for the actual establishment of an anti-Japanese national united front.

5. Owing to the presence of the pro-Japanese group inside the Kuomintang, it made no definite or thoroughgoing change in its policy at the Third Plenary Session of its Central Executive Committee and did not concretely solve any problem. However, owing to the pressure of the people and to developments in its own ranks, the Kuomintang had to begin to change its wrong policy of the previous ten years, that is, it had to turn away from the policy of civil war, dictatorship and non-resistance to Japan and to move in the direction of peace, democracy and resistance to Japan, and it had to begin accepting the policy of an anti-Japanese national united front; this initial change revealed itself at the Third Plenary Session of its Central Executive Committee. From now on the demand must be for a thorough change in Kuomintang policy. In order to attain this goal our Party and the people throughout the country must develop the movement for resistance to Japan and for democracy still more extensively, must go a step further in criticizing the Kuomintang, pushing it into action and keeping up the pressure, must unite with all those within the Kuomintang who stand for peace, democracy and resistance to Japan, and must help the hesitant waverers forward and throw out the pro-Japanese elements.

6. The present stage is the second one in the new period. Both the previous and present stages are stages of transition towards nationwide armed resistance to Japan. If in the previous stage the principal task was the fight for peace, then in the present stage the principal task is the fight for democracy. It must be understood that just as a genuine and solid anti-Japanese national united front cannot be established without internal

peace, so it cannot be established without internal democracy. Hence at the present stage of development the fight for democracy is the central link in the revolutionary task. If we fail to see the importance of democracy clearly and slacken our fight for it, we shall be unable to establish a genuine and solid anti-Japanese national united front.

THE STRUGGLE FOR DEMOCRACY AND FREEDOM

7. Japanese imperialism is now intensifying its preparations for the invasion of China south of the Great Wall. In concert with the intensified preparations of Hitler and Mussolini for predatory war in the West, Japan is exerting every ounce of energy in the East in order to prepare the ground, according to a definite plan, for the subjugation of China at a single stroke--she is creating the military, political, economic and ideological conditions at home and the diplomatic conditions internationally, and fostering the pro-Japanese forces in China. Japan's propaganda about "Sino-Japanese collaboration" and a certain relaxation in her diplomatic measures stem precisely from the tactical needs of her policy of aggression on the eve of war. China is now approaching the critical moment of decision between survival and extinction and must rush preparations for resisting Japan and saving the nation. We are certainly not against preparation; what we are against is the doctrine of protracted preparation and the frivolous, dissipated and gluttonous life of civil and military officialdom which imperils the nation; such things actually help the enemy and must be quickly swept away.

8. Political, military, economic and educational preparations for national defence are all necessary for armed resistance to save the nation, and none of them should be delayed for a moment. But the key that will ensure victory for our armed resistance is the winning of political democracy and freedom. Armed resistance requires domestic peace and unity, but the peace already won cannot be consolidated and internal unity cannot be strengthened without democracy and freedom. Armed resistance requires the mobilization of the people, but there is no way of mobilizing them without democracy and freedom. Unless peace and unity are consolidated, unless the people are mobilized, our armed resistance will meet the same fate as Abyssinia's. Abyssinia was defeated mainly because her feudal regime could not achieve solid internal unity and rouse the initiative of her people. Without democracy, a genuine and solid national united front against Japan cannot be established in China and its goals cannot be attained.

9. China must at once start democratic changes in the two following respects. First, in the matter of the political system, the reactionary

Kuomintang dictatorship of one party and one class must be changed into a democratic government based on the co-operation of all parties and all classes. In this respect, a start should be made by changing the undemocratic procedures for electing and convening the national assembly, and by holding democratic elections to the assembly and ensuring freedom in the conduct of its meetings, after which it will be necessary to go on to framing and adopting a truly democratic constitution, convening a truly democratic parliament, and electing a genuinely democratic government that will carry out genuinely democratic policies. Only thus can internal peace be truly consolidated, internal armed hostilities ended and internal unity strengthened, enabling the whole nation to unite and resist the foreign foe. It is possible that Japanese imperialism will attack us before the changes are completed. Therefore, in order to be able to resist and thoroughly crush the Japanese attack when it comes, we must quickly go ahead with the reforms and be prepared to accomplish them fully in the course of our armed resistance. The people of the whole country and the patriots of all parties should throw off their former indifference towards the question of a national assembly and a constitution, and should concentrate on the movement for a national assembly and a constitution, a movement that is important for national defence; they should subject the Kuomintang, the party in power, to severe criticism, and press and impel it to give up its one-party, one-class dictatorship and act according to the opinions of the people. In the next few months of this year, a broad democratic movement must be set going throughout the country, with the immediate objective of completely democratizing the national assembly and the constitution. The second matter concerns freedom of speech, assembly and association for the people. Without such freedom, it will be impossible to carry out the democratic reconstruction of the political system, mobilize the people for the war of resistance and victoriously defend the motherland and recover the lost territories. In the next few months the nation-wide democratic movement should strive for at least a minimal achievement of such freedoms, which must include the release of political prisoners, the removal of the ban on political parties, etc. Democratic reconstruction of the political system and freedom and rights for the people constitute an important part of the programme of the anti-Japanese national united front; at the same time they are prerequisites for the establishment of a genuine and solid anti-Japanese national united front.

10. Our enemies--the Japanese imperialists, the Chinese traitors, the pro-Japanese elements and the Trotskyites--have been doing their utmost to wreck every move for peace and unity, democracy and freedom in China and for armed resistance to Japan. In the past, while we were fighting

strenuously for peace and unity, they were doing all they could to foment civil war and splits. At present and in the near future, while we fight strenuously for democracy and freedom, they will no doubt resort to their wrecking again. Their general objective is to thwart us in our task of armed resistance in defence of the motherland and to accomplish their aggressive plan for subjugating China. From now on, in the struggle for democracy and freedom, we must not only exert ourselves in propaganda, agitation and criticism directed towards the Kuomintang die-hards and the backward sections of the people, but must also fully expose and firmly combat the intrigues of the Japanese imperialists and of the pro-Japanese elements and Trotskyites who serve as their running dogs in the invasion of China.

11. For the sake of internal peace, democracy and armed resistance and for the sake of establishing the anti-Japanese national united front, the Chinese Communist Party has made the following four pledges in its telegram to the Third Plenary Session of the Central Executive Committee of the Kuomintang:

(1) the Communist-led government in the Shensi-Kansu-Ningsia revolutionary base area will be renamed the Government of the Special Region of the Republic of China and the Red Army will be redesignated as part of the National Revolutionary Army, and they will come under the direction of the Central Government in Nanking and its Military Council respectively;

(2) a thoroughly democratic system will be applied in the areas under the Government of the Special Region;

(3) the policy of overthrowing the Kuomintang by armed force will be discontinued; and

(4) the confiscation of the land of the landlords will be discontinued.

These pledges are necessary as well as permissible. For only thus can we transform the state of antagonism between the two different regimes within the country and achieve unity for common action against the enemy, in line with the changes in the relative political importance of China's external and internal contradictions. These are principled and conditional concessions, made with the aim of obtaining in return what the whole nation needs--peace, democracy and armed resistance. Moreover, the concessions have limits. The preservation of the Communist Party's leadership over the Special Region and in the Red Army, and the preservation of the Communist Party's independence and freedom of criticism in its relations with the Kuomintang--these are the limits beyond which it is impermissible to go. Concessions mean concessions by both parties: the Kuomintang abandons the policy of civil war, dictatorship and non-resistance to the foreign foe, and the Communist Party abandons the policy of maintaining antagonism between the two regimes. We exchange the latter for the former and resume our co-operation with the Kuomintang to fight for national salvation. To describe this as capitulation by the Communist Party is nothing but Ah Q-ism [14] or malicious slander.

12. Does the Communist Party agree with the Three People's Principles? Our answer is, Yes, we do. [15] The Three People's Principles have undergone changes in the course of their history. The revolutionary Three People's Principles of Dr. Sun Yat-sen won the people's confidence and became the banner of the victorious revolution of 1924-27 because they were resolutely applied as a result of his co-operation with the Communist Party. In 1927, however, the Kuomintang turned on the Communist Party (the party purge [16] and the anti-Communist war) and pursued an opposite policy, bringing the revolution down in defeat and endangering the nation; consequently the people lost confidence in the Three People's Principles. Now that there is an extremely grave national crisis and the Kuomintang cannot continue to rule in the same old way, the people of the whole country and the patriots within the Kuomintang are urgently demanding co-operation between the two parties. Consequently, it is completely in keeping with the historical requirements of the Chinese revolution that the essence of the Three People's Principles should be revived and restored, and that the two parties should resume their co-operation, in accordance with the Principle of Nationalism, or the struggle for national independence and liberation, the Principle of Democracy, or the attainment of internal democracy and freedom, and the Principle of People's Livelihood, or the promotion of the people's welfare, and they should lead the people to put these principles resolutely into practice. This ought to be clearly grasped by every member of the Communist Party. Communists will never abandon their ideal of socialism and communism, which they will attain by going through the stage of the bourgeois-democratic revolution. The Chinese Communist Party has its own political and economic programme. Its maximum programme is socialism and communism, which is different from the Three People's Principles. Even its programme for the period of the democratic revolution is more thoroughgoing than that of any other party in China. But the Communist Party's programme for the democratic revolution and the programme of the Three People's Principles as proclaimed by the Kuomintang's First National Congress are basically not in conflict. Therefore, far from rejecting

76

the Three People's Principles, we are ready staunchly to put them into practice; moreover, we ask the Kuomintang to implement them together with us, and we call upon the whole nation to put them into effect. We hold that the Communist Party, the Kuomintang and the people of the whole country should unite and fight for these three great objectives of national independence, democracy and freedom, and the people's livelihood.

13. Was our past slogan of a workers' and peasants' democratic republic wrong? No, it was not. Since the bourgeoisie, and particularly the big bourgeoisie, withdrew from the revolution, became retainers of imperialism and the feudal forces and turned into enemies of the people, the only remaining motive forces of the revolution were the proletariat, the peasantry and the urban petty bourgeoisie, and the only remaining revolutionary party was the Communist Party, which, as such, inevitably had to shoulder the responsibility for organizing the revolution. The Communist Party alone continued to hold aloft the banner of revolution, preserved the revolutionary tradition, put forward the slogan of a workers' and peasants' democratic republic and fought hard for it for many years. This slogan was not in conflict with the task of bourgeois-democratic revolution but signified that we were resolutely carrying out this task. Not a single item of policy adopted in our actual struggle was out of keeping with this task. Our policy, including the confiscation of the land of the landlords and the enforcement of the eight-hour working day, never went beyond the bounds of capitalist private ownership; our policy was not to put socialism in practice then. What will be the composition of the new democratic republic? It will consist of the proletariat, the peasantry, the urban petty bourgeoisie, the bourgeoisie, and all those in the country who agree with the national and democratic revolution; it will be the alliance of these classes in the national and democratic revolution. The salient feature here is the inclusion of the bourgeoisie; the reason is that in the present circumstances there is a possibility that the bourgeoisie will once again co-operate with us and join in the resistance to Japan, and the party of the proletariat should therefore not repel but welcome them and revive its alliance with them for the common struggle, so as to help the Chinese revolution forward. In order to end the internal armed conflict, the Communist Party is willing to discontinue the policy of forcible confiscation of the land of the landlords and is prepared to solve the land problem by legislative and other appropriate means in the course of building the new democratic republic. The first question to be settled is whether China's land will be owned by the Japanese or by the Chinese. Since the solution of the land problem of the peasants is predicated on the defence of China, it is absolutely necessary for us to turn from the method of forcible

confiscation to appropriate new methods.

It was correct to put forward the slogan of a workers' and peasants' democratic republic in the past, and it is correct to drop it today.

14. To establish the national united front for joint resistance to the enemy, it is necessary properly to resolve certain internal contradictions, the principle here being that the solution should help strengthen and extend the anti-Japanese national united front and not weaken or narrow it. During the stage of the democratic revolution, it is impossible to avoid contradictions and struggles between classes, parties and political groupings, but it is both possible and essential to put an end to such struggles as are detrimental to unity and to resisting Japan (the civil war, the antagonistic conflict between the political parties, provincial separatism, feudal political and economic oppression on the one hand, and the policy of insurrection and excessive economic demands harmful to the resistance on the other, etc.), and to continue such struggles as benefit unity and resistance to Japan (for freedom of criticism, for the independence of the political parties, for the improvement of the political and economic life of the people, etc.).

15. Within the over-all task of fighting for an anti-Japanese national united front and a unified democratic republic, the tasks of the Red Army and the anti-Japanese base area are:

(1) To suit the circumstances of war against Japan, the Red Army should immediately be reorganized into the National Revolutionary Army and become a model army in that war by raising the level of its military, political and cultural education.

(2) Our base area should become a component part of the state, apply its democratic system under the new conditions, reorganize its peace preservation corps, clear out traitors and saboteurs, and become a region that is a model of resistance and democracy.

(3) Essential economic construction should be conducted in this area and the livelihood of the people should be improved.

(4) Essential cultural work should be carried out.

OUR RESPONSIBILITY TO LEAD

16. It is a law confirmed by Chinese history that the Chinese bourgeoisie, which may participate in fighting imperialism and feudalism in certain

historical circumstances, vacillates and turns traitor in others, because of its economic and political flabbiness. Thus it is history's verdict that China's bourgeois-democratic revolution against imperialism and feudalism is a task that can be completed, not under the leadership of the bourgeoisie, but only under that of the proletariat. What is more, it is possible to overcome the bourgeoisie's inherent vacillation and lack of thoroughness and to prevent the miscarriage of the revolution only by bringing the perseverance and thoroughness of the proletariat in the democratic revolution into full play. Is the proletariat to follow the bourgeoisie, or is the bourgeoisie to follow the proletariat? This question of responsibility for leadership in the Chinese revolution is the linchpin upon which the success or failure of the revolution depends. The experience of 1924-27 shows how the revolution forged ahead when the bourgeoisie followed the political leadership of the proletariat and met defeat when the proletariat became the political tail of the bourgeoisie through the fault of the Communist Party. [17] This piece of history should not be allowed to repeat itself. In the present circumstances, without the political leadership of the proletariat and its party it is impossible to establish an anti-Japanese national united front, to attain the objectives of peace, democracy and armed resistance and to defend the motherland, and impossible to set up a unified democratic republic. Today the bourgeoisie, represented by the Kuomintang, is still very passive and conservative, and the proof of this is its long hesitation about accepting the anti-Japanese national united front initiated by the Communist Party. This situation increases the responsibility of the proletariat and its party for giving political leadership. To function as the general staff in resisting Japan and saving the nation is a responsibility the Communist Party cannot relinquish, an obligation it cannot decline.

17. How does the proletariat give political leadership through its party to all the revolutionary classes in the country? First, by putting forward basic political slogans that accord with the course of historical development and by putting forward slogans of action for each stage of development and each major turn of events in order to translate these political slogans into reality. For instance, we have put forward the basic slogans for "an anti-Japanese national united front" and for "a unified democratic republic", but we have also put forward the slogans, "end the civil war", "fight for democracy" and "carry out armed resistance", as specific objectives for concerted action by the entire nation; without such specific objectives political leadership is out of the question. Second, the proletariat, and especially its vanguard the Communist Party, should set an example through its boundless enthusiasm and loyalty in achieving the specific objectives when the whole country goes into action for them. In the fight to fulfil all the tasks of the anti-Japanese national united front and the

democratic republic, Communists should be the most far-sighted, the most self-sacrificing, the most resolute, and the least prejudiced in sizing up situations, and should rely on the majority of the masses and win their support. Third, the Communist Party should establish proper relations with its allies and develop and consolidate its alliance with them, while adhering to the principle of never relinquishing its defined political objectives. Fourth, it should expand the ranks of the Communist Party and maintain its ideological unity and strict discipline; It is by doing all these things that the Communist Party gives effect to its political leadership of the people throughout China. They constitute the foundation for guaranteeing our political leadership and for ensuring that the revolution will win complete victory and not be disrupted by the vacillations of our allies.

18. When internal peace is achieved and co-operation is established between the two parties, changes will have to be made in the forms of struggle, organization and work which we adopted when the line was one of maintaining a regime antagonistic to that of the Kuomintang. They will mainly be changes from military to peaceful forms and from illegal to legal forms. It will not be easy to make these changes and we shall have to learn afresh. The retraining of our cadres thus becomes a key link.

19. Many comrades have been asking questions about the nature of the democratic republic and its future. Our answer is: as to its class nature, the republic will be an alliance of all revolutionary classes, and as to its future, it may move towards socialism. Our democratic republic is to be established in the course of national armed resistance under the leadership of the proletariat and in the new international environment (with socialism victorious in the Soviet Union and the approach of a new period of world revolution). Therefore, though it will still be a bourgeois-democratic state socially and economically, yet it will be different from the general run of bourgeois republics because, in concrete political terms, it will have to be a state based on the alliance of the working class, the peasantry, the petty bourgeoisie and the bourgeoisie. Thus, as to the future of the democratic republic, though it may move in a capitalist direction, the possibility also exists that it will turn towards socialism, and the party of the Chinese proletariat should struggle hard for the latter prospect.

20. The fight against closed-doorism and adventurism and also against tailism is essential to the accomplishment of the Party's tasks. In the mass movements our Party has a traditional tendency towards rank closed-doorism, haughty sectarianism, and adventurism; this ugly tendency hinders the Party in establishing an anti-Japanese national united front and

winning over the majority of the masses. It is absolutely necessary to wipe out this tendency in each and every field of work. What we ask is: rely on the majority and take the whole situation into account. There must be no revival of the Chen Tu-hsiu type of tailism, which is a reflection of bourgeois reformism in the ranks of the proletariat. To debase the class stand of the Party, to obscure its distinctive features, to sacrifice the interests of the workers and peasants to suit the needs of bourgeois reformism, is sure to lead the revolution to defeat. What we ask is: carry out firm revolutionary policies and strive for complete victory in the bourgeois-democratic revolution. To overcome the undesirable tendencies we have described, it is absolutely necessary to raise the Marxist-Leninist theoretical level of the whole Party, for Marxism-Leninism alone is the compass which can guide the Chinese revolution to victory.

NOTES

1. The Northern China Incident took place in 1935 when the Japanese carried on aggression against northern China and the Kuomintang government headed by Chiang Kai-shek betrayed our sovereignty and humiliated our nation. In May of that year, the Japanese demanded that the Kuomintang government grant them administrative authority over northern China, and in June Ho Ying-chin the Kuomintang government's representative there, submitted and signed an agreement with Yoshijiro Umezu, commander of the invading forces in northern China which became known as the "Ho-Umezu Agreement". By its terms China forfeited much of her sovereignty in the provinces of Hopei and Chahar. In October at the instigation of the Japanese invaders, some Chinese traitors staged a revolt in Hsiangho, Hopei Province, and seized the county town. In November, a number of Chinese traitors were put up by the Japanese invaders to start a self-styled movement of autonomy in the five provinces of northern China, and a puppet "Anti-Communist Autonomous Administration" was established in eastern Hopei To meet the Japanese demand for "special administration for northern China" the Kuomintang government appointed Sung Cheh-yuan and others to form a "Political Council for Hopei and Chahar".

2. This declaration was issued by the Chinese Communist Party on August 1, 1935. Its main points are contained in the following extracts:

"At this moment when our country and our people are threatened with imminent destruction, the Communist Party once again appeals to all fellow countrymen: whatever the past or present differences of political opinion and of interests among the political parties, whatever the differences of view and of interests among our countrymen in their various walks of life, whatever the past or present hostilities between the various armies, we should truly awaken to the realization that 'brothers quarreling at home, join forces against attacks from without' and, first and foremost, we should stop the civil war so as to concentrate the nation's resources (manpower, material and financial resources, and the armed forces) on the fight for the sacred cause of resisting Japan and saving the nation. Once again the Communist Party solemnly declares if the Kuomintang troops cease their attacks on the Red Army and if any units carry out resistance to Japan, then the Red Army, regardless of any old feuds or present conflicts or differences on domestic issues, will not only immediately cease its hostile actions against these units, but willingly work closely with them to save the nation."

"The Communist Party is willing to initiate a national defence government of this kind; for the joint formation of such a national defence government it is ready to hold immediate talks with all those willing to join the cause of resisting Japan and saving the nation--all political parties, all organizations (trade unions, peasant associations, student unions, chambers of commerce educational associations, journalists' societies, associations of teachers and other staff of schools, fellow-townsmen's associations, the Chih Kung Tang the Association for National Armed Self-Defence, the Anti-Japanese Association the Association for National Salvation, etc.), all prominent public figures, scholars and statesmen and all local military and administrative bodies The national defence government emerging out of these negotiations should be a provisional organ of leadership for saving the nation from subjugation and ensuring its survival. It should endeavour to convene a delegate body truly representative of all our countrymen (with delegates democratically elected by all the various circles of workers, peasants, soldiers, government personnel, businessmen and students, by all parties and all organizations willing to resist Japan and save the nation, and by all overseas Chinese and all the nationalities within China's boundaries) to discuss all problems relating to armed resistance and national salvation in more specific terms. The Communist Party will do its very best to help convene such an assembly of representatives of the people and to carry out all its decisions."

"An anti-Japanese united army should be formed of all troops willing to fight Japan. A single general headquarters of this army should be set up under the leadership of the national defence government. The question of whether this headquarters should be composed of representatives elected by the officers and men of the various anti-Japanese army units or be formed in some other way should be decided by the representatives of all circles and by the will of the people. The Red Army will unreservedly be the first to join this united army and fulfil its duty in resisting Japan and saving the nation. To enable the national defence government and the anti-Japanese united army effectively to discharge their immense responsibilities for national defence and for resisting Japan, the Communist Party hereby appeals to the whole nation: those who have money give money, those who have guns give guns, those who have grain give grain, those who have labour power give labour power, and those who have special skill contribute special skill, so that all our fellow-countrymen will be mobilized and all weapons, old or modern, will be used to arm the people in millions upon millions."

3. The December resolution was the "Resolution on the Present Political Situation and the Tasks of the Party", adopted at the meeting of the Political Bureau of the Central Committee of the Chinese Communist Party at Wayaopao, northern Shensi, on December 25, 1935. It made a comprehensive analysis of the current internal and international situation and the changes in class relations in China, and formulated the Party's policy. The resolution runs in part as follows:

The present situation shows that the attempts of Japanese imperialism to annex China have shocked the whole country and the whole world. Changes have taken place or are taking place in the relations between all classes, strata, political parties and armed forces in China's political life. There is a realignment of forces in both the national revolutionary front and the national counter-revolutionary front. Therefore, the Party's tactical line is to arouse, unite and organize the revolutionary forces throughout the country and among all the nationalities to oppose the chief enemy confronting them, namely, Japanese imperialism and the arch-traitor Chiang Kai-shek. All people, all parties, all armed forces and all classes, in so far as they are opposed to Japanese imperialism and the traitor Chiang Kai-shek, should unite and wage the sacred national revolutionary war, drive the Japanese imperialists out of China, overthrow the rule of their running dogs in China, achieve the complete liberation of the Chinese nation and safeguard China's independence and territorial integrity. Only by establishing the broadest anti-Japanese national united front (embracing the lower and upper strata) can we defeat Japanese imperialism and its running dog, Chiang Kai-shek. Of course, different individuals, different organizations, different social classes and strata and the various armed forces join the anti-Japanese national revolution from different motives and with different class standpoints. Some do so in order to hold on to their positions, some to gain leadership in the movement so that it will not go beyond, the limits they allow, and some genuinely to work for the complete liberation of the Chinese nation. Precisely because their motives and their standpoint differ, some will vacillate or turn traitor at the very start of the struggle, some will become indifferent or withdraw from the fight midway and some will determinedly fight to the end. Nevertheless, our task is to unite not only al possible basic forces but also all potential allies likely to resist Japan and enable the people throughout the country who have labour power to give labour power, those who have money to give money, those who have guns to give guns, and those who have knowledge to contribute knowledge, leaving no patriotic Chinese outside the anti-Japanese front. Such is the general line of e Party's tactics for the broadest possible national united front. Only by pursuing this line can we mobilize the forces of the whole people to deal with the common enemy, Japanese imperialism and the traitor Chiang Kai-shek. The Chinese working class and peasantry remain the basic motive forces of the Chinese revolution. The broad masses of the petty bourgeoisie and the revolutionary intellectuals are their most reliable allies in the national revolution A solid alliance of the workers, the peasants and the petty bourgeoisie is the basic force for defeating Japanese imperialism and the traitors and collaborators When a section of the national bourgeoisie and the warlords gives moral support, maintains benevolent neutrality or directly participates in the struggle against Japan and the traitors and collaborators, this will serve to expand the anti-Japanese front, however much it may disapprove of the agrarian revolution an Red political power. For the total strength of the counter-revolution will thus be reduced and the total strength of the revolution increased. To this end the Party should adopt appropriate ways and means to win these forces over to the anti-Japanese front. Moreover, unity is by no means prevalent even in the camp of the landlord and comprador classes. Since the contention for China among many imperialist powers has generated contending groups of traitors in their service with contradictions and conflicts among them, the Party should employ a variety of methods to ensure that for the time being some of these counter-revolutionary forces do not actively oppose the anti-Japanese front The same tactics should be applied in dealing with the imperialist powers other than Japan. In arousing, uniting and organizing the forces of the people through out the country to fight the common enemy, the Party should resolutely and unswervingly combat all tendencies towards vacillation, compromise, capitulation and betrayal within the anti-Japanese united front. Those who disrupt the Chinese people's anti-Japanese movement are traitors or collaborators whom we should all join in hitting hard. The Communist Party should win the leadership of the anti-Japanese front by being resolute and right in its words and deeds against the Japanese imperialists and the traitors and collaborators Only under the Communist Party's leadership can the anti-Japanese movement be completely victorious. With regard to the masses in the anti-Japanese war, it is necessary to satisfy their demands in matters affecting their basic interests (the demand of the peasants for land and the demand of the workers the soldiers the urban poor and the intellectuals for better living). Only by satisfying their demands will we be able to mobilize still broader sections of the masses to join the anti-Japanese ranks, keep up the anti-Japanese movement, and lead the movement to complete victory. And only thus can the Party win leadership in the anti-Japanese war.

See "On Tactics Against Japanese Imperialism", pp. 153-78 of this volume.

4. The Red Army sent an open telegram on May 5, 1936 demanding that the Nanking government end the civil war, conduct peace negotiations with the Communists for unity against Japan. The text reads as follows:

To the Military Council of the Nanking National Government; to all land, sea and air forces, to all parties, all political groups; all public bodies, all newspapers; and to all fellow-countrymen refusing to be slaves to a foreign nation.

After crossing the Yellow River on its eastward expedition, the Anti-Japanese Vanguard of the Chinese People's Red Army, organized by the Revolutionary Military Commission of the Chinese Red Army, was everywhere victorious and won support from all over the country. But when it occupied the Tatung-Puchow Railway and was energetically preparing to drive eastward into Hopei to engage the Japanese imperialists directly, Chiang Kai-shek sent more than ten divisions into Shansi and co-operated with Yen Hsi-shan in barring its advance against the Japanese. He also ordered the troops under Chang Hsueh-liang and Yang Hu-cheng, as well as the troops in northern Shensi, to march on the Shensi-Kansu Red area to harass our anti-Japanese rear In order to be able to reach and fight the Japanese, the people's Anti-Japanese Vanguard should have concentrated its entire strength and wiped out Chiang's troops blocking the way. But after much deliberation, the Revolutionary Military Commission of the Red Army decided that a battle to the finish between the two sides in the present national crisis would only damage China's strength for national defence and delight the Japanese imperialists, whichever side emerged victorious Furthermore, there are quite a number of patriotic officers and men in Chiang Kai-shek's and Yen Hsi-shan's armies who are willing to end the civil war and unite to resist Japan, and it is really against their consciences to obey Chiang's and Yen's orders and block the Red Army on its way to fight the Japanese. Therefore, in spite of its numerous victories in Shansi, the Revolutionary Military Commission of the

Red Army has withdrawn the people's Anti-Japanese Vanguard to the west of the Yellow River in order to preserve China's strength for national defence and thereby help to bring nearer the war of resistance against Japan, resolutely carry out our repeated declarations to the nation on ending the civil war and uniting to resist Japan, and hasten the final awakening of Chiang Kai-shek and the patriotic officers and men in his army. With this demonstration of our good faith to the Nanking government, to all the country's land, sea and air forces and to the whole nation, we are ready to arrange a cease-fire with all the armed units attacking the and-Japanese Red Army within one month and to enter into peace negotiations with them in order to end the civil war and resist Japan. The Revolutionary Military Commission of the Red Army hereby solemnly advises the gentlemen of the Nanking government at this critical juncture, when our country and people are threatened with imminent destruction, to make a determined effort to atone for past misdeeds and end the civil war in the whole country, to join forces against attacks from-without in the spirit of brothers quarreling at home, and first of all end the civil war in Shensi, Kansu and Shansi, whereupon both sides should appoint delegates to discuss specific measures for resisting Japan and saving the nation. This will be a blessing to the nation and the country as well as for your own good. However, if you obstinately refuse to listen to reason and prefer to be traitors and collaborators, your rule will surely collapse in the end and you will be spurned and overthrown by the whole nation. The old saying runs, "A thousand pointing fingers accuse, and a man dies even without a sickness." Or as another saying goes, "The butcher who lays down his knife at once becomes a Buddha." These are words for you gentlemen to digest and ponder. And the Revolutionary Military Commission of the Red Army calls upon all organizations all parties and all people in the country, who refuse to be slaves to a foreign nation, to support our proposal for a cease-fire and peace negotiations, and for unity against Japan, to organize committees for hastening the cessation of the civil war and to send representatives to the front to stop the firing on both sides and to supervise the full implementation of this proposal.

5. See "A Statement on Chiang Kai-shek's Statement' Note 7, pp. 259-61 of this volume.

6. The slogan of "A people's republic" was first put forward in the "Resolution on the Present Political Situation and the Tasks of the Party", adopted at the meeting of the Political Bureau of the Central Committee of the Chinese Communist Party held in December 1935 and in the report by Comrade Mao Tse-tung "On Tactics Against Japanese Imperialism". Later circumstances made it necessary for the Party to adopt the policy of

forcing Chiang Kai-shek to resist Japan and, as the slogan would have been unacceptable to the Chiang Kai-shek clique, it was changed into "A democratic republic" in the Party's letter of August 1936 to the Kuomintang The slogan of a democratic republic was subsequently explained in more concrete terms in the "Resolution on the New Situation in the Movement to Resist Japan and Save the Nation, and on the Democratic Republic", which the Central Committee of the Party adopted in September of the same year. Though different in form the two slogans are in essence the same. The following two extracts concerning the democratic republic are from the September 1936 resolution of the Party's Central Committee:

"The Central Committee holds that in the present situation it is necessary to put forward the slogan of 'establish a democratic republic', because this is the best way to unite all the anti-Japanese forces to safeguard China's territorial integrity and avert the calamity of the destruction of China and of the subjugation of her people, and also because this is the most fitting slogan for the formation of a united front based on the democratic demands of the broad masses of the people. By 'a democratic republic' we mean a democracy which is geographically more extensive than that of the workers' and peasants' democratic dictatorship in one part of China and a political system which is far more progressive than the one-party dictatorship of the Kuomintang in the main parts of China; it will therefore offer a better guarantee of the wide development of armed resistance to Japan and the achievement of complete victory. Moreover, the democratic republic will not only enable the broadest sections of the Chinese people to take pare in the country's political life and enhance their political consciousness and organized strength, but also give the Chinese proletariat and its leader, the Communist Party, scope for activity in the struggle for the future victory of socialism. Therefore, the Chinese Communist Party proclaims its active support of the movement for a democratic republic. It also declares that when the democratic republic is established through the length and breadth of China and a parliament elected by universal suffrage is convened the Red areas will at once become an organic part of the republic, the people of the Red areas will elect their representatives to the parliament, and the same democratic system will be put into practice in the Red areas."

"The Central Committee stresses that we shall impel the Kuomintang government m Nanking to resist Japan and we shall create the prerequisites for the democratic republic only by extending the Chinese people's movement of armed resistance and national salvation. by broadening the anti-Japanese national united front of all political parties, people of all walks of life and all armies, by strengthening the Chinese Communist Party's's role of political leadership in the national united front, by greatly consolidating the Red political power and the Red Army, and by waging a determined struggle against all words and deeds which betray our sovereignty and humiliate our nation or weaken the forces of the national united front. It is impossible for the democratic republic to become a reality without bitter and sustained struggles, without the mobilization of the entire Chinese nation, and without a high tide of revolution. In the course of the struggle for the democratic republic, the Chinese Communist Party should insist that the democratic republic should begin by carrying out the Ten-Point Programme for Resisting Japan and Saving the Nation proposed by our Party's and go on until it finally fulfils the basic tasks of the Chinese bourgeois-democratic revolution."

7. This telegram was dispatched on February 10, 1937. The full text reads as follows:

To the Third Plenary Session of the Central Executive Committee of the Kuomintang

Gentlemen:

It is a matter of national rejoicing that the Sian Incident has been settled peacefully. From now on it will be possible for the policy of internal peace and for unity and solidarity against foreign aggression to be carried out; this is a blessing to the nation and the country. At this moment when the Japanese invaders are running amuck and the survival of the Chinese nation hangs by a thread, our Party's eagerly hopes that, in accordance with this policy, the Third Plenary Session of the Central Executive Committee of your party will decide on the following as the national policy:

(1) end all civil wars and concentrate the country's strength in a united effort to meet the foreign aggression;

(2) guarantee freedom of speech, assembly and association, and release all political prisoners;

(3) call a conference of representatives of all political parties, people of all walks of life and all armies, and concentrate the radon's talents in a common endeavour to save the country;

(4) speedily complete all preparations for resisting Japan; and

(5) improve the livelihood of the people.

If the Third Plenary Session of your Central Executive Committee can succeed in resolutely and firmly deciding on this as the national policy, our Party will pledge the following as an expression of our good faith in solidarity against foreign aggression:

(1) the policy of armed insurrection to overthrow the National Government will be discontinued throughout the country;

(2) the Workers' and Peasants' Democratic Government will be renamed the Government of the Special Region of the Republic of China and the he Red Army will be redesignated as part of the National Revolutionary Army, and they will come under the direction of the Central Government t in Nanking and its Military Council respectively;

(3) a thoroughly democratic system based on universal suffrage will be put into effect in the areas under the Government of the Special Region; and

(4) the policy of confiscating the land of the landlords will be discontinued and the common programme of the anti-Japanese national united front resolutely carried out.

8. In November and December 1936, big strikes broke out among 45,000 workers in twenty-six Japanese and Chinese-owned textile mills in Shanghai. In December all the workers of the Japanese-owned textile mills in Tsingtao struck in sympathy. The Shanghai workers won their strike, their wages were increased five per cent retrospectively from November, and the employers undertook not to sack workers arbitrarily or assault or abuse them. But the strike in Tsingtao was suppressed by Japanese marines.

9. Britain and the United States began to change their attitude towards Japan and exerted some influence on the Chiang Kai-shek government in its policy towards Japan after Japanese imperialism occupied Shanhaikuan and penetrated into northern China in 1933, and especially after the conclusion of the "Ho-Umezu Agreement" (see Note I, p. 276) in 1935, which directly jeopardized their imperialist interests in northern and central China. During the Sian Incident of 1936, Britain suggested rejection of Japanese demands prejudicial to British interests in China and even intimated that, provided the Chiang Kai-shek government maintained its rule over the Chinese people, it would not be a bad thing for it to "form some sort of alliance with the Communist Party" so as to deal a blow to the

Japanese policy of aggression.

10. In June 1936, Li Tsung-jen and Pai Chung-hsi, warlords of Kwangsi, and Chen Chi-tang, warlord of Kwangtung, jointly declared their opposition to Chiang Kai-shek under the pretext of "resisting Japan and saving the nation". In August their opposition mated away before Chiang Kai-shek's tactics of bribery and divide and rule.

11. The Japanese forces and puppet troops began to invade Suiyuan in August 1936. In November, the Chinese troops there fought back and the people throughout the country started a movement in support of their fight.

12. After the "Ho-Umezu Agreement" of 1935, the Nanking Kuomintang government took a firmer attitude towards Japan under the pressure of the people's rising anti-Japanese sentiment and under the impact of the stiffer policy the British and U.S. imperialists were adopting towards Japan. The Kuomintang government used stalling tactics in the negotiations with Japan from September to December 1936, which ended without result.

13. This was the meeting of the Central Executive Committee of the Kuomintang on February 15,1937 after the peaceful settlement of the Sian Incident.

14. Ah Q is the leading character in The True Story of Ah Q, the famous nova by the great Chinese writer Lu Hsun. Ah Q typifies all those who compensate themselves for their failures and setbacks in real life by regarding them as moral or spiritual victories.

15. In the stage of China's bourgeois-democratic revolution, the Communists agreed with the basic points of Sun Yat-sen's programme and co-operated with him, which did not mean that they agreed with the bourgeois and petty-bourgeois world outlook or ideological system of which he was the exponent. As the vanguard of the Chinese proletariat, the Chinese Communists had an entirely different world outlook or ideological system and theoretical approach to the national and other problems, from those of Sun Yat-sen.

16. Reorganized by Sun Yat-sen in 1924, the Kuomintang became a revolutionary alliance of several classes, which members of the Communist Party joined in their individual capacity. After its betrayal of the revolution in 1927, the Kuomintang carried out what it called a "party purge" throughout the country, butchering the Communists and many of its own

left-wingers who genuinely supported Dr. Sun Yat-sen's Three Great Policies. From then on the Kuomintang became the counter-revolutionary political party of the big landlords and big bourgeoisie.

17. This refers to the situation created by the opportunist leadership of the Central Committee of the Party in the first half of 1927.

WIN THE MASSES IN THEIR MILLIONS FOR THE ANTI- JAPANESE NATIONAL UNITED FRONT

May 7, 1937

[This was the concluding speech made by Comrade Mao Tse-tung at the National Conference of the Communist Party of China, held in May 1937.]

Comrades! In the course of the discussions of the last few days you have expressed agreement with my report, "The Tasks of the Chinese Communist Party in the Period of Resistance to Japan"; only a few comrades expressed different views. As these dissenting views were rather significant, I shall discuss them first in my concluding speech before dealing with certain other problems.

THE QUESTION OF PEACE

For nearly two years out Party has fought for internal peace. After the Third Plenary Session of the Kuomintang Central Executive Committee, we declared that peace had been attained, that the stage of "fighting for peace" was over, and that the new task was to "consolidate the peace". We also pointed out that this new task was linked with "fighting for democracy", i.e., consolidating the peace by fighting for democracy. However, some comrades argue that this view of ours is untenable. It follows that they must either arrive at the opposite view or hover between the two. For they argue, "Japan is retreating [1] and Nanking is wavering more than ever; the contradiction between the two countries is becoming weaker and the contradiction within the country is growing sharper." Naturally, according to this appraisal, there is no new stage or new task, and the situation has reverted to its old stage or even deteriorated. I think this view incorrect

In saying that peace has been attained, we do not mean that it is consolidated; on the contrary, we have said that it is not consolidated. Bringing about peace and consolidating it are two different things. History might reverse its course for a while and peace might meet with setbacks because of the existence of Japanese imperialism, traitors and the pro-Japanese group. But the fact is that peace was attained after the Sian Incident and was the product of several factors Japan's fundamental policy of invasion, the favourable attitude of the Soviet Union and also Britain, the United States and France towards internal peace in China, the pressure of the Chinese people, the Communist Party's peace policy during the Sian Incident and its policy for ending the antagonism between the two regimes, the differentiation within the bourgeoisie, the differentiation within the Kuomintang, and so on); peace cannot be made or unmade by Chiang Kai-shek alone. To unmake it, he would have to fight against many forces and draw closer to the Japanese imperialists and the pro-Japanese group. There is no doubt that the Japanese imperialists and the pro-Japanese group are still endeavouring to prolong civil war in China. That is precisely why peace is not yet consolidated. Such being the case, we have come to the conclusion that, instead of reverting to the old slogans of "end the civil war" and "fight for peace", we should take a step forward and adopt the new slogan of "fight for democracy", for this is the only way to consolidate internal peace and bring the war of resistance against Japan into being. Why do we put forward the three closely related slogans of "consolidate the peace", "fight for democracy", and "carry out armed resistance"? The answer is that we desire to push the wheel of revolution forward and that circumstances allow us to do so. Those who deny the new stage and the new task, who deny that the Kuomintang has "begun to change" and by the same logic also deny the achievements of all the forces that have been struggling for peace during the last year and a half will remain where they were before, without advancing an inch.

Why do these comrades make such an unsound appraisal? Because in weighing up the current situation they start not from fundamentals but from a number of limited and transient phenomena (Sago's diplomacy, the Soochow trial, [2] the suppression of strikes, the eastward transfer of the Northeastern Army, [3] General Yang Hu-cheng's journey abroad, [4] and so on); hence their dismal picture. We say that the Kuomintang has begun to change and we also say that it has not changed completely. It is inconceivable that the Kuomintang's reactionary policy over the past ten years will completely change without new efforts--without more and greater efforts--on our part and on the part of the people. Quite a number of reputedly "Left" people, who often bitterly denounce the Kuomintang and who during the Sian Incident advocated putting Chiang to death and "fighting our way out through Tungkuan", [5] are now astonished when events like the Soochow trial occur immediately after peace is attained, and ask, "Why does Chiang Kai-shek still do such things?" They ought to understand that neither the Communists nor Chiang Kai-shek are gods, nor are they isolated individuals, but members of a party or a class. The Communist Party can push the revolution forward by degrees but cannot clear away all the evils in the country overnight. Chiang Kai-shek and the Kuomintang have begun to change, but the accumulated filth of the past ten years will certainly not be rapidly removed without great effort on the part of the whole people. We maintain that the trend is towards peace, democracy and resistance, but this does not imply that the old evils--civil war, dictatorship and non-resistance--will be swept away without any effort. It is only through struggle and hard work, and over a long period too, that we can eliminate the old evils, the old filth, and prevent setbacks or even reversals in the revolution.

"They are bent on destroying us." Quite true, they are always trying to destroy us. I fully admit the soundness of this appraisal, and indeed one would have to be fast asleep to overlook the point. But the question is whether there has been any change in the way they are trying to destroy us. I think there has been. The change is from war and massacre to reform and deceit, from a tough policy to a soft one, from a military to a political policy. Why has there been such a change? Confronted with Japanese imperialism, the bourgeoisie and the Kuomintang are temporarily forced to seek an ally in the proletariat, just as we are seeking an ally in the bourgeoisie. We should take this as our point of departure in considering the question. Internationally, for a similar reason, the French government has changed from hostility towards the Soviet Union to alliance with it.[6] Our domestic task has changed from a military to a political one. We for our part have no use for plotting or scheming; our aim is to defeat Japanese imperialism in a common effort by uniting with all those members of the bourgeoisie and the Kuomintang who favour resistance.

THE QUESTION OF DEMOCRACY

"To put the emphasis on democracy is wrong, the emphasis should be solely on resistance to Japan. Without direct action against Japan, there can be no movement for democracy. The majority of the people want only resistance to Japan, not democracy, and what is needed is another December 9th Movement." [7]

Let me first put a few questions. Can it be said that what the majority of the people wanted in the previous stage (i.e., from the December 9th Movement of 1935 to the Third Plenary Session of the Kuomintang Central Executive Committee in February 1937) was merely resistance to Japan and not internal peace? Was it wrong to emphasize internal peace then? Was it impossible to have a movement for internal peace without direct action against Japan (the Sian Incident and the Third Plenary Session of the Kuomintang Central Executive Committee took place after the resistance in Suiyuan ended, and today, too, there is as yet nothing equivalent to the Suiyuan resistance or the December 9th Movement)? Everybody knew that in order to resist Japan there had to be internal peace, that without internal peace there could be no resistance to Japan, and that internal
94

peace was a condition for resistance. All the anti-Japanese activities in the previous stage, whether direct or indirect (beginning with the December 9th Movement and ending with the Third Plenary Session of the Kuomintang Central Executive Committee), were centred on the struggle for internal peace which was then the central link, the most essential thing, in the anti-Japanese movement.

Similarly today, in the new stage, democracy is the most essential thing for resistance to Japan, and to work for democracy is to work for resistance to Japan. Resistance and democracy are interdependent, just as are resistance and internal peace, democracy and internal peace. Democracy is the guarantee of resistance, while resistance can provide favourable conditions for developing the movement for democracy.

We hope there may be--and indeed there will be--many direct and indirect struggles against Japan in the new stage, and these will give an impetus to the war of resistance and greatly assist the movement for democracy. But the core and essence of the revolutionary task history has set us is the winning of democracy. Is it, then, wrong to keep stressing democracy? I do not think so.

"Japan is stepping back, Britain and Japan are virtually inclined to strike a balance, and Nanking is wavering more than ever." Ignorance of the laws of historical development has given rise to this needless anxiety. If there were a revolution in Japan and she really withdrew from China, it would help the Chinese revolution and would be just what we want, marking the beginning of the collapse of the world front of aggression. What room for anxiety would there be then? But as a matter of fact, this is not what is happening; Sago's diplomatic moves are preparations for a major war, and a major war confronts us. Britain's policy of wavering can get her nowhere, her clash of interests with Japan making this certain. If Nanking continues to waver for long, it will become the enemy of the whole nation, and its own interests do not allow it to keep on wavering. A temporary retrogression cannot change the general law of history. Hence one should not deny the existence of the new stage or the necessity of setting the task of winning democracy. In any case, moreover, the slogan of democracy is appropriate, because it is obvious to everybody that the Chinese people have far too little democracy, and not too much. Actual events have also shown that to define the new stage, and to set the winning of democracy as our task, is to move a step closer to resistance. Events have moved forward; let us not put the clock back!

"Why do we place so much emphasis on a national assembly?" Because it is something which can affect every aspect of life, because it is the bridge from reactionary dictatorship to democracy, because it is connected with national defence, and because it is a legal institution. To recover eastern Hopei and northern Chahar, to combat smuggling, [8] to oppose "economic collaboration",[9] etc., as many comrades have proposed, is quite correct, but this complements rather than in any way conflicts with the fight for democracy and a national assembly; the essential thing is still the national assembly and freedom for the people.

It is correct and indisputable that the day-to-day struggle against Japan and the people's struggle for a better life must be linked up with the movement for democracy. Nevertheless, the central and essential thing in the present stage is democracy and freedom.

THE QUESTION OF THE FUTURE
OF THE REVOLUTION

Some comrades have raised this question, and here I can only give a brief answer.

In the writing of an article the second half can be written only after the first half is finished. Resolute leadership of the democratic revolution is the prerequisite for the victory of socialism. We are fighting for socialism, and in this respect we are different from those who confine themselves to the revolutionary Three People's Principles. It is the great future goal to which our present efforts are directed; if we lose sight of the goal, we cease to be Communists. But equally we cease to be Communists if we relax our efforts of today.

We are exponents of the theory of the transition of the revolution [10] and we are for the transition of the democratic revolution in the direction of socialism. The democratic revolution will develop through several stages, all under the slogan of a democratic republic. The change from the predominance of the bourgeoisie to that of the proletariat is a long process of struggle, of struggle for leadership in which success depends on the work of the Communist Party in raising the level of political consciousness and organization both of the proletariat and of the peasantry and urban petty bourgeoisie.

The staunch ally of the proletariat is the peasantry, and next comes the urban petty bourgeoisie. It is the bourgeoisie that will contend with us for leadership.

To overcome the vacillation of the bourgeoisie and its lack of revolutionary thoroughness we must rely on the strength of the masses and on the correctness of our policy, or otherwise the bourgeoisie will come out on top.

A bloodless transition is what we would like and we should strive for it, but what will happen will depend on the strength of the masses.

We are exponents of the theory of the transition of the revolution, and not of the Trotskyite theory of "permanent revolution". [11] We are for the attainment of socialism by going through all the necessary stages of the democratic republic. We are opposed to tailism, but we are also opposed to adventurism and impetuosity.

To reject the participation of the bourgeoisie in the revolution on the ground that it can only be temporary and to describe the alliance with anti-Japanese sections of the bourgeoisie (in a semi-colonial country) as capitulation is a Trotskyite approach, with which we cannot agree. Today such an alliance is in fact a necessary bridge on the way to socialism.

THE QUESTION OF CADRES

A great revolution requires a great party and many first-rate cadres to guide it. In China, with a population of 450 million, it is impossible to carry through our great revolution, which is unprecedented in history, if the leadership consists of a small, narrow group and if the Party leaders and cadres are petty-minded, short-sighted and incompetent. The Chinese Communist Party has been a large party for a long time and it is still large despite the losses during the period of reaction; it has many good leaders and cadres, but still not enough. Our Party organizations must be extended all over the country and we must purposefully train tens of thousands of cadres and hundreds of first-rate leaders. They must be cadres and leaders versed in Marxism-Leninism, politically far-sighted, competent in work, full of the spirit of self-sacrifice, capable of tackling problems on their own, steadfast in the midst of difficulties and loyal and devoted in serving the nation, the class and the Party. It is on these cadres and leaders that the Party relies for its links with the membership and the masses, and it is by relying on their firm leadership of the masses that the Party can succeed in defeating the enemy. Such cadres and leaders must be free from selfishness, from individualistic heroism, ostentation, sloth, passivity, and sectarian arrogance, and they must be selfless national and class heroes; such are the qualities and the style of work demanded of the members, cadres and leaders of our Party. Such is the spiritual legacy handed down to us by the tens of thousands of members, the thousands of cadres, and the scores of first-rate leaders who have laid down their lives for the cause. Beyond any doubt, we ought to acquire these qualities, do still better in remoulding ourselves and raise ourselves to a higher revolutionary level. But even this is not enough; we must also regard it as our duty to discover many more new cadres and leaders in the Party and the country. Our revolution depends on cadres. As Stalin said, "Cadres decide everything." [12]

THE QUESTION OF DEMOCRACY WITHIN THE PARTY

To attain this aim, inner-Party democracy is essential. If we are to make the Party strong, we must practice democratic centralism to stimulate the initiative of the whole membership. There was more centralism during the period of reaction and civil war. In the new period, centralism should be closely linked with democracy. Let us apply democracy, and so give scope to initiative throughout the Party Let us give scope to the initiative of the whole Party membership and so train new cadres in great numbers, eliminate the remnants of sectarianism, and unite the whole Party as solidly as steel.

UNITY IN THE CONFERENCE
AND IN THE WHOLE PARTY

After explanation, the dissenting views on political issues voiced at this conference have given way to agreement, and the earlier difference between the line of the Central Committee and the line of retreat adopted under the leadership of certain comrades, has also been settled; [13] this shows that our Party is very solidly united. This unity provides the most important basis for the present national and democratic revolution, because it is only through the unity of the Communist Party that the unity of the whole class and the whole nation can be achieved, and it is only through the unity of the whole class and the whole nation that the enemy can be defeated and the national and democratic revolution accomplished.

WIN THE MASSES IN THEIR MILLIONS
FOR THE ANTI-JAPANESE NATIONAL UNITED FRONT

The aim of our correct political policy and of our solid unity is to win the masses in their millions for the anti-Japanese national united front. The broad masses of the proletariat, the peasantry and the urban petty bourgeoisie need our work of propaganda, agitation and organization. Further efforts on our part are also needed to establish an alliance with those sections of the bourgeoisie which are opposed to Japan. To make the policy of the Party the policy of the masses requires effort, long and persistent effort, unrelenting and strenuous, patient and painstaking

98

effort. Without such effort, we shall achieve nothing. The formation and consolidation of the anti-Japanese national united front, the accomplishment of the task incumbent on it and the establishment of a democratic republic in China are absolutely inseparable from our effort to win over the masses. If we succeed in bringing millions upon millions of the masses under our leadership by such effort, our revolutionary task can be speedily fulfilled. By our exertions we shall surely overthrow Japanese imperialism and attain complete national and social liberation.

NOTES

1. The Japanese imperialists made temporary conciliatory gestures after the Sian Incident in order to induce the Kuomintang authorities to disrupt the internal peace which was being restored and to break up the anti-Japanese national united front which was taking shape. They arranged for the bogus autonomous government of Inner Mongolia under their control to release two messages, one in December 1936 and another in March 1937, pledging allegiance to the Kuomintang government in Nanking. And the Japanese foreign minister, Sago himself, publicly wooed Chiang Kai-shek, slyly declaring that Japan would improve its relations with China and help China achieve political unification and economic recovery. Furthermore, Japan sent a so-called Economic Study Group, headed by Kenji Kodama, a Japanese financial magnate, ostensibly to help China "complete the organization of a modern state". These were schemes for aggression and were known as "Sago's diplomacy"; they were called a "retreat on the part of Japan" by those people who were deluded by the Japanese imperialist make-believe.

2. In "April 1937, the Kuomintang High Court in Soochow tried Shen Chun-ju and six other leaders of the Resist Japan and Save the Nation Movement who had been arrested in November 1936 in Shanghai. The charge was "endangering the Republic", the usual trumped-up indictment the reactionary Kuomintang authorities used to stigmatize all patriotic movements.

3. Prior to the Sian Incident, the Northeastern Army was stationed on the border between Shensi and Kansu Provinces and was in direct contact with the Red Army in northern Shensi. Greatly influenced by the Red Army, it subsequently staged the coup in Sian. In March 1937, the Northeastern Army was forced to go east to Honan and Anhwei Provinces, a move taken by the Kuomintang reactionaries to cut it off from contact with the Red Army and at the same time to sow discord in its ranks.

4. General Yang Hu-cheng was a military leader in China's Northwest who

staged the Sian Incident together with Chang Hsueh-liang. Thus the prime movers in this incident were popularly linked together in the double-barrelled surname "Chang-Yang". When Chiang Kai-shek was released. Chang accompanied him to Nanking but was immediately placed under detention. In April 1937 Yang, too, was ousted from his post by the Kuomintang reactionaries and had to take leave of absence abroad. When the War of Resistance began, Yang returned to China to offer his services, only to be interned by Chiang Kai-shek for the rest of his life In September 1949, when the People's Liberation Army was driving forward near Chungking, the Kuomintang had him murdered in a concentration camp.

5. Tungkuan is a strategically important gateway on the borders of Shensi, Honan and Shansi. At the time of the Sian Incident the Kuomintang troops were mainly quartered east of it. Certain reputedly "Left" people in the Party, like Chang Kuo-tao, then urged that the Red Army should "fight its way out through Tungkuan", which meant that the Red Army should mount an offensive against the Kuomintang troops. This proposal ran counter to the Central Committee's policy for a peaceful settlement of the Sian Incident.

6. For a long time after the October Revolution, the French imperialists pursued a hostile policy towards the Soviet Union. From 1918 to 1920, the French government took an active part in the armed intervention by 14 powers against the Soviet Union and continued its reactionary policy of isolating the Soviet Union even after the intervention failed. It was not until May 1935 that, under the influence of the Soviet Union's peace policy among the French people and because of the German fascist menace, France concluded a treaty of mutual assistance with the Soviet Union, though her reactionary government failed to observe it.

7. The students' patriotic demonstration in Peking on December 9, 1935, led by the Chinese Communist Party. The movement called for the cessation of civil war and armed resistance to Japan and won nation-wide support.

8. The smuggling of Japanese goods into China.

9. This refers to the self-styled Sino-Japanese economic collaboration.

10. See Karl Marx and Frederick Engels, Manifesto of the communist Party, Part IV; V. I. Lenin, two Tactics of Social-Democracy in the Democratic Revolution, Part XII and Part XIII; History of the Communist Party of the Soviet Union (Bolsheviks), Short Course, Chapter 3, Section 3.

11. See J.V. Stalin, "The Foundations of Leninism", Part m, "The October Revolution and the Tactics of the Russian Communists", Part II; "Concerning Questions of Leninism", Part III.

12. See J. V. Stalin, "Address Delivered in the Kremlin Palace to the Graduates from the Red Army Academies" in May 1935, in which he said: ". . . of all the valuable capital the world possesses, the most valuable and most decisive is people, cadres. It must be realized that under our present conditions 'cadres decide everything.'"

13. This difference was between the line of the Party's Central Committee and Chang Kuo-tao's line of retreat in 1935-36. See "On Tactics Against Japanese Imperialism", Note 22, pp. 175-76 of this volume. In stating that "the earlier difference ... has ... been settled", Comrade Mao Tse-tung was referring to the fact that the Fourth Front Army of the Red Army had joined forces with the Central Red Army. Chang Kuo-tao's subsequent open betrayal of the Party and his degeneration into a counter-revolutionary was the act of an individual traitor and no longer a question of differences over Party line.

LETTER TO THE SPANISH PEOPLE

May 15, 1937

[Extracted from a letter dated 15 May 1937, published in Chieh-fang, no. 4, June 1937.]

People of Spain, Comrades in arms:

We, the Chinese Communist Party, the Chinese Red Army, and the Chinese Soviets, regard the war fought by the Spanish Republican Government as the most sacred war in the world. This war is being waged not only for the life of the Spanish people, but also for the oppressed peoples of the world, because the Spanish Government is resisting German and Italian fascism, which, with their Spanish accomplices. are destroying the culture, civilization, and justice of the world. The Spanish Government and the Spanish people are fighting the German and Italian fascists, who are in league with and giving support to the Japanese facial invaders of China in the Far East...Were it not for the support received from German and Italian fascism, Japanese fascism could not, as it is now doing attack us like a mad dog...

We do not believe that the struggle of the Chinese people can be separated from your struggle in Spain. The Communist Party of China is supporting and encouraging you, the Spanish people, by struggling against Japanese fascism. The Communist Party of China, the Chinese Soviets, the Chinese Red Army, and the Chinese people are greatly moved by your defence of Madrid and by your victories on the northern and southern fronts. Each day our press here in the Soviet regions publishes reports and articles about your heroic struggle... We firmly believe that the unity of your various parties in the People's Front is the basis for your final victory...

We know that your victory will directly aid us in our fight against Japanese fascism. Your cause is our cause. We read with emotion of the International Volunteers organized by people from every land, and we are glad that there are Chinese and Japanese in their ranks. Many comrades of the Chinese Red Army also wish to go to Spain to join you. . . Were it not that we are face to face with the Japanese enemy, we would join you and take our place in your front ranks.

As many of you know, the Chinese Red Army has carried on a ceaseless and hard struggle for ten years. We fought without resources, through hunger and cold, with insufficient arms, ammunition, and medical supplies, until at last we won our victories. We know that you and your army are also passing through great hardships such as we also have passed through, and we are certain that you will be victorious. Our ten years' struggle has proved that if a revolutionary people and their revolutionary army are not afraid of suffering, but continue to fight heroically and unyieldingly against the enemy, they will be victorious.

The People of China Express Solidarity With Spain

1937

To the Spanish people – Comrades-in-arms.

We, the Chinese Communist Party, the Chinese Red Army, and the Chinese Soviets, regard the war led by the Spanish Republican government as the most holy war in the world. This war is being fought not only for the life of the Spanish nation, but also for the oppressed nations of the world because the Spanish government is fighting German and Italian fascism which, with their Spanish henchmen, are destroying the culture and civilisation, and the human justice of the world. The Spanish government and the Spanish people are fighting German and Italian fascists who are actively in league with and giving support to the Japanese fascist invaders of China in the Far East. Japanese fascists are directing their full strength against China. After the occupation of our Manchurian Provinces, they advanced into North China. Were it not for the support they receive from German and Italian fascism they would never be so mad, so wild, as they are today in their invasion of our country.

The Communist Party of China fully sympathises with the different political parties united in the Spanish People's Front, and is now calling on the different political parties in China to join in a national united front against Japanese fascism. Our work is advancing rapidly and, if we succeed, China can deal a blow to Japanese fascism which will be of great help to the Spanish government and people.

We do not believe that the struggle of the Chinese people can be separated from your struggle in Spain. The Communist Party of China is now supporting and emulating you, the Spanish people, by struggling against Japanese fascism. The Communist Party of China, the Chinese Soviets, the Chinese Red Army and the Chinese people are greatly encouraged by your defence of Madrid, and of your northern and southern fronts. Each day our press here in the Soviet regions publishes reports and articles about your struggle. Through our radios we receive the latest daily news about you. We firmly realise that the unity of your various parties in the People's Front is the basis for your final victory. We have also read and fully support the ten-point programme proposed by the Spanish Communist Party and expressed in your manifesto.

Your struggle is similar to our own in the Far East because, apart from other similarities already mentioned, there are traitors and Trotskyists hiding in our ranks, just as they hide in yours. Only by the most determined measures against such traitors can we consolidate our Front. In struggling against our own enemies in China, we are giving support to you in Spain.

In China there are now over one hundred magazines and newspapers which publish regular reports, articles and pictures sympathetic to you in your heroic struggle for democracy and liberation. We know that your victory will directly aid us in our fight against Japanese fascism. Your cause is our cause. We read with enthusiasm of the International Volunteers organised by people from every land, and we are glad that there are Chinese and Japanese in their ranks. Many comrades of the Chinese Red Army also wish to go to Spain to join you, and not a day passes but that they discuss your struggle and the whole Spanish situation. Were it not that we are face to face with the Japanese enemy, we would join you and take our place in your front ranks.

As many of you know, the Chinese Red Army has carried on a ceaseless and hard struggle for ten years. We fought without resources, through hunger and cold, without arms and ammunition save that which we captured, until at last we won our present victory. We know that you and your army are also passing through great hardships such as we also have passed through, and that you will be victorious. Our ten years' struggle has proved that if a revolutionary people and their revolutionary army are not afraid of suffering, but continue to fight heroically against the enemy, they will be victorious.

We, the Communist Party of China, the Chinese Red Army, the Chinese Soviets and the Chinese people, express our deepest solidarity and comradeship with you, the heroic men and women fighting for Spanish democracy. Also, we express our deepest solidarity and comradeship for the International Volunteers who are offering their lives for the emancipation of their Spanish brothers and sisters and, through them, for the oppressed nations of the world. As in the past, we will follow your struggle with daily and hourly interest, rejoicing in all your victories, confident that final victory will be yours.

Mao Tse-tung
Chairman, Chinese Soviet Government, Yenanfu (Fushin), North Shensi, China
15 May 1937

Letter to Earl Browder, General Secretary of the Communist Party of the USA

Source: Earl Browder, China and the U.S.A., Workers Library, New York, October 1937, pages 10-11. Transcribed and prepared by Juan Fajardo, 8 August 2020.

[Just before 24 June 1937]

My dear Comrade Browder:

Taking advantage of the comrade's visit, I am sending this letter to you, our respected Comrade Browder, good friend of the Chinese people and leader of the American people.

Both the Communist Party of China and the Communist Party of U.S.A. are confronted with a historic task, the task of resisting and overthrowing the aggressive policy of Japanese imperialism. The Chinese Party is endeavoring to bring about an anti-Japanese national united front.

Although our work is passing through a difficult period, we have already made progress and we are doing our best to bring about the desired result.

From several American friends, and from other sources, we learned that the Communist Party of the United States and the masses of the American people are deeply concerned with China's struggle against Japan and have given us assistance in many ways. This makes us feel that our struggle is by no means isolated and we are heroically assisted from abroad. At the same time we feel that when we achieve victory, this victory will be of considerable help to the struggle of the American people for liberation. The world is now on the eve of a great explosion. The working class of the world and all the peoples who desire liberation must unite for the common struggle.

Revolutionary greetings,

MAO TSE-TUNG

INSCRIPTION FOR THE FOUNDING OF THE NORTH SHENSI PUBLIC SCHOOL
1937

We must educate a lot of people — the sort of people who are the vanguard of revolution, who have political farsightedness, who are prepared for battle and sacrifice, who are frank, loyal, positive, and upright; the sort of people who seek no self-interest, only national and social emancipation, who show, instead of fear, determination and forwardness in the face of hardships; the sort of people who are neither undisciplined nor fond of limelight, but practical, with their feet firmly on the ground. If China possesses many such men, the tasks of the Chinese revolution can easily be fulfilled.

SPEECH AT THE MEETING CELEBRATING THE COMPLETION OF THE BUILDING OF THE ANTI-JAPANESE MILITARY AND POLITICAL UNIVERSITY

1937

What I want to say to you, Comrades, is that, in short. the success of this great enterprise is due to [our] overcoming difficulties and uniting with the masses. The experience of the struggle in the past ten years. the cave [-buildings] you have dug, and the future course of the Resistance War have proved or will prove that if we continue to overcome difficulties and unite with the masses we shall be ever victorious!

To overcome natural difficulties by defeating the foes and to overcome military difficulties by defeating the Japanese bandits have something in common but quite a lot of differences. The latter is harder and more arduous. Therefore in addition to orienting oneself towards overcoming difficulties and uniting with the masses, the Resistance War requires skills in strategy and tactics, in mobilizing, organizing, and leading the masses, and in winning allies.

You have now the spirit to overcome difficulties and unite with the masses. If you can use your talents to develop from this basis, it is entirely possible to defeat Japan and drive the Japanese out of China.

ON LU HSUN
1937

魯迅 一九三〇年九月
二十五日攝于上海，
時年五十。

[Speech at the meeting Commemorating the First Anniversary of the Death of Lu Hsun held in the North Shensi Public School on 19.10.1939. Reproduced from the fortnightly July (Chi-yueh), March 1938.]

Comrades,

Our main tasks at the present moment are those of the vanguard. At a time when the great national Resistance War is making rapid progress, we need a large number of activists to play the leading role [in it] and a large number of vanguards to find the path. Vanguards must be frank, positive, and upright people. They seek no self-interest, only national and social emancipation. They fear no hardships, instead, in the face of hardship they are determined and forever moving forward. Neither undisciplined nor fond of limelight, they have their feet firmly on the ground and are realistic. They are the guides on the road of revolution. In the light of the present state of the war, if the Resistance is the concern only of the government and armed forces, without the participation of the broad masses, we cannot be certain that we shall win the final victory. We must now train a large number of vanguards who will fight for our national liberation and can be relied upon to lead and organize the masses for the fulfilment of this historic mission. First of all, the numerous vanguards of the whole country must urgently organize themselves. Our communist party is the vanguard of national liberation. We must fight to the bitter end in order to accomplish our tasks.

Today we commemorate [the death] of Lu Hsun. We must first of all understand him and his place in the history of our revolution. We commemorate him not only because he was a distinguished writer but also because he, at the forefront of national emancipation, dedicated all his strength to the revolutionary struggle. (We commemorate him not only because he wrote well, becoming a great literary figure, but also because he was a vanguard for national liberation and gave tremendous help to the revolution.) Although he did not belong to the communist party organization, his thinking, action, and writing were all Marxianized. He showed more and more youthful energy as his life drew to its end. He fought consistently and incessantly against feudal forces and imperialism. Under despicable circumstances of enemy pressure and persecution, he struggled (suffered) and protested. In a similar way, Comrades, you can also study revolutionary theories diligently while [living] under such adverse material conditions [because] you are full of militant spirit. The material arrangement of this school is poor, but here we have truth, freedom, and a place to train revolutionary vanguards.

Lu Hsun emerged from the decaying feudal society. But he knew how to fight back against the rotten society and the evil imperialist forces of which he had had so much experience . He used his sardonic, humorous, and sharp (powerful) pen to depict the force(s) of the dark society (and of the ferocious imperialists). He was really an accomplished 'painter'. In his last years he fought for truth and freedom from the standpoint of the proletariat and national liberation.

Lu Hsun's first characteristic was his political vision. He examined society with both a microscope and a telescope, hence with precision and farsightedness. As early as 1936 he pointed out the dangerous tendencies of the criminal Trotskyites. Now the clarity and correctness of his judgement have been proved beyond doubt by the facts—the obvious fact that the Trotskyite faction has turned into a traitorous organization subsidized by Japanese special agents.

In my view, Lu Hsun is a great Chinese saint—the saint of modern China, just as Confucius was the saint of old China. For his immortal memory, we have established the Lu Hsun Library and the Lu Hsun Teachers' Training School in Yenan So that future generations may have a glimpse of his greatness.

His second characteristic was his militancy, which we mentioned a moment ago. He was a great steadfast tree, not a blade of wavering grass, against the onslaught of dark and violent forces. Once he saw a political destination clearly he strove to reach it, never surrendering or compromising half way. There have been half-hearted revolutionaries who fought at first but then deserted the battlefield. Kautsky and Plekhanov of foreign countries (Russia) were good examples [of this]. Such people are not infrequently found in China. If I remember correctly, Lu Hsun once said that at first all [of them] were 'left' and revolutionary, but as soon as pressure came, [they] changed and presented their comrades [to the enemy] as a gift. Lu Hsun bitterly hated this sort of people. While fighting against them, he educated and disciplined the young writers who followed him. He taught them to fight resolutely, to be vanguards, and to find their own way .

His third characteristic was his readiness to sacrifice himself, completely fearless of enemy intimidation and persecution and utterly unmoved by enemy enticement. With merciless pungency his sword-like pen cut all those he despised. Among the bloodstains of revolutionary fighters he showed his tenacious defiance and marched ahead while calling [the others to follow him]. Lu Hsun was an absolute realist, always uncompromising, always determined. In one of his essays he maintained that one should [continue to] beat a dog after it had fallen in water. If you did not, the dog wound jump up either to bite you or at least to shake a lot of dirty water over you. Therefore the beating had to be thorough. Lu Hsun did not entertain a speck of sentimentalism or hypocrisy.

Now the mad dog, Japanese imperialism, had not been beaten in water yet. We must learn this 'Lu Hsun spirit' and apply it to the whole country.

These characteristics are the components of the great 'Lu Hsun spirit'. Throughout his life Lu Hsun never deviated from this spirit and that is why he was an outstanding writer in the world of letters and a tough, excellent vanguard in the revolutionary ranks. As we commemorate him, we must learn his spirit. [We] must take it to all the units engaged in the Resistance War and use it in the struggle for our national liberation.

BASIC TACTICS
1937

CHAPTER I

INTRODUCTORY REMARKS

1. HOW THE POPULAR MASSES CARRY OUT MILITARY ACTION.

How is it that the bare-handed masses, banded together in ill-armed military units without guns or bullets, are able to charge the enemy, kill the enemy, and resolutely carry out effective action in the war? This is a very widespread and very reasonable query. But if we know the function of the weapons used by an army and the aim of an army's action, we can then understand how our popular masses, although bare-handed, still have weapons and can engage in action to subdue the enemy.

The principal function of an army's weapons is simply to kill the enemy, and an army's final aim is simply to reduce or destroy the enemy's fighting strength. Well, in our daily life, is there any object that cannot be used to kill the enemy or any type of action that cannot reduce or destroy his fighting strength? For example, a kitchen knife, a wooden cudgel, an axe, a hoe, a wooden stool, or a stone can all be used to kill people. Such actions as cutting electric lines, destroying bridges, starting rumors, spreading poison, or cutting off supplies can everywhere inconvenience the enemy or reduce his fighting strength. All these are methods we may be unwilling to utilize or unable to employ. If we really want to kill and exterminate the enemy, there are weapons for us everywhere and work for us to be doing at all times, in order to ensure effective united action by the army and the people.

2. POINTS OF SPECIAL ATTENTION.

After from this, we must pay special attention to the present war on the national level, which has become cruel beyond our imagination and has also lasted a long time. We must not, because we are undergoing the suffering of a war more cruel than any seen in the past, immediately capitulate; nor must we, under the influence of a long war, suddenly lose our endurance and give way to lassitude. We must inspire ourselves with the most resolute spirit of unyielding struggle, with the most burning patriotic sentiments, and with the will to endurance, and carry out a protracted struggle against the enemy. We must know that, although the circumstances and the duration of the war are cruel and protracted, this is nothing compared to what would happen if the war were lost; if our country were destroyed and the whole of our people reduced to a position of irretrievable ruin, the suffering would be even more cruel and would never come to an end. Therefore, however cruel the war may be, we must absolutely and firmly endure until the last five minutes of struggle. This is especially the case with our present enemy, who finds his advantage in a rapid decision in the war, whereas our advantage is to be found in the strategy of a protracted war.

3. WE MUST NOT FEAR THE ENEMY.

When we see the enemy, simply because he has a weapon in his hands, we must not be frightened to death like a rat who sees a cat. We must not be afraid of approaching him or infiltrating into his midst in order to carry out sabotage. We are men; our enemies are also men; we are all men, so what should we fear? The fact that he has weapons? We can find a way to seize his weapons. All we are afraid of is getting killed by the enemy. But when we undergo the oppression of the enemy to such a point as this, how can any one still fear death? And if we do not fear death, then what is there to fear about the enemy? So when we see the enemy, whether he is many or few, we must act as though he is bread that can satisfy our hunger, and immediately swallow him.

4. DEFINITION OF GUERRILLA WARFARE

When it is not advantageous for our main land army to meet the enemy in large-scale engagements and we, therefore, 'send' out commando units or guerrilla units, which employ the tactics of avoiding strength and striking at weakness, of flitting about and having no fixed position, and of subduing the enemy according to circumstances, and when we do not oppose the enemy according to the ordinary rules of tactics, this is called employing guerrilla tactics.

CHAPTER II

TACTICS

At a time when our country's national defense preparation are not completed, and when our weapons are inferior to the excellent equipment with which the enemy has provided himself, we must observe the following principles whenever we wish to wage a battle with the enemy:

1. PRECAUTIONS WHEN ON THE MARCH.

When we are on the march, we must send plainclothes units armed with pistols ahead of our vanguard, behind our rear guard, and to the side of our lateral defenses, in order to spy out the situation and to forestall unexpected attacks by the enemy, or superfluous clashes.

2. PRECAUTIONS DURING HALTS.

When we encamp, if there is a presumption that the enemy may be near, we should send every day a guerrilla company—or at least a platoon— toward the enemy's defenses to carry out reconnaissance at a distance (from 20 to 30 li) or to join up with the local forces and carry out propaganda among the masses, in order to inspire them to resist the enemy. If this unit discovers the enemy, it should, on the one hand, resist him and, on the other hand, report to us so that we can prepare to meet the foe or to retreat without being drawn into an unnecessary battle.

3. WE MUST NOT ATTACK STRONG POSITIONS.

If the enemy guards his position firmly or defends a strong strategic point, then, unless we have special guarantees of success. we must not attack him. If we attack him, we will waste considerable time, and our losses in killed and wounded will certainly be many times those of the enemy. Moreover, in guerrilla warfare, our artillery is not strong: if we recklessly attack a strong position, it will be very difficult to take it rapidly, at one stroke, and, meanwhile, it will be easy for the enemy to gather his forces from all sides and surround us. On this point, the army and the people must be absolutely firm of purpose and cannot act recklessly in a disorderly fashion because of a moment's anger.

4. DO NOT FIGHT HARD BATTLES.

If we do not have a 100 per cent guarantee of victory, we should not fight a battle, for it is not worth while to kill 1,000 of the enemy and lose 800 killed among ourselves. Especially in guerrilla warfare such as we are waging, it is difficult to replace men, horses, and ammunition; if we fight a
116

battle and lose many men, and horses, and much ammunition, this must be considered a defeat for us.

5. WE MUST NOT FIGHT IF THE SITUATION OF THE ENEMY IS NOT CLEAR.

When we are encamped in a certain place and suddenly discover the enemy but are not informed regarding his numbers or where he is coming from, we must absolutely not fight, but must resolutely retreat several tens of li. It is only if we are right up against the enemy that we should send covering units, for, if the enemy comes to attack us, it is certainly because his forces are superior or he has a plan, and we must under no circumstances fall into his trap. If the enemy is in force, it is obviously advantageous to retreat. If his numbers are small and we retreat, nothing more than a little extra fatigue is involved, and there will always be time to return and attack him again later.

6. WE MUST ORGANIZE THE MASSES AND UNITE WITH THEM.

Modern warfare is not a matter in which armies alone can determine victory or defeat. Especially in guerrilla combat, we must rely on the force of the popular masses, for it is only thus that we can have a guarantee of success. The support of the masses offers us great advantages as regards transport, assistance to wounded, intelligence, disruption of the enemy's position, etc. At the same time, the enemy can be put into an isolated position, thus further increasing our advantages. If, by misfortune, we are defeated, it will also be possible to escape or to find concealment. Consequently, we must not lightly give battle in places where the masses are not organized and linked to us.

7. USING THE MASSES TO MAKE A SURPRISE ATTACK AND BREAK A BLOCKADE.

When the enemy surrounds us and blockades us, we should rouse the popular masses and cut the enemy's communications in all directions, so that he does not know that our army is already near him. Then, we should take advantage of a dark night or of the light of dawn to attack and disperse him.

8. SURPRISE ATTACKS ON ISOLATED UNITS.

When we have reconnoitered the enemy's position and have kept our men at a distance of several li and when he has unquestionably relaxed his precautions, then we advance rapidly with light equipment, before dawn when the enemy does not expect us, and exterminate him.

9. USING THE POPULAR MASSES TO HARRY THE ENEMY.

On the basis of a decision by the main force of the army, in time of battle, we send out part of our forces, divided into several units—the smallest element being a platoon—to lead the local militia, police, volunteer army, or other popular masses of the peasantry and the workers. These groups use a great variety of flags, occupy mountaintops or villages and market towns, use brass gongs, spears, rudimentary cannon, swords and spikes, trumpets, etc. They scatter all over the landscape and yell, thus distracting the enemy's eyes and ears. Or, both night and day, on all sides, they shoot off isolated shots to cause panic among the enemy soldiers and fatigue their spirit. Then, afterward, our army appears in full strength when the enemy does not expect it and disperses him by a flank attack.

10. CIRCLING AROUND TO GET AWAY FROM THE ENEMY.
When we are faced with a large enemy force and do not have sufficient strength to meet its attack, we use the method of circling around. We hasten to a place where there are no enemy troops, and we use mountain trails so that the enemy cannot catch up with us. At the same time, along the way, we utilize the popular masses, getting them to carry on reconnaissance work in the front and the rear, so that we are not attacked, by the enemy from either direction.

11. GETTING OUT OF DIFFICULT SITUATIONS.
Presume that in the rear there is a pursuing army and in the front an obstacle, or that the pursuing army is too strong for us. As a plan to get out of such a difficult situation, we can send a part of our forces 4 or 5 li off, to lure the enemy up a big road, while our main force follows a side road and escapes the enemy. Or we can make a detour around to the enemy's rear and attack him there by surprise. Or we can use the local militia and the police to go along another route, leaving some objects, making footprints in the road, sticking up notices etc., so as to induce the enemy to follow them. Then, our main force suddenly rushes out from a side road, striking at the enemy from the front and the rear, encircles him on all sides, and annihilates him.

12. "CAUSE AN UPROAR IN THE EAST, STRIKE IN THE WEST."
When the army wants to attack a certain place, it does not advance there directly but makes a detour by some other place and then changes its course in the midst of its march, in order to attack and disperse the enemy. "The thunderclap leaves no time to cover one's ears."

13. CONCEALED ATTACKS FROM AMBUSH.
When the enemy is pursuing us in great haste we select a spot for an ambush and wait until he arrives. Thus, we can capture the enemy all at one stroke.

14. AMBUSHING THE ENEMY IN THE COURSE OF HIS MARCH.

When we learn from reconnaissance that the enemy plans to advance from a certain point, we choose a spot where his path is narrow and passes through confusing mountainous terrain and send a part of our troops—or a group of sharpshooters— to lie hidden on the mountains bordering his path, or in the forest, to wait until his main force is passing through. Then we throw rocks down on his men from the mountains and rake them with bullets, or shoot from ambush at their commanding officers mounted on horseback.

15. MAKING A STRONG DEFENSE BY EMPTYING THE COUNTRYSIDE.

When our spies have informed us that the enemy is about to arrive, and if our force is not sufficient to give battle, we should then carry out the stratagem of "making a strong defense by emptying the countryside." We hide the food, stores, fuel, grain, pots and other utensils, etc., in order to cut off the enemy's food supply. Moreover, as regards the popular masses of the area in question, with the exception of old men, women, and children, who are left behind to provide reconnaissance information, we lead all able-bodied men to hiding places. Thus, the enemy has no one to serve as porters, guides, and scouts. At the same time, we send a few men to the enemy's rear communication lines, to cut off his supplies, capture his couriers, and cut or sabot age his communications facilities.

16. MEETING A SUPERIOR ENEMY.

(1) When the enemy advances, we retreat. If the enemy's forces were weaker than ours, he would not dare advance and attack us. So, when he advances toward us, we can conclude that the enemy is certainly coming with superior force and is acting according to plan and with preparation. It is, therefore, appropriate for us to evade his vanguard, by withdrawing beforehand. If we meet with the enemy in the course of our march and either do not have clear information regarding him or know that his army is stronger than ours, we should, without the slightest hesitation, carry out a precautionary withdrawal.

As to the place to which we should withdraw, it is not appropriate to go long distances the main roads, so that the enemy follows us to the end. We should move about sinuously in the nearby area, winding around in circles. If the enemy appears ahead of us, we should circle around to his rear, if the enemy is on the mountains, we should descend into the valleys; if the enemy is in the middle, we should retreat on the two sides ; if the enemy in on the left bank of the river, we should retreat on the right bank ; if the enemy is on the right bank, we should retreat on the left bank.

Moreover, in withdrawing, when we come to a crossroads, we can deliberately leave some objects in the branch of the road we do not take or send a small fraction of our men horses that way, in order to leave some tracks or write symbols. Or we can write some distinguishing marks on the road we do take to indicate that it is closed. Thus, we induce the enemy to direct his pursuit and attack in the wrong direction.

At such times, it is best to evacuate the popular masses and such armed forces as the militia, police, volunteer army, etc., by various routes in all directions, in order to confuse the enemy's eyes and ears. We can leave behind part of our men, who bury their uniforms and weapons and disguise themselves as merchants, street vendors, etc. They spread rumors or pretend to be obliging in order to spy out information regarding the enemy's numbers, his plans, the location and routine of his camps, and the precautions he is taking. If the enemy questions them about the direction in which we have withdrawn and the strength of our force, they should talk incoherently, pointing to the east and saying the west, pointing to the south and saying the north, replacing big by small and small by big, talking at random and creating rumors. They wait until our army is about to attack, and then they dig up their uniforms and put them on, take out their weapons, and attack the enemy from his midst, thus completely routing him and leaving him with nowhere to turn.

(2) When the enemy retreats, we pursue. When the enemy army retreats, it is appropriate to take advantage of the situation to advance. On such an occasion, the enemy's military situation must have undergone a change, otherwise he would not have retreated, and he is certainly not prepared to join battle against us with any resolution. If we take advantage of the situation and make a covering attack on his rear, the enemy's covering units will certainly not be resolved to fight, and in the context of the enemy's over-all plan it will be difficult for his forward units to return and join in the fray. In rough mountainous terrain, where the paths are narrow and rivers and streams intertwined so that there are many bridges, even if the enemy's forward forces were to turn back, this move would require much time. So, by the time he turns back, his rear will already have been annihilated and he will already have been disarmed.

At this time, the organizations of the popular masses, should devise methods for destroying the bridges on the route over which the enemy is retreating, or cutting the wires of his communications system. Or, best of all, they should wait until the bulk of the enemy's army have retreated and, taking advantage of the protection afforded by our guards and army, block the enemy's path of retreat, so that, although his forces may want to turn back, they cannot do it, and, although they yearn for help, they cannot obtain it.

But, at such a time, the most important task of the popular masses is to spy out the direction in which the enemy is withdrawing, in order to ascertain whether or not there may be an ambush or a feigned retreat intended to encircle us from two sides, and report to us immediately so that our army can pluck up courage and pursue the enemy or devise a method of evading him.

(3) When the enemy halts, we harass him. When the enemy is newly arrived in our territory, is not familiar with the terrain, does not understand the local dialect, and is unable to gain any information from the scouts he send out, it is as though he had entered a distant and inaccessible land. At such a time, we should increase our harassment— shooting off guns everywhere, to make him ill at ease day and night, so exercising a great influence on both his mind and body under such circumstances, I fear that any army, however overbearing, will begin to waver and will become weary. We need only await the time when his spirits are wavering and his body weary, and then, if our armies rush in all together, we can certainly exterminate him completely.

17. DEALING WITH A WEAK ENEMY.
Fighting as we are for the existence of our nation and the achievement of the aims of guerrilla warfare—which are to destroy the enemy and to stir up the courage of the popular masses— when we are faced with a weak enemy, naturally we should unite with the popular masses of the place in question to surround him and exterminate him at one stroke.

18. AROUSING THE MASSES.
There are always a good many among the popular masses who forget the great cause for the sake of petty advantage. Frequently having received great favors from the enemy, they act contrary to conscience and aid the forces of evil. For this reason, before the arrival of the enemy in a given place, we must do our utmost to whip up the spirits of the popular masses, to rouse their will to resist and to endow them with an unshakable resolve to fight to the end. without seeking advantage, without compromise or surrender. We must induce them to follow our orders sincerely and to cooperate with our army to resist the enemy. At the same time, we should also organize "resist-the-enemy associations", "associations for national salvation", and other types of professional bodies to facilitate the transmission of orders and the evacuation of villages in time of necessity

and to clean out traitors and prevent their utilization by the enemy.

CHAPTER III

THE AIM OF THE WAR

The ultimate aim of guerrilla warfare is certainly to disarm the enemy, to destroy his fighting strength, to get back the territories he has occupied and to save our brethren whom he is trampling under foot! But when, because of objective circumstances and other factors of various kinds, it is impossible to attain this goal, it sometimes happens that the areas unaffected by the fighting are controlled by the enemy in all tranquility. This should not be. Because of this possibility, we must think up methods for inflicting economic and political damage in these areas and destroying communication facilities, so that, although the enemy has occupied our territory, it is of no use to him and he decides to withdraw on his own initiative.

In guerrilla warfare, we must observe the principle "To gain territory is no cause for joy, and to lose territory is no cause for sorrow." To lose territory or cities is of no importance. The important thing is to think up methods for destroying the enemy. If the enemy's effective strength is undiminished, even if we take cities, we will be unable to hold them. Conversely, when our own forces are insufficient, if we give up the cities, we still have hope of regaining them. It is altogether improper to defend cities to the utmost, for this merely leads to sacrificing our own effective strength.

CHAPTER IV

ORGANIZATION

1. OPPORTUNITIES FOR ORGANIZATION.

(1) When we are devoting ourselves to warfare in an open region, it is the sparsely populated areas, with a low cultural level, where communications are difficult and facilities for transmitting correspondence are inadequate, that are advantageous.

(2) Narrow mountainous regions, rising and falling terrain, or areas in the vicinity of narrow roads—all of which are inconvenient for the movement of large bodies of troops— are also advantageous.

Opportunities also exist:

(3) When the people in the enemy's rear are in sympathy with our army.

(4) When the enemy is well-armed, and his troops numerous and courageous, so that we have to evade direct clashes.

(5) When the enemy has penetrated deeply into our territory and we are preparing everywhere to carry out measures of harassment and obstruction against him.

(6) Dense forests or reedy marshes, in the depths of which we can disappear, are most advantageous for this purpose, especially in the late summer and autumn, when we find ourselves behind a curtain of green.

2. FORMS OF ORGANIZATION.
The action of a guerrilla unit takes one of the following forms:

(1) We send out a large cavalry unit from our main force, together with mounted artillery, or cavalry accompanied by a platoon or more armed with light automatic weapons. They penetrate as rapidly as possible into the enemy's rear destroy there all his communications links, and carry out the thorough and complete destruction of all his storehouses of food, grain for his horses, and ammunition. Moreover, they send out a small group of their forces to destroy all places of military significance in the enemy's rear. Once these forays have been carried out, the group fights its way out in another direction and rejoins the main force.

(2) We send out cavalry or a special task group of infantry. Their strength should be from a platoon to a few companies. They should penetrate as deeply as possible into the enemy's rear and, moving rapidly and unpredictably, should carry the battle from one place to another. When there is no alternative, or when the enemy is not expected to arrive before a certain time, they can also dwell temporarily in secret where they are. As required by the exigencies of the situation, they can employ either all or a part of their forces. They return when the time comes that they can no longer stay in the enemy's rear, or when the task entrusted to them is completed, or because the enemy has already discovered our traces and our intentions, and has taken effective measures of defense.

(3) In the enemy's rear, we choose some young, strong, and courageous elements among the local population and organize some small groups who will accept the leadership of the experienced and trained persons we send out or of experienced persons whom we had trained previously in the place in question. The secret activity of these small groups involves moving from their own area to another one, changing their uniforms, unit numbers, and external appearance, and using every method so as to cover

their tracks to the utmost.

(4) Or we seek volunteers from our army and provide them with high-quality light weapons, in order to form them into special guerrilla units under the leadership of such officers as have benefited from experience and study.

(5) Guerrilla units can be classified according to their nature. Those formed of selected volunteers are called special guerrilla units. Those organized generally from a part of our army are called basic guerrilla units. Those organized from the local population are called local guerrilla units. When basic and local guerrilla units engage in combined actions, they are subject to the unified command of the commander of the basic unit.

(6) As for the choice of the members of a guerrilla unit, the members of a basic guerrilla unit should be taken from among those soldiers who are healthy, firm of purpose, patient, courageous, and quick-witted. Moreover, the soldiers themselves be willing to join the group in question. In the case of the independent actions carried out by these men in the course of guerrilla operations, there is generally no way to verify whether or not their tasks are executed in accordance with orders, and frequently they act beyond the knowledge of the responsible commander. For this reason, the choice and training of members of guerrilla units should have as its central theme "faithfully carrying out one's task. "

(7) The choice and the nomination of the commander of a guerrilla task group or small group requires even greater forethought and reflection. The capacity of the commanders for faithful and courageous action, their military knowledge-especially their knowledge of guerrilla tactics-their possession of a lively intelligence and the ability to adapt rapidly to changing circumstances, their loyalty, and their daring are indispensable conditions for carrying out plans and completing our tasks.

3. NUMBER OF TROOPS
The number of men belonging to a guerrilla unit is determined by the tasks, but it commonly ranges from five or ten men to something over a thousand. However, the maximum strength of such a unit may not exceed one regiment. If the number of soldiers is too large, the movements of our forces will be encumbered, there will be greater difficulties regarding food supply, and it will be difficult to conceal the troops by the use of false uniforms. Because of these problems, our plans may be discovered or revealed before they have been carried out. Moreover, replenishing our supplies of ammunition will be a problem. Furthermore, we will often have

difficulties because of poor roads, with the result that not only will all our plans prove merely illusory, but also we will often fall into difficulties to no good purpose in going and returning.

The great superiority of a small guerrilla unit lies in its remarkable mobility. With very little expenditure of time and effort, one can get food, and it is also easy to find a place to rest, for one does not need much in the way of rations or a place of shelter to camp. Still less is one held up by bad roads, and supplies of ammunition and medicine are also easy to replenish. If we do not succeed in our operation, we can retreat in good order.

4. TYPES OF SOLDIERS.
As for the type of soldiers employed in guerrilla units, cavalry, engineers, and highly mobile infantry troops are excellent. Cavalry is entrusted with the task of creating disorder on the enemy's flanks, and also, when we are pursuing the enemy, with that of maintaining pressure on his rear guard and creating confusion on his flanks and in his rear. Moreover, at all times, cavalry is the guerrilla unit's only instrument for transmitting correspondence and for reconnoitering. Hence, the cavalry is indispensable to any guerrilla unit. Engineers are used for destroying communications in the enemy's rear (such as railroads, telephone and telegraph lines, bridges, etc.) As for the highly mobile infantry units, they are useful to startle the enemy and produce in him a feeling of insecurity night and day.

5. WEAPONS.
Apart from the rifles of the infantry and the cavalry, light machine guns, hand grenades, etc., guerrilla units should also be supplied with pistols and submachine guns.

To the extent that the terrain permits it, one can also add heavy machine guns, mortars, and small cannons.

6. MEN AND BAGGAGE
Convenience of movement and agility being the characteristics of a guerrilla unit, the baggage train, cases of equipment and ammunition, etc., should all be kept as simple as possible for the sake of convenience. The combatant and noncombatant members of the unit should all be organized as most appropriate for guerrilla warfare, and all other persons who are not indispensable should be kept to the strict minimum.

(1) The officers and men in each guerrilla squad should not exceed 8; each platoon should not exceed 26; and each company should not exceed 100.

(2) When automatic weapons are somewhat more numerous, the number of men can be still further reduced, and guerrilla units composed of 5 or 6 men can be sent out repeatedly, in order to achieve the greatest results in terms of harassing the enemy or securing intelligence.

(3) Each commanding officer of a unit should have only one orderly at most. Apart from this according to the complexity of the tasks, two or three officers should share the services of one orderly. Even more attention should be accorded to not abusing this rule by unnecessarily increasing the number of couriers as a substitute for orderlies and to seeing that an unnecessarily large number of men are not sent to carry out a given task, thereby reducing the fighting strength of one's own unit. Hence, when one sends out couriers, one must reflect carefully on whether they can accomplish their task or not.

(4) It is preferable that each mass unit should not carry bundles of food. When the dry rations carried separately by each soldier are exhausted, one should take advantage of opportunities to borrow the pots and pans of the population so as to prepare supplementary rations. If it is necessary to carry bundles, each unit should not carry more than two.

(5) Bundles of writing materials should not be carried in excess of needs. Normally, two bundles per regiment, one per battalion, and one per company are permissible. The weight of each bundle should not exceed 40 kilograms.

(6) Each officer and soldier should carry his own bedding, knapsack, etc. Bearers should not be engaged to transport these items. This rule should be firmly established in advance.

7. OBJECTS TO BE CARRIED.
A guerrilla unit preferably should have the following things:

(1) Equipment and explosives for destroying railroads, telephone and telegraph lines, arsenals, etc.

(2) Medicines. Those needed in case of emergencies should be carried according to the season, but dressings, etc., should be provided on a permanent basis.

(3) A compass, and maps of the area in which the guerrilla unit operates.

(4) Light radio equipment, which is especially important in order to be able

to report at all times on the situation of the enemy and to listen in on the enemy's reports.

(5) A certain quantity of gold coins, to provide for unexpected needs and for buying food.

8. DISCIPLINE.
Whether or not the military discipline of a guerrilla unit is good influences the reputation of our whole army and its ability to secure the sympathy and support of the popular masses. Only strict discipline can assure the complete victory of all our independent actions. Consequently, our attitude toward those persons who violate military discipline, harm the people's interest, and do not resolutely execute the orders of their superiors, should consist in punishing them severely without the slightest regard for politeness. The application of military discipline in a partisan unit does not aim exclusively at punishment. Rather, it aims at strengthening the political instruction of the officers and men and raising their level of political consciousness, thereby indirectly eliminating a large number of actions contrary to military discipline and causing the officers and soldiers to understand the psychology of the masses, so that at appropriate times they can unite effectively with the common people.

9. POLITICAL ORGANIZATION.
(1) Each guerrilla task group and small group should have a political director, and in the headquarters of the guerrilla unit there should be a political training department, for directing the political work of officers and soldiers and dealing with the human problems of all the political instructors.

(2) Each mess unit of a guerrilla unit should establish a special commissioner in order to guard against the infiltration and activity of reactionary elements and to encourage those soldiers without clear ideological consciousness who are wavering in their purposes.

(3) In order to prevent desertion by the soldiers, a committee against desertion, as well as "groups of ten," should be organized in each guerrilla unit. The groups of ten and the committee against desertion are negative methods for preventing desertion. Their organization and work should be carried out roughly as follows:

a. In order to prevent desertion, every guerrilla unit should establish a desertion committee and every mess unit should organize a group of ten.

b. The committee against desertion should be composed of from seven to nine people, one of them being the chairman and the others members. It should be composed of lower-level cadres who can endure difficulties and whose thinking is friary, as well as heads of the groups of ten. The groups of ten are composed of ten men in all, one of them being the head and the others members. They are made up of faithful and reliable soldiers.

c. The over-all activity of the groups of ten is subordinated to the committee against desertion. As regards military matters, it is subordinated to the commander of the unit and to the committee against desertion. In other work, it is subordinated to the political training department. Both groups of ten and committees against desertion must accept the guidance of their commanding officer.

d. The work of the group of ten should take account of all the actions and talk of the officers and soldiers, especially of "camp idlers" and such. Unstable elements should be secretly watched, even if they are members of the group of ten or their friends.

e. Meetings should be held once a week to review the work and to report to the commanding officer and the committee against desertion regarding the situation in general at all times. After each extreme difficulty or when our army has suffered a slight defeat and is staying in its base camp, special attention should be paid to unfavourable attitudes that may develop among the soldiers and to conversations that may endanger the morale of the soldiers.

f. The work of the committee against desertion consists above all in reviewing the work of the groups of ten and in admonishing and guiding them at the appropriate times. The committee may also call conferences of the heads of all the groups of ten, or plenary conferences of all the members of the groups, to discuss the progress of the work as a whole.

The soldiers' life is rather like living in the desert, and every day the men undergo the fatigue of political study and training in the art of combat. This may easily engender feelings of disgust and opposition. In order to provide entertainment for the army and to compensate for a dull life, one should establish in a guerrilla unit clubs or amusement rooms. (For details of the organization and activities of such clubs, see the account in Chap. XV, 10.)

10. SPECIAL FORMS OF MILITARY ORGANIZATION.
(1) In order to make up for insufficient supplies of ammunition and poor marksmanship, every company should have: from three to nine

sharpshooters, to be employed exclusively for shooting from ambush at long distances or for shooting at special targets (enemy officers, machine-gunners or artillery-men, couriers, etc.) .

(2) The commander of each task group and small group should choose particularly sharp-eyed couriers to serve as observes. Normally, a task group commander should have two of these, and a small group commander one. These men serve exclusively to remedy the insufficiency of battlefield observation.

(3) Each task group and small group of a guerrilla unit should have two nurses, who devote themselves exclusively to emergency care of sick officers and soldiers and to instruction in hygiene.

(4) In order to obtain reliable information regarding the enemy's disposition, so as to be able to oppose him without losing any opportunities, all guerrilla units should establish groups of scouts. Normally, it will be sufficient if each unit has one platoon, each task group has one squad, and each small group a smaller element. A network of local scouts should also be established by the group of scouts wherever they go, or by scouts concealed in advance.

CHAPTER V

TASKS

The principal object of the action of a guerrilla unit lies in dealing the enemy the strongest possible blows to his morale, and in creating disorder and agitation in his rear, in drawing off his principal force to the flanks or to the rear, in stopping or slowing down his operations, and ultimately in dissipating his fighting strength so that the enemy's units are crushed one by one and he is precipitated into a situation where, even by rapid and deceptive actions, he can neither advance nor retreat.

1. Destroy railroads and highways within the area of action, as well as important structures along the roads. Telephone lines and telegraph systems are especially important.

2. Destroy the enemy's principal or secondary supply depots.

3. Destroy the enemy's storehouses of food and military equipment.

4. Strike in the enemy's rear, at his baggage train, or at his mounted and unmounted couriers, as well as at his mounted scouts, etc. Also seize the provisions and ammunition that the enemy is bringing up from the rear to

the front.

5. Strike at the enemy's independent task groups and at the inhabited areas that he has not yet solidly occupied.

6. Mobilize and organize the popular masses everywhere and aid them in their own self-defense.

7. Destroy airfields and military depots of the air force in the enemy's rear.

CHAPTER VI

OPERATIONS

1. ACTION.

1. The first principle lies in careful and secret preparation, and in rapid and sudden attack. Fierce wind and heavy rain offer a favorable occasion for a guerrilla attack, as do thick fog, the darkness of night, or circumstances in which it is possible to strike at an exhausted enemy.

2. The operations of a guerrilla unit should consist in offensive warfare. Whether its numbers be great or small, such a unit can nonetheless appear where it is not expected and, in its attacks, take advantage of the enemy's lack of preparation. But when there are indications that the situation is unfavourable, or when there is no certainty of victory, it is appropriate to withdraw rapidly, so as not to suffer damaging losses. If the attack originally planned by the guerrilla unit fails to give an advantageous result, and, the enemy goes over to the offensive, a guerrilla unit should withdraw quickly. Only when the enemy pursues us, and it is impossible to evade his attacks, can we fight a defensive action and then gradually withdraw.

2. THE USE OF TACTICS.

1. The redoubtable force of a guerrilla unit definitely does not depend exclusively on its own numerical strength, but on its use of sudden attacks and ambushes, so as to "cause an uproar in the east and strike in the west," appearing now here and now there, using false banners and making empty demonstrations, propagating rumors about one's own strength, etc., in order to shatter the enemy's morale and create in him a boundless terror. In addition, we must pay attention to such principles as: "The enemy advances, we retreat, the enemy retreats, we advance, the enemy halts, we harass him," camouflaged attacks, etc.

2. A really excellent stratagem for bringing the enemy to his destruction lies in mobilizing the popular masses, in making a strong defense by emptying the countryside, in luring the enemy to penetrate our lines

deeply, in cutting his communications, in placing him in a position where he has difficulties with his food supply, where his men are weary and the terrain is unfavorable and then launching an attack.

3. By such tactics as sudden attacks, ambushes, making a strong defense by emptying the countryside, etc., a guerrilla unit should make every effort to avoid positional warfare, and all frontal engagements. Before the local guerrilla units have received regular military training. they should not be launched against the enemy in a regular and prolonged battle. For this reason, when local guerrilla units are first formed, they should be used only in conjunction with actions by basic or special guerrilla units. It is only after a certain period that they can act independently.

4. If we strike at the point where the enemy feels the greatest difficulties, in order to draw his main force to come to the relief of the position, then, afterward, we send our main force somewhere else, either to attack other isolated and weak forces of the enemy or to attack his reinforcements on the march.

3. ADVANTAGEOUS AND DISADVANTAGEOUS TERRAIN.
1. Because open terrain affords very little good cover, it is slightly disadvantageous for us when guerrilla units operate there. Covered, mountainous, or broken terrain are advantageous for us.

2. A guerrilla unit should be thoroughly familiar with the terrain in its region of action and should think frequently about the ways in which it can appear from a place where the enemy army does not expect it, following secret and hidden routes such as valleys, forests, or narrow winding paths, so as to approach close to the enemy army and take advantage of a situation in which the enemy, persuaded he is quite secure, has taken no measure of defence whatsoever. Then, following the principle that the "thunderclap leaves no time to cover one's ears," the unit can strike sudden blows and then vanish into hiding without a trace, thus reducing the enemy to a level where he does not feel secure whether he is withdrawing or advancing, attacking or defending, moving or remaining still, sitting or lying down.

3. Relatively large villages, market towns, and places where there is a reasonably large amount of grain and other moveable property are frequently the objects of enemy attack and harassment. A guerrilla unit should regularly spy out the enemy's traces, and prepare an ambush so as to attack him when he is in the midst of his march.

131

4. A guerrilla unit should use every method, within its area of action, to prevent the enemy's small units from entering. and his main force from concealing itself there. In case of necessity, a guerrilla unit should also strive to unmask the military strength, disposition, and plans of the enemy operating outside its area of action.

4. SEASONS.
A guerrilla unit must consider the seasons (winter, summer, or autumn are suitable for operations), with reference to the strength of our forces and those of the enemy, and especially with reference to the weapons of war; it must also be thoroughly familiar with the organization of the enemy's rear. Whether or not each season is favourable to us is also determined with reference to the terrain.

5. SECRET ACTION
The peculiar quality of the operations of a guerrilla unit lies entirely in taking the enemy by surprise. Consequently, we must take every possible measure to preserve military secrecy, as described in detail below:

1. The commander of the unit should explain to his subordinates their tasks and the plan for the operation only just before the action begins, or while they are advancing. In case of necessity, he should explain the whole plan only by stages, so that others learn about each stage only when required.

2. The best method for the transmission of orders in a guerrilla unit is by oral explanations from the commander to his subordinates. It is necessary to limit written orders insofar as possible, in order to avoid leakage of military secrets.

3. One should not discuss the whole of one's actions and plans with guides or the local population. This is the case even with regard to local populations favourable to us; it is even more necessary to forbid such talk when we are about to attack a certain place.

4. We should send out faithful and reliable scouts in advance to observe the point where we are going to camp or to lie in ambush along important roads in the enemy's rear, in order to cut off his information.

5. When we advance, our rear guard should take full responsibility for obliterating and removing all secret signals and road signs. We should also advance by circuitous route, so that the enemy does not know the direction of our advance.

6. Fixed code names should be used in place of all unit designations, and the use of the real names of units should be strictly prohibited.

7. Except in case of necessity, all documents should be burned immediately after they have been read.

8. Apart from the methods already enumerated, the true plans of a guerrilla unit can also be obscured in certain cases by using the local population for the deliberate propagation of false information about the operations of the guerrilla unit, in order to deceive the enemy.

6. ARRANGEMENTS AND PREPARATIONS FOR MOVEMENT.
In order that our movements may be rapid, apart from doing our utmost to simplify all our organization, we should at all times maintain excellent preparations for action (investigation and intelligence regarding the front, care of sick soldiers, preparation for guides, preferably employing local peasants whose sympathies lie with the guerrillas, or other reliable persons), and we should also preferably carry three days' dry rations. If this is done, then when we want to move, we move, and when we want to stop, we stop, and there is no need for special arrangements.

7. THE CONDITIONS FOR VICTORY.
1. A condition for the victory of a guerrilla unit is that the officers and soldiers have an absolutely courageous and resolute spirit. They must also be filled with a spirit of action in common, and be thoroughly alert and resolved to carry out their own tasks. Apart from this, they must have healthy bodies and be able to endure boundless hardships, be good at the use of their weapons, etc.

2. A guerrilla unit should not lose heart in difficult times, nor should it cease its activity if it encounters difficult circumstances. As regards their confidence in ultimate victory, their confidence in the success of their cause, and especially their hatred of our national enemy, such circumstances should only strengthen their purpose to advance courageously in spite of all obstacles.

8. UNITED ACTIONS.
If a small guerrilla unit, because its numbers are insufficient, cannot carry out a task assigned to it, it can unite temporarily with a few other guerrilla units, in order to fulfill its task.

Guerrilla operations are best carried out under cover of night.

CHAPTER VII

SURPRISE ATTACKS

1. POINTS THAT SHOULD BE CAREFULLY CONSIDERED REGARDING OUR TASKS BEFORE A SURPRISE ATTACK.

When a guerrilla unit has finished concentrating for an attack, and when plans for scouts, courier service etc., have all been satisfactorily completed, and one is preparing a surprise attack on a certain inhabited place, the commander of the guerrilla unit must first form a clear idea about each of the following points.

1. What is the strength of the military forces defending the given inhabited place? How are they deployed? How are they armed? What is their fighting capacity? How many scouts to sound a warning have they sent out?

2. Is there any other enemy nearby? If there is, how far away is he? Can he quickly come to the aid of the defending forces? Can we imagine how he would come to aid them? From what direction he would come?

3. What sort of roads are there that could be followed by the guerrillas and by the enemy? What hidden roads are there in the vicinity of the place we intend to attack by surprise? What route will we take to get to the place we are attacking? The preceding three points are not only things we should know in view of carrying out a surprise attack; we must also not fail to consider them with reference to our withdrawal after the attack.

4. As for fixing the time of a surprise attack, it is best to carry it out at night, for, under the cover of darkness, even if the attack should fail, it can still inspire panic in the enemy. But we can attack at night only if we are thoroughly familiar with the terrain, and have clearly understood the enemy's dispositions or have extremely good guides. Otherwise, we should choose instead to carry out such surprise attacks at daybreak. If a surprise attack is to be directed against a supply depot, it should be carried out in the dead of night, for the men, horses, and military equipment in such a depot will be on the move again very early, at daybreak.

5. Can the population of the given inhabited place aid the enemy or not? How can we prevent the population from bringing trouble on itself in this way?

While we should think through our plans at length, we should avoid overly subtle plans.

2. POINTS FOR ATTENTION BEFORE SETTING OUT.

1. Before setting out, a guerrilla unit should complete all its preparations for the march (see below). Moreover, it should consider taking stretchers for transporting wounded soldiers.

2. The method for a surprise attack on the enemy should be thoroughly understood beforehand not only by the commander of the unit and the commanders of each task group, but also by all the members of each independent task group. The best mode of transmitting this information is through oral explanations by the commander and his staff. Written orders of all kinds should be held to a minimum, in order to avoid having their contents divulged by loss or mistake.

3. Prior to setting out, all officers at every level should appoint a replacement, in order, on the one hand to express their resolution to sacrifice themselves and, on the other hand, to avoid the risk that, if they are wounded or killed, the action of the guerrilla unit may fail to attain its objective because of them, thus influencing the whole situation.

3. POINTS FOR ATTENTION WHILE ON THE MOVE.

1. We must make the greatest efforts to conceal the movements of a guerrilla unit and to prevent discovery by the enemy. Consequently, while advancing, we must leave the highroads and avoid large villages, and choose out-of-the-way places or even places where there are no roads at all, advancing along narrow winding trails. But we should keep away from miry roads, so as to avoid excessive fatigue.

2. When advancing, we should not proceed for long time on the same road, for this makes it easy for the enemy to discover our tracks. From the standpoint of keeping our movements secret, it is also generally appropriate to move by night, even when we are advancing a long distance.

3. When we are advancing, for the sake of concealing ourselves, we should hold the number of people we send out for reconnaissance to the very lowest level. In general, it will be sufficient to send just a few scouts along the road, but we must have very good guides.

4. If we are not absolutely certain that there are no enemy spies coming to observe us, it is best to divide our forces into small groups, which advance separately in different directions and then concentrate at a point which has been secretly designated.

5. When a guerrilla unit is on the move, it should be constantly prepared for a meeting with the enemy. For this reason, the commanding officer of a guerrilla unit generally advances, accompanied by his staff, just behind the scouts, behind the elite soldiers, or ahead of the staff of the unit (the staff is entrusted to the leadership of the second in command). Thus, it is easy to obtain a clear picture of the situation, and decisions can be taken very rapidly. If the commander sees that it is possible to advance, he advances; if he becomes aware of difficulties, he withdraws. All that is required is for two or three officers to hold a discussion, and then the decision can be made. Thus, we avoid sending orders back and forth, with the consequent wasting of opportunities, and we diminish command form the rear, and its attendant evil of taking action not in keeping with the circumstances.

6. Apart from the scouts sent out along the road, the soldiers of the guerrilla unit should not load their rifles, so as to avoid accidental discharges during the march and discovery by the enemy.

4. MEASURES TO BE TAKEN IF THE ENEMY IS ENCOUNTERED WHILE ON THE MARCH.
1. Under no circumstances should a guerrilla unit provoke a pointless battle before it has reached its objective. Even though a guerrilla unit may encounter the enemy in the course of its march, it should devise a way for getting around him—if necessary, departing from the original plan. If there is no way of avoiding battle, we should emerge from ambush, after rapid preparations, so as to appear where the enemy does not expect us and annihilate him by a surprise attack. At the same time, when we are carrying out such a maneuver, we should pay attention to whether the enemy halts or advances, and send out scouts to reconnoiter from all directions. If the enemy army is not prepared for battle or if, although he is in some strength, he is not on the alert, we should charge him immediately. Otherwise, we should remain in hiding and quietly await an opportunity.

2. When, in the course of our march, we encounter enemy outposts or scouts, we should avoid being seen by them and circle past them in strict silence. But it we encounter a situation in which we judge there is an opportunity to be grasped, we should act rapidly and capture them without firing a shot.

5. DISPOSITION OF TROOPS DURING A SURPRISE ATTACK.
When a guerrilla unit carries out a surprise attack, the disposition of its troops should be more or less as follows:

1. We should launch a fierce attack by our main force on the point in the enemy's disposition where it hurts the most — a really swift and resolute sudden blow. We should also send another force around to carry out energetic action on the enemy's flanks and in his rear, in order to confuse his judgement, and prevent him from fathoming where our main force is located.

2. We should attack one point in the enemy's disposition with all our might, but we should also carry out feigned deployments in other places and make an empty demonstration with a few scattered soldiers, so as to confuse the enemy's eyes and ears, and disperse his forces.

3. If we can determine beforehand the enemy's line of retreat, then we should, within the limits of what is possible, send a part of our forces to intercept him. Ii the enemy has his heavy artillery and logistic supply installed outside the village, then we should designate a special small group to seize them.

4. If the guerrilla unit is numerically strong, it should be divided into several columns and should carry out the attack from two, three, or several directions, attempting to cut off the enemy's retreat, But we should consider the matter thoroughly, so as to avoid causing confusion in our own ranks, which might result in erroneously taking our own troops for those of the enemy. Because of this possibility, it is necessary, in advance of the action, to agree on signals.

5. In the case of a surprise attack on the enemy, if there is reason to fear that enemy reinforcements may arrive from a certain direction, we should send a small body of troops in advance of the action to the route where the reinforcements may arrive, so as to obstruct their advance, or report this peril to the main force.

6. At the time of a surprise attack, the choice of the point on which the brunt of the attack will fall, and the geographical distribution of our forces (in general, two-thirds of our men are used for the principal direction of attack, and only one-third for the auxiliary directions of attack) must absolutely be such as to prevent the enemy forces from spreading out or receiving reinforcements and to make it possible for us to smash them one by one.

7. The various task groups making up a guerrilla unit should divide their forces within a very short distance of the point where the attack is to be made, and from there make a separate but coordinated advance. The best

place for this is the point from which the charge will be made. In this way, we can avoid such misfortunes as losing our way, or the premature division of our forces, and we can also. guard against the danger of surprise attacks by the enemy. For the farther apart are the various independent columns or groups, the more likely they are to be separated by the terrain, and the more difficult it will be to expect them all to strike at the same moment.

6. THE SUCCESS OF A SURPRISE ATTACK.

In general, we charge the enemy when he is not prepared, in circumstances where he is frightened and flustered. If we really want to strike when the enemy is not expecting us and attain success, the following points should be attended to:

1. We must act rapidly and secretly and not allow our plans to be revealed prematurely.

2. We must strike at a time when the enemy's warning system is not very alert.

3. We must make an empty display, and attack in several places at once, so that the enemy's reaction is confused, his forces are frightened and hamper one another, and he cannot use all his strength to resist us stubbornly.

4. In carrying out the surprise attack, we must attack at the appointed hours; there must be no noise; no shots must be fired; there must be no battle cries. We must make every soldier understand the use of the arms employed in a surprise attack, which are the bayonet and the hand grenade. We must not return fire simply because we hear the gunfire of the enemy. It is only when we have an opportunity to take advantage of the situation to attack the enemy that we should launch our attack, with our vanguard well supported by our rear guard, choosing frontal, flanking, or direct blows.

7. DISPOSITIONS FOLLOWING THE SUCCESS OF A SURPRISE ATTACK.

1. As soon as the tasks of a surprise attack have been carried out, a guerrilla unit should rapidly withdraw. Before withdrawing, it is best to go a few li in a false direction, and then afterward turn and go in our true direction, so that the enemy will be unable to discover our tracks, and will not be able to follow us.

2. It is not appropriate for a guerrilla unit to take along prisoners, or to acquire large amounts of booty, which hinder our movement. It is best to

require the prisoners first to hand over their weapons, and then to disperse them or to execute them. As for booty, it should be dispatched by the local government, or by the population.

3. During the battle, three officers and men out of every company should be given the exclusive task of picking up and gathering together abandoned rifles and ammunition. After a victorious battle, we should devote all our efforts to collecting everything on the battlefield, and we can also call upon the population of nearby areas to gather such things together, so that not the smallest trifle is left behind.

8. DISPOSITIONS FOLLOWING THE DEFEAT OF A SURPRISE ATTACK.
If a surprise attack is defeated, we should rapidly withdraw to the place of assembly designated in advance. The usual assembly point is in the place where we encamped the previous night. If our forces are sufficient, we can leave a reserve unit along the designated withdrawal route, to look out for prisoners and wounded men.

CHAPTER VIII

ESPIONAGE

1. POINTS FOR ATTENTION WHEN CARRYING OUT ESPIONAGE.
1. All reports on the situation should be transmitted without loss of time to one's superiors or to friendly armies.

2. The reports which we collect absolutely must be in full detail. All sloppy and negligent reporting must be severely prohibited.

3. The scope of espionage is not limited merely to the situation of the enemy; spies should also pay attention to the terrain. We should be informed of all aspects of the terrain that are disadvantageous to us, especially those aspects favourable to the enemy, such as narrow roads, river crossings, circuitous routes for avoiding these river crossings and narrow roads, etc.

4. We should bend every effort to obtain complete and detailed information regarding all matters having any relation to our guerrilla unit; our efforts should never cease until we understand the situation thoroughly.

5. We should pay attention to the sentiments of the people toward ourselves and the enemy. Are the people actively aiding us? How is their positive attitude manifested?

2. METHODS OF ESPIONAGE.

Apart from sending out courageous and intelligent individuals (i.e., spies) to carry out espionage on every hand, a guerrilla unit must unite closely with the popular masses of the place in question. Moreover, in strategically important places, we use reliable local inhabitants or those among the people who sympathize with the guerrilla unit (for example, we can make use of feudal relationships and find a relative, or someone belonging to the family of person who has been executed by the enemy; we can also employ those among the people who hate the enemy, etc.). We give these people a relatively good salary, establish a secret espionage network, as well as a system of sentries, so that we can transmit information with facility.

3. ESPIONAGE REGARDING THE NUMBER OF THE ENEMY'S TROOPS, HIS TACTICAL SKILL, AND HIS ARMAMENT.

1. Where are so and so many enemy infantrymen, cavalrymen, artillery-men, and other units to be found? How many armored cars and trains, tanks and air planes does the enemy have? And where are they?

2. What kind of defensive works does the enemy have in his front, in his rear, and around his cities and other places? What kind of forces are defending?

3. Where are the enemy's encampments and arsenals?

4. What about the enemy's reserves and flanking troops? Where are they?

5. How is the morale of the enemy soldiers? Are they prepared to fight or not? What are their relations with the people and with their own officers?

6. What about the enemy army's supplies of military equipment, bedding and clothes, food, and other items?

4. ESPIONAGE REGARDING THE TERRAIN.

1. First of all, we must pay attention to the important roads within this area, as well as their direction, their width, their type of surface, whether or not they are muddy, etc., and whether or not they are suitable for use by all types of forces.

2. Are there any forests or not? If there are, we must pay attention to the kinds of trees, and to their area.

3. We must consider rivers, their width and depth, their rate of flow, the slope and type of soil of the banks. Are there bridges, ferries, or other means for crossing the river? If there are bridges, will they bear up under artillery, the baggage train, and other types of unit?

4. Are there any marshes? Where? What is their area? Can they be crossed or not? If so, we must note what kinds of troops can get through them.

CHAPTER IX

AMBUSHES

1. TYPES OF AMBUSH.

When we emerge suddenly from hiding, and strike a sudden blow at the enemy who is just passing by, this is called an ambush. The sole habitual tactic of a guerrilla unit is the ambush. By means of an ambush it is extremely easy to obtain a good result, and as a general rule they are always advantageous. Such action is divided into the following types:

1. Ambush by luring the enemy. This occurs when our troops, so to speak, prostrate themselves and hold out both arms, enticing the enemy to penetrate deeply. It is carried out by first placing our main force in ambush along the two sides of the road, or in a hiding place on one side, and then attacking the enemy with a small force. This force then feigns defeat and withdraws, luring the enemy deep into our lines, after which the main force rushes out from one side or both sides and carries out a surprise attack.

2. Waiting ambushes. These are very similar to ambushes by luring the enemy, but it is not necessary for a part of our forces to feign defeat. Instead, we establish an observation post on some height, to observe the movements of the enemy army, and when his main force has reached the appropriate point, we rush out and attack him by surprise.

2. SPOTS FOR CARRYING OUT AMBUSHES, AND OBJECTIVES TO BE ATTACKED.

Ambushes can be carried out against a variety of objectives such as isolated enemy soldiers, couriers, whole mobile units, logistic convoys, transport columns, trains, etc. Further details are given below.

1. When ambushing the enemy's cavalry or infantry, we should choose a spot where they cannot use their weapons and where it is not easy for them to manifest their full strength.

2. Ambushes against logistic convoys or transport columns should be

carried out in the midst of a forest or in the countryside.

3. Ambushes of small enemy units, or whole mobile units or motorized transport columns are most valuable. But we must first understand their plans, the direction in which they are advancing, and the time it will take them to pass. We must also reflect in detail on the location for the ambush and carefully seek out a place likely to contribute to a favourable result. At the same time, we must carefully select in advance the route for our own withdrawal.

4. When a guerrilla unit carries out an ambush against a railroad train, our forces can be split into three parts. The first part should take up battle positions near the railroad, to guard against resistance from the train. The second part should take up a position on the two sides of the train, and shoot into the carriage. The third part has the task of charging and boarding the train to make a search, unloading the cargo, taking charge of the weapons, etc .

3. THE TERRAIN IN AMBUSHES.
The point at which an ambush is carried out must have the following features:

1. It must have good cover, in order to prevent our being observed by the enemy and, at the same time, permit us to observe the enemy.

2. It must permit us to employ our maximum fire power.

3. It must allow us to leap out rapidly at one bound from ambush and come to grips with the enemy. Hence, between the point where we lie in ambush and the enemy, there should be a dense forest, a damp depression, a narrow road, or some other intervening ground.

4. THE DISTANCE FROM WHICH AN AMBUSH SHOULD BE CARRIED OUT.
If the guerrilla unit which carries out a surprise attack is in sufficient strength so that it wants to come to grips with the enemy at one bound, then it should stage its ambush near the side of the road. If, on the other hand, the enemy is in considerable strength, and our plan is merely to harass him and cause confusion, then we should remain in a place some distance from the road.

5. IMPORTANT TRICKS FOR AN AMBUSH.
1. An ambush can most advantageously be carried out in silence. Whether by day or night, loud talking should be absolutely forbidden, as should

patrolling along the front.

2. Remaining a long time in ambush can easily lead to discovery of our plans and an increase in the danger. Because of remaining too long in ambush, the state of tension of our men is gradually weakened, and they can no longer maintain their vigilance. Hence, one can easily be discovered by the enemy. A point that especially merits attention is that, if we have already been discovered by the enemy, we should immediately either launch our attack or withdraw.

CHAPTER X

SURPRISE ATTACKS ON THE ENEMY'S FORAGING UNITS

1. OCCASIONS FOR SURPRISE ATTACKS.

A charge against the enemy's foraging units should be carried out under the following circumstances:

1. It can be executed when the enemy unit is nearing a village.

2. We can wait until the enemy enters a village and has scattered in all directions to forage from door to door, and then carry it out.

3. We can wait until the enemy has finished foraging and is returning loaded with booty, and then attack by surprise from ambush.

4. Which of the above types of attack is most appropriate should be determined with reference to the circumstances, by the persons who are responsible for the guerrilla unit. They should carefully evaluate all the factors and make arrangements adapted to circumstances.

2. SURPRISE ATTACKS IN A VILLAGE.

It is most advantageous to attack the enemy's foraging units in a village. At such a time the greater part of the enemy's foraging unit is scattered all over the place, and it is not easy for them to gather together quickly. But, in carrying out this type of surprise attack we must steal by the enemy's warning outposts or capture his sentinels without the slightest sound; only then can we make our attack.

3. SURPRISE ATTACKS OUTSIDE A VILLAGE.

It the force carrying out a surprise attack is especially weak, it must wait until the foraging is completed and until the foraging column has reached a place favourable to a surprise attack— such as when it is passing through a

143

forest, across a bridge, or along a narrow road—before attacking.

4. THE OBJECTIVES OF THE SURPRISE ATTACK.

When a guerrilla unit has attacked and dispersed the enemy unit covering a foraging operation, it can reckon only that it has completed part of its attack. It must also destroy or capture all of their wagons. Consequently, the guerrilla unit should first engage the enemy covering unit in combat and then attack the logistic convoy with its main force and capture it.

5. POINTS TO WHICH THE GUERRILLA UNIT SHOULD PAY ATTENTION.

It is easy to obtain the assistance of the local population when attacking one of the enemy's foraging units. Hence, within the limits of what is possible, part of the property seized should be given to the popular masses, to heighten their courage.

CHAPTER XI

SURPRISE ATTACKS ON ENEMY'S TRANSPORT UNITS

An attack on a transport column is one of the most advantageous forms of action for a guerrilla unit, since we can obtain in this manner the weapons, food, and supplies we need.

1. SUDDEN SURPRISE ATTACKS.

With such attacks, we can frighten the enemy out of his wits, and precipitate him into a state of complete confusion. The coolies of the transport units are, in large part, timid peasants forcibly impressed. Moreover, the size of the covering force is limited, and it is generally spread out over a very long distance. If we overturn one of the wagons, we can make all the wagons behind it stop too.

2. METHODS OF ATTACK.

1. The guerrilla unit must not forget that its task is not to defeat the enemy, but to capture the enemy's wagons. Consequently, we should detail only a part of our forces to do battle with the enemy's covering unit. The rest of our men should be ordered to plunder, pursue, and demolish the materials he is transporting. Hence, whenever we carry out such a surprise attack, we should do our best to contrive matters so as to open fire rapidly against the transport unit and cause them to stop, in order to increase their confusion and fear.

2. In order to stop the whole transport column, it is only necessary to shoot at the front part of it, because, under conditions of mass anxiety and bewilderment, when the wagons in front stop, they will interfere with one another, fall over on the side of the road, and bring about a situation of

extreme confusion. If there are a large number of transport wagons, and if, because the front of the column is under fire, the wagons at the rear endeavor to turn around and escape, the guerrilla unit should send out a small number of riflemen to shoot furiously from cover at the tail end of the column, so that it does not dare turn around.

3. If the unit carrying out the surprise attack is in an inferior position, and the covering unit is taking active precautionary measures, the guerrilla unit should exhaust the enemy by incessant false alarms, and then when the transport column is passing through a forest or valley or along a narrow road in some other type of terrain, where the enemy's logistic convoy cannot easily turn around, the attack should be swiftly carried out.

It is not often advantageous to carry out a surprise attack on a baggage train in a village, for the covering unit and the logistic convoy can easily make use of the houses and other cover, and offer strong resistance.

4. If the covering unit has already been dispersed by our attack, the resistance of the transport unit has also been overcome, and enemy reinforcements cannot arrive in time, the guerrilla unit can then destroy the wagons and the goods they are carrying or destroy completely whatever the guerrillas cannot carry away or have no use for.

CHAPTER XII

THE CORRESPONDENCE NETWORK OF A GUERRILLA UNIT AND THE DESTRUCTION OF COMMUNICATIONS FACILITIES IN THE REAR

1. THE OBJECT OF THE NETWORK.

So that they may be able to call upon one another for aid and receive information at all times regarding the situation of the enemy, guerrilla units should do their utmost to maintain the closest and most solid relations with the local population for the exchange of correspondence.

2. MEANS FOR MAINTAINING RELATIONS.

In order to set up such a correspondence network, we should, in addition to utilizing the telephone in the greatest possible measure, employ all means at hand. These include runners, messengers on horseback, messengers on bicycles, secret couriers posted in advance for transmitting information, as well as transmittal by sentries, and even signals and pre-established signs, etc.

3. METHODS FOR TRANSMITTING REPORTS.

1. A network for important correspondence should be set up. Reports of

an urgent character can best be transmitted by messengers on horseback. When this is impossible, we should send out reliable individuals particularly good at going on foot. It is also possible to arrange in advance for the transmittal of secret letters. There are times, too, when we must send out several men, each of them taking a different route, to make certain that the report in question will reach its destination. (This method should be limited to the most important reports.)

2. As for ordinary reports that are not particularly important, they are commonly transmitted by runners or messengers on bicycles. There are times when one can also use faithful individuals from among the local population who are thoroughly familiar with the routes to carry such reports.

4. SIGNALS FOR COMMUNICATIONS.
For the sake of convenience in guiding each guerrilla group or unit by day or by night, in its actions in mountainous terrain or in forests, the commander of a guerrilla unit should establish in advance a certain number of basic signals and signs (such as signals fires at night, smoke signals by day, coloured pennants, flags, semaphore signaling by flags, paper signals, whistles, bugle calls, etc.).

5. DISPOSITIONS REGARDING ROUTES OF COMMUNICATION IN THE REAR.
Should we or should we not destroy the routes of communication in the enemy's rear? We must reflect in detail about this problem. If we conclude that, in the future, our own army will not need to utilize these roads, or will not be able to utilize them, then we can destroy them.

6. POINTS FOR ATTENTION IN DESTROYING ROUTES OF COMMUNICATION.
If we want to destroy routes of communication, we must be thoroughly familiar with the terrain. It is only then that, moving rapidly and elusively, we appear suddenly and quickly withdraw. In eliminating the enemy's sentries, we must not fire a shot, in order not to alert them and give them a chance to flee.

7. PRECAUTIONS WHEN BEGINNING THE DESTRUCTION OF ROUTES OF COMMUNICATION.
When we begin the destruction of routes of communication, we must first send out a detachment to the place where the presence of the enemy has been reported, in order to keep an eye on the enemy's patrols and his small detachments, so that they cannot quickly and secretly get close to the point where our own unit is at work. If, while beginning work, we are discovered by the enemy, we should shoot at him to keep him from

coming nearer.

8. METHODS OF DESTROYING WORKS ON THE GROUND.

1. Railroads should be destroyed at the points where they are most difficult to repair, such as at curves, at points where the railway is hidden from view, where the enemy's precautions are lax, where we can work under cover, or where we can destroy a large length of track. When destroying the rails, we should bend them, or hollow out the ground beneath them. In low-laying places we should dig ditches. As for tunnels, we should obstruct them.

2. Railroad ties, wooden bridges, telegraph and telephone poles, etc., should be burned up. Wires should be carried away or dropped into the water.

3. Signals switches, semaphores, railroad carriages, etc., located in the stations should be destroyed, preferably by blowing them up with explosives.

4. In destroying cobblestone roads, highways, bridges, and other constructions, we must in all cases choose a method of destruction appropriate to the nature of the construction.

CHAPTER XIII

REGULAR HIDING PLACES AND PRECAUTIONS TO BE TAKEN WHEN WE HALT

1. MARSHALING OUR TROOPS.

The problem is not merely one of resting and marshaling out troops. We require a place that can also be used for conserving ammunition and food and for receiving and looking after wounded and sick soldiers. Hence, the place in question commonly serves also as a supporting point in time of battle. As soon as we are the objects of the enemy's pursuit and attack, we withdraw there, and secretly hide, so as to await an opportunity to act or to begin resisting the enemy again.

2. THE CHOICE OF A SPOT.

1. A hiding place where we can rest for a long time may conveniently be found deep in the forest, in a thatched hut near a marsh, in a cave under the ground or in a mountainside, on a lonely farm, or in a small and secluded hamlet. Because of the sympathy it enjoys a small guerrilla unit normally has no difficulty at all in finding a regular hiding place.

2. A guerrilla unit must absolutely maintain the strictest secrecy regarding the hiding places it has selected. Even one's closest friends and relatives must not be informed if they have no connection with the guerrilla unit in question. If our original hiding place has been discovered by the enemy, then, in general, we should not wait for the enemy to come and attack us but must quickly remove elsewhere.

3. Sometimes such hiding places also serve as storehouses for military equipment, powder, and provisions, and also for receiving wounded and sick soldiers. More often, a separate secret location in the vicinity of the hiding place is selected for each type of storehouse because there are people continually going in and out of a hiding place and it can very easily be discovered by the enemy.

4. The more individuals there are among the people who support the guerrillas, so that the guerrilla unit can also maintain a communications network among the people, the easier it is for the guerrilla unit to find a hiding place. There are times when, in order to evade the enemy's pursuit and attack, and find a good place to hide, a given guerrilla unit must be split up, each of its members being obliged to find a way to hide himself in one of the houses of the local population. In such circumstances, the local population is the only hope of salvation of the members of the guerrilla unit.

3. THE QUESTION OF PROVISIONS.
In places where the local population is hostile to the guerrillas, there is no alternative to foraging backed by force, but one should send reliable people from among the detachment, in order to guard against pillaging.

When the guerrilla unit does not fear discovery, it can send out a special small unit to forage for food, to collect contributions of food, or to demand food supplies from the local authorities.

4. CHANGING ONE'S HALTING PLACE.
The best method by which a guerrilla unit can maintain its own security is through the agility of its action. In case of necessity, the unit can make a habit of changing its halting place every night (if, during the day, it has been in village A, at twilight it moves to village B).

5. OCCUPYING A HALTING PLACE.
When a guerrilla unit encamps, the arrangement of its forces should be determined entirely by the nature of its action, but it should not occupy a

large village that its own forces are insufficient to hold. If a guerrilla unit cannot do otherwise, and finds itself in such a place, it should occupy only a few collective dwellings situated apart and convenient for defense. The best thing is to be located in a village where one can keep a lookout in all directions, especially on the road along which the enemy might come. We must absolutely not disperse the members of the unit to stay in different houses, acting, for the sake of individual convenience, in a way of which the enemy could take advantage. In order to keep the enemy from knowing where we are staying, the best method is to enter the village only late at night. Moreover, we should look about carefully and all sides of the village and not allow anyone at all to come out.

6. THE DEGREE OF PRECAUTIONS.

In order to avoid excessive fatigue to the members of a guerrilla unit, and to assure them of a real rest, it is not necessary to send out large numbers of scouts to sound a warning. It suffices to arrange for military outposts and concealed scouts in all adjoining places and along all roads (those which the enemy must take, or those related to us). We should also send out spies to places from 2 to 4 li away. This distance will be sufficient.

Whether or not the enemy attacks us, we must always fix an assembly point at a distance of from 10 to 16 li, for use in case of withdrawal. Moreover, the roads leading to the assembly point should be designated and marked in advance (but there must be at least two roads giving access to such a place) .

7. PREPARATIONS.

When a guerrilla unit is staying in a place, all its members, whether they be officers or soldiers, must at all times take measures to prepare for battle. Especially after twilight, every officer and soldier must gather together the arms and other equipment he carries with him, and arrange them in proper order, so that it will be convenient, in case there is an alarm in the dark, for him to go out quickly and meet the attack.

8. WHEN THERE IS ANXIETY ABOUT A SURPRISE ATTACK BY THE ENEMY.

1. If the guerrilla unit itself is especially alert, if its intelligence network is organized with exceptional discretion, and if the people of the area are in sympathy with us, so that they regularly report all movements to us, then it is extremely difficult for the enemy to mount sudden surprise attacks. But whatever the circumstances may be, we must always exercise due caution.

2. In order to prevent the enemy relying on a hostile population from

coming and making a surprise attack on us, we must take special precautionary measures. Thus by methods of intimidation we warn the local population, we arrest and detain people. But at the same time, the unit must exercise caution and be prepared.

3. If there is an alarm, we should assemble the whole unit in a building that has been prepared for defense. We should dispatch to this building advance sentries and observers as required. The entrance to the building should be closed by movable obstacles, and we should establish in advance signals for the defense. Weapons and other equipment should be properly prepared and placed within reach of each man.

4. When circumstances are extremely critical, part of a friendly unit should take over responsibility for the security of our position and the place in which our army is staying, as well as for sending out spies far and wide to add to the warning system. They report constantly to the guerrilla task group on the situation of nearby enemy forces.

5. When we use artificial obstacles to block the roads, we must make provision for communication with our first line and reserves, as well as with the local population and our correspondence network.

6. In case of necessity, the roads within villages can be completely blocked off, or we can leave a way through. Whenever possible, each guerrilla task group should have a prepared position.

9. DISPOSITIONS IN CASE OF AN ENEMY SURPRISE ATTACK.

1. When we discover that the enemy is moving toward us, if we find out from reconnaissance that he is not in strength, we should annihilate him with one sudden blow. If the enemy forces are several times more numerous than ours, we should rapidly withdraw. But while we are withdrawing we should give the enemy a false impression of the direction in which we are moving, so as to conceal our actual route of withdrawal.

2. If the enemy attacks us by surprise and we do not succeed in evading him, we should exploit in full measure the advantages of a village for defensive action, resist him firmly, and then later take advantage of an opportunity to withdraw.

3. If we have already lost a village, we should reply by a counterattack or counterblows in order to take it back quickly and save our captured

comrades, or those comrades who are clinging to a position and defending it stubbornly to the death. If our action is rapid, we can always attain such objectives, because after a victory the enemy is often in great confusion and lax in his precautions.

4. The best occasion for carrying out such counterblows, or such a counteroffensive, is just after the victory of the enemy's surprise attack. The sacrifices of a charge under such circumstances are less than those from running away, or from stopping and giving battle in unfavourable terrain following the enemy' s attack.

CHAPTER XIV

TRAINING

1. THE SCOPE OF TRAINING.

Training is not limited to the military arts; we must also pay attention to political training, to the literacy movement, to training in hygiene, etc. Consequently, when a guerrilla unit is engaged in drill, literacy training should represent an appropriate part of the whole, and can be given in all places and at all times.

For the purpose of achieving a full and satisfactory result from all the kinds of training carried out in a guerrilla unit, we must increase the will to study on their own initiative among the officers and soldiers. Apart from the political aspect, and in addition to increasing political consciousness, we must also promote amusements for the army, mitigate a painful and tedious existence, assist the people in their own self-defense, and cause the armed force of the popular masses to unite closely with us.

2. TRAINING IN ALL SUBJECTS.

The consequence of training in all subjects, though it is difficult to reduce it to uniformity, is, as regards methods in general, to proceed from the superficial to the profound, first the broad and then the rigorous, from the simple and easy to the complex and difficult, first the partial and then the universal. In all fields, one must demonstrate one's theories by concrete experience, so as to strengthen the students' confidence.

3. CULTIVATING THE PEOPLE'S CAPACITY FOR SELF-DEFENSE.

The most pressing and most important task of a guerrilla unit is to carry out guerrilla attacks without ceasing in the places occupied by the enemy, to seize and kill all traitors and reactionaries, and to protect the popular masses. At the same time, a guerrilla unit must investigate the concrete offenses of the enemy and use every possible method to discover and smash his tricks and plots. Therefore:

1. It is advantageous to make known our good government, to make great efforts to unite with the popular masses, and to support the forces of the popular masses. Such actions can also be carried out on the territory of the enemy. We should also use every possible method and devote all our strength to encourage the people to imitate our own actions, stimulate them to fight the enemy actively, and guide their combat.

2. Our action in supporting the people's capacity for self-defense should be of long duration, and not ephemeral. We must do the best we can to let people know that, at all times, a guerrilla unit struggles and sacrifices itself for the popular masses and, even in the case of the most dangerous crisis, will absolutely not harm the popular masses. If the local population meets with a defeat in its first military action, after we have drawn it into the war, its spirit of struggle will necessarily be dissipated to some extent. When the masses falter in this way, we must devise a way to rouse their enthusiasm and to bring their spirit of struggle to a high level once more.

3. A guerrilla unit constitutes the most conscious and advanced segment of the people. Hence, they should first unite those among the popular masses who are dissatisfied with the enemy and who accept the leadership of those we send among them. We must also aid the people to establish plans, to get arms, and to establish liaison and mutual assistance with mass organizations in neighboring villages and even in other cities that are victims of the enemy's oppression. But, in carrying out all such work, we must maintain the strictest secrecy.

4. TRAINING IN HYGIENE.
1. In order to strengthen its own fighting capacity, every mess unit should designate one or two soldiers as nurses, to treat the ailments of the officers and soldiers when they arise and, also to explain the rudiments of hygiene, as well as to assist, direct, supervise, and encourage all matters of hygiene in the unit.

2. Replenishing stocks of medicines is an extremely difficult matter in a guerrilla unit. Hence we should, in accordance with the seasons etc., prepare certain medicines especially for emergency care, and other normally indispensable medicines. As regards wounded and seriously ill members of the unit, when there is no alternative, they are entrusted to fellow soldiers with some slight medical knowledge or to local inhabitants sympathetic to us.

5. MILITARY TRAINING.

Military training all relates to the enemy army. Its purpose is to create greater skill than that of the enemy in each specialized art.

1. Subjects. The items requiring particular attention are dispersing, assembling, marksmanship, maneuvering an army, mountain climbing, construction of military works, night fighting, mountain fighting, fighting on narrow roads, espionage and security measures, searches, liaison, and other such actions.

2. Methods. In carrying out military instruction, particular attention should be paid to all methods of teaching and explanation, which should be more or less as described below:

a. For theoretical instruction one can employ the method of giving suggestions and the method of questions and answers. All methods of teaching that adopt the style of speechmaking and injecting [ideas into the students' heads] should be eliminated in so far as possible.

b. When explaining actions, we should pay attention to linking our talks with the living reality, so that it will be easy for the soldiers to understand us.

c. We should devote more time to concrete demonstrations of actions and less time to talking about empty theories. Consequently, the greatest effort should be made to diminish the duration and number of classroom sessions and the numbers of practical exercises should be increased.

d. All explanations in the classroom should in so far as possible correspond to the exercises outside.

e. All demonstrations of actions should be carefully prepared in advance before they are executed. All negligent and perfunctory behaviour—doing things any old way—must absolutely be eliminated.

f. With respect to all activities, we should devise a way to incite the officers and soldiers to carry out a competition, in order to increase the spirit of initiative and the positive attitude they manifest in their work, and to speed up the work.

g. Increase applied training, diminish training according to a fixed pattern, and correct the erroneous idea that training according to a fixed pattern is useful in maintaining military discipline.

h. The plan of training should be suited to the circumstances, time, and place in which it is to be carried out. The training plan must absolutely not be rigid; we must seize every occasion and strive to give training adapted to the circumstances. This is done more or less as indicated below:

i. We utilize the time when the army is on the march to carry on direction finding, recognizing differences in terrain, estimating distances, reconnaissance action, and designating objectives and the utilization of terrain.

i. When we are in camp, we utilize preparations for security measures in order to carry out exercises in all kinds of observation and precautions, beginning with the role of advanced sentries. We also provide training in construction of military works.

ii. We utilize the opportunity provided by a battle, and before setting out or before the fighting begins, we explain, on the basis of the tasks we have been ordered to perform, such forms of action as ambushes, surprise attacks, main attacks, and supporting attacks, etc.

iii. We utilize the opportunity, when we are awaiting the moment for action, to explain in practical terms how we resist the charges of the enemy, as well as shooting and other such military actions.

iv. We utilize post-battle exposition and criticism (such exposition and criticism should be based on a minute investigation of the facts, carried out beforehand) to point out the strength and weaknesses in our actions during the battle and what was appropriate and inappropriate in the individual commands, thus giving a concrete lesson to all of officers and men.

v. We utilize the time offered by morning and evening roll calls to give various kinds of talks.

vi. We utilize the occasion offered by the recreation period to put on games, dances, and modern-style plays, having military significance, thus imperceptibly increasing the officers' and soldiers' desire to correct themselves, and increasing their willingness to follow good examples.

vii. We utilize each occasion of reward and punishment to carry out thorough propaganda among the officers and soldiers, in order to increase the soldiers' sense of achievement and their shame in doing evil, and thus, little by little, fostering a good military discipline.

6. POLITICAL TRAINING.
In order to assure that all the independent actions of a guerrilla unit attain complete victory, apart from reinforcing military training, the most important thing is that we must make certain that the officers and soldiers have a high level of "political consciousness" and of "devotion" to their own cause. Political training is the only method by which this objective can be attained. Its content is described in detail later on.

7. THE LITERACY MOVEMENT.
In order to increase the cultural level of the officers and soldiers, so that they may more easily absorb all kinds of training, each mess unit must carry out literacy training. The methods are as follows:

1. The "A" class includes all those who know about fifty characters.

2. The "B" class includes those who know above twenty characters.

3. The "C" class includes those who know no characters at all.

4. The teachers of the various classes consist of those in the unit with a relatively high cultural level.

5. When we halt, there should be an hour each day devoted to the study of characters. When we are on the march, we can carry out instruction either while moving or during rest periods. In such training, the important thing is regularity rather than speed. In general, if the soldiers learn two words a day, it is excellent.

CHAPTER XV
POLITICAL WORK
1. THE AIM OF THE POLITICAL WORK OF A GUERRILLA UNIT.
This aim lies in strengthening and raising to a higher level the fighting capacity of each member of the unit. The fighting capacity of a guerrilla unit is not determined exclusively by military arts, but depends above all on political consciousness, political influence, setting in motion the broad popular masses, disintegrating the enemy army, and inducing the broad popular masses to accept our leadership. All the plans of a guerrilla unit, whether they be political. military, or of any other nature, are all directed toward this single end.

2. THE MAIN CONTENT OF POLITICAL WORK.

We must carry out political instruction directed toward the resurrection of our people (stimulate the soldiers' national consciousness, their patriotism, and their love for the people and for the masses) and see to it that every officer and soldier in a guerrilla unit understands not only the national tasks for which he is responsible but also the necessity of fighting in defense of our state.

We must also pay attention to supporting the leaders, to maintaining the solidarity of the unit with real sincerity, to carrying out to the end the orders of one's superiors, and to maintaining an iron military discipline. We must see to it that the multitude of the soldiers are of a single mind and endowed with the resolve and the will to save our country together.

Apart from strengthening its own fighting capacity, a guerrilla unit must also carry out propaganda among the masses regarding the plots of the invaders and of the enemy.

3. DISCUSSIONS IN SMALL GROUPS.

These are excellent activities to unite our walls, to strengthen confidence, and to proclaim our doctrine.

1. We collect the view of all the comrades, in order to avoid feelings of alienation and to achieve the effect of gathering together ideas and obtaining greater advantage.

2. By the cadres, we increase their capacity for work and give them more practice in techniques for holding meetings and in methods of speaking. We will also be able to solve problems more quickly, investigate the past, and transform the future.

3. We can thus verify the fellowship existing among the members of the unit, and draw new comrades into the party.

4. This method is convenient for training, and makes it possible to understand completely each comrade's circumstances, capacity, and knowledge.

5. According to their character, these activities can be divided into discussion meetings, review meetings, and criticism meetings.

4. METHODS

Before the meeting we must prepare for it. These preparations consist in informing the members of the group, establishing the essential subject matter of the discussion, and, at the same time, reporting to the next higher echelon.

1. As regards the number of participants, from three to five represents the optimum.

2. One should not be bound by any rigid pattern. Discussion meetings can be held at all times and in all places.

3. As for the time limit, it is not desirable that the meetings should last too long. One hour is the maximum permissible.

4. It is appropriate to hold one meeting a week. The order of procedure consists in a report by the chairman, discussion of the report by the participants, and a conclusion entrusted to the leader of the group. The record of the meeting should indicate in detail the name of the chairman, the subjects of discussion, the number of those present and absent, and the place where the meeting was held.

5. Not more than two problems at most should be discussed. The discussion should have as its starting point the individual problems of the participants.

6. As for the manner of speaking, it is appropriate that the remarks of the participants should deal with essentials and be simple and clear. They should be systematic and not repetitive. They should be persuasive in content and presented in a friendly and agreeable manner. In answering questions, one should avoid any hint of mockery and pay attention to what the others say. At the same time, one should arrive at a decision concerning the topic discussed.

7. As regards the leader of the group, his report should be simple. He should not give a long and repetitive presentation but seize the occasion to induce the participants to speak.

8. The conclusion should follow the inductive method. It should include a criticism of the whole of the discussions. If there are dissident conclusions, they may also be expressed

5. CARRYING OUT POLITICAL WORK.
One should not merely rely on a few political workers. The best thing is to be able to attract and train conscious elements, or interested officers and

soldiers, to participate in the work and to train the whole personnel of the unit so that they can all carry on effective political work.

6. TYPES OF POLITICAL WORK.

In broad terms, political work can be divided into three categories according to whether it is carried out in ordinary times, during battle, or after a battle. As for propaganda destined to encourage the troops, the various aspects are as indicated below:

1. Political work in ordinary times. We intensify political training in order to raise the level of political consciousness, create unity in thought, word, and deed, maintain an iron military discipline, and unite closely with the popular masses. The methods are roughly as follows:

a. We must really put into practice the principles of not disturbing or harming the people (such as "Pay fairly for what you buy," "Speak politely," "Return everything you borrow", and "Pay for anything you damage").

b. At all times and in all places, aid the popular masses and help them to solve their difficulties (for example, help the popular masses to gather the harvest or to cultivate their land and send our army doctors to prevent epidemics or treat the people's ailments, or to enquire after people who have suffered difficulties and devise methods to aid them), maintain the unity of the army and the people, and encourage the spirit of sharing both good fortune and adversity together.

c. Chat frequently with the popular masses and let them know about our military discipline and our affection for them, and also learn in detail about the hunger and suffering among the people.

d. Frequently hold joint entertainment sessions for the soldiers and the people, so as to smooth over any feelings of alienation between the army and the people and increase the affection of the army and the people for one another.

2. Resolving any feelings of alienation between the lower and higher ranks of officers and soldiers. The methods employed are roughly as follows:

a. Persons engaged in political training, apart from sharing the good fortune and adversity of the soldiers, should also frequently chat with the soldiers, carefully investigate all their deep grieves and report their problems at all times to their superior officers, and devise methods for improving the situation.

b. As regards all the opinions of higher and lower ranks, we should take our stand on a position of pure rational knowledge, convince them by an attitude of sincere entreaty, and explain things to them. We must make absolutely certain that higher and lower ranks unite solidly as one man, and we must strengthen their capacity to unite.

c. With respect to soldiers who violate discipline, we should use educational methods to persuade them. All corporal punishment and insults must absolutely be reduced.

d. We should frequently hold meetings at which officers and soldiers can enjoy themselves together, in order to heighten the affection between officers and soldiers.

3. Augmenting the officers' and soldiers' hatred of the enemy, and increasing their resolve to fight to the death to kill the enemy. Increasing the common hatred of the enemy is an important factor in strengthening the soldiers' morale. Consequently, a guerrilla unit should pay particular attention to all the atrocities of the enemy, and to all the instances in which he massacres our army or our people, and carry out propaganda generally among the army regarding these atrocities, so as to heighten the courage of the officers and soldiers to fight to the death and harden their resolve to fight the enemy to the death, since either we or they must perish.

4. Strengthening confidence in the inevitable victory of our war against the enemy. The methods are more or less as follows:

a. We must frequently avail ourselves of the tales of the glorious feats of arms in our past, in order to carry out propaganda among our officers and soldiers and inspire them.

b. We put forward examples of the enemy's defects (such as difficulties, collapses, and other problems that he has recently encountered), in order to demonstrate that in the end the enemy must be defeated.

c. We must put forward examples of our own strong points (such as the support of the popular masses, transmission of information, familiarity with the terrain) and the present victorious circumstances, in order to demonstrate that we must ultimately triumph.

d. By exposing the clever tricks habitually used by the enemy, we make known the points to which our army should pay particular attention, in order to prevent the emergence of a mentality of fearing or underestimating the enemy.

After we have suffered an attack, we sink for a time into a situation characterized by difficulties and painful effort, and as a consequence we underestimate ourselves, exaggerate the enemy's strength, and lose our confidence in victory.

7. POLITICAL WORK IN TIME OF BATTLE.
Political work before we set out is carried on as described below.

1. The commander in chief of the unit first calls a meeting of the cadres. He explains in what respects the existing political situation is favorable to us, as well as the conditions of victory and the significance of the battle. He also explains the methods and points for attention in attaining our goal, but without infringing military secrecy.

2. On the basis of the meeting of the cadres, the political training section immediately calls meetings of political workers at all levels, at which the essential points and the methods of propaganda are explained and concrete tasks are assigned.

3. The various groups immediately call meetings of all the officers and soldiers, at which, in addition to reporting on the current political situation and the guarantees of our victory, conditions for competition are also put forward. ("He who is lightly wounded should not leave the firing line, he who is seriously wounded should not cry out in pain"; "Let us see who can hand in the most weapons"; or "Let us see who can take the most prisoners,") At the same time, tasks are distributed to all political workers and activists (supervision, leadership, or propaganda).

4. Political workers should be sent to the local population to gather them together, call meetings, and give talks, inspiring them to participate in the battle or to join the ranks of the porters or the transport units. As regards the organizations of the popular masses, we should guide them in methods of calling meetings, of fighting, and of preparing mobilization.

5. After the battle has begun, the most important political training workers should be sent to inspire the units responsible for the main attack or for particularly important actions. The less important political training workers should be sent to inspire the less important fighting units.

6. Propaganda units and groups of singers and dancers (all composed of lively and lovable boys in uniform and attractive clothing) should be sent in advance to positions along the side of the roads where the army will advance, to give short talks, sing, dance, or shout slogans, so as to inspire the maximum of courage in the officers and soldiers.

8. POLITICAL WORK AFTER THE BATTLE HAS BEGUN.

1. After the battle has begun, we should pay attention to calling out slogans to the soldiers of the other side, so as to dissipate their morale. This is one of the forms taken by our work of sabotage.

2. When the situation on the battlefield enters the stage of an encounter at close range or from positions arrayed opposite one another, we devise a method for holding a joint meeting with the soldiers of the opposite side and take advantage of this opportunity to give them food, in order to gladden their hearts. After this, we carry on more propaganda work, which must be prepared in advance.

3. After the battle has begun, we must assuredly carry out propaganda directed toward those outside our army. It is even more important to inspire those within our army. The methods for this work are diverse and are determined primarily by what is adapted to the circumstances. For example:

a. On the attack:

i. When we suffer a surprise attack by the enemy while advancing to attack, we should give an explanation such as the following "Comrades! Airplanes cannot decide a battle. We must seize this opportunity, advance rapidly, and quickly come to grips with the enemy on the ground. Charge the enemy with your bayonets!"

ii. When firing begins, we should encourage the soldiers in the following terms: "Comrades! Don't shoot at random, shoot only when you have taken careful aim. We must try to kill an enemy with every bullet."

iii. When we are near the enemy and are about to charge, the method for inspiring the soldiers is as follows:
"Comrades! The time to dispose of the enemy has come. We shall pay no attention to sacrifice, we shall summon up our courage, defeat the enemy and annihilate him. Let our victory inspire the whole army! Forward

quickly! Charge!"

iv. When the first charge is repelled and we charge a second time, we should encourage the soldiers as follows: "Comrades! We are an invincible iron army, we are a mighty unit victorious in every battle, we are absolutely resolved to destroy this enemy and preserve our glorious reputation."

v. When officers are wounded or killed in battle, we should exhort the troops as follows: "Comrades! Our officers (So-and-so) and (So-and-so) have already sacrificed themselves gloriously. Let us tread in their bloody footsteps, complete their task, and annihilate the enemy before us. Let us go and avenge them!"

vi. If the enemy shows signs of wavering, we should exhort the soldiers as follows: "Comrades! The enemy is wavering. Charge quickly and capture his commander in chief alive!"

vii. When we pursue the enemy, we should exhort the soldiers as follows: "Comrades! The enemy has retreated. Pursue him quickly! Charge and smash the enemy's holding units, finish off his main force, annihilate his whole force. Let us see who can hand in the most arms, and who can take the most prisoners. To win a battle and not to pursue the enemy is a great pity."

b. On the defence:

i. When the order has been received, we should carry out propaganda as follows: "Comrades! The enemy has arrived. This is the best opportunity to annihilate the enemy. Make skillful use of natural obstacles, and shoot with sang-froid. The more of the enemy we kill and wound, the easier it will be for our main attack to progress and obtain results."

ii. When the enemy charges, we should exhort the troops as follows: "Comrades! The enemy is about to charge. Fix your bayonets, and prepare your hand grenades. Let us summon up our awe-inspiring reputation, preserve the glory we have already won, and annihilate the enemy in front of our position."

iii. When we are surrounded by the enemy, we should exhort the soldiers as follows: "Comrades! We are an ever-victorious unit. We are a courageous and invincible iron army. We will wage a bloody battle to the end for our people and our country, shed our last drop of blood, hold onto

162

our rifles to the death, and die rather than surrender. To hand over one's rifle is suicide, to surrender is the supreme shame. Let us smash their lines at one point and break through."

iv. At the time of the counterattack or when the order to go over to the offensive is received: "Comrades! We are counterattacking. Let us take away the enemy's rifles, let us capture the enemy officers, let us see who is most courageous!"

v. Propaganda when we retreat: "Comrades! Let us keep our movements secret and baffle the enemy in his calculations. Let us open wide our arms and lure the enemy to penetrate deep. Do not break ranks, do not fall behind, do not waver, do not succumb to panic, do not fear sacrifice, execute resolutely to the end the orders of your superiors. Final victory will be ours!"

vi. When we cover the withdrawal of our forces, the methods for exhorting them are similar to those indicated above.

9. POLITICAL WORK FOLLOWING A BATTLE.
After the battle has been concluded, political work continues.

1. In order to avoid the appearance of attitudes of slighting the enemy or fearing the enemy, we should pay attention to the following points:

a. We should correctly point out the causes of victory and defeat. We must not become puffed up because of a small victory; still less can we lose our confidence in victory because of a small setback.

b. We must establish the attitude that should be adopted henceforth, or the points requiring attention.

2. We should collect materials and anecdotes concerning our victory, as well as the names of units, individual officers, and soldiers who have fought courageously. We should then use these materials to compose propaganda outlines, songs, dances, old- and new-style plays, etc.

3. We should print large numbers of victory announcements and slogans and stick them up everywhere. At the same time, we should organize a roving propaganda unit, which spreads out toward areas established in advance, to carry out propaganda and to call the popular masses together and hold meetings to celebrate the victory.

4. When meetings are held to celebrate the victory, one should pay attention to the following points:

a. Report on the significance of the victory, and the tasks now before us, as well as the concrete methods to be employed to carry out these tasks.

b. Report on units that have fought courageously, as well as individual officers and soldiers. As for officers and soldiers wounded or killed, one can select the most valuable among them and report about them.

c. Put on new versions of classic plays, as well as songs and dances.

While the reports indicated under a and b above are being delivered, or the play is being put on, the units participating in such a meeting should shout out slogans in accompaniment. We should also bring up the methods for providing pensions to the members of the families of the soldiers killed in battle.

Moreover, we should bring together the prisoners and booty in the sight of the masses, thus further increasing the courage and the spirit of struggle of our soldiers and of the people.
5. At meetings to celebrate the victory, all organizations should also launch a consolation movement. The main points for attention in this respect are:
a. As regards material consolation, the important thing is not the quantity, but the significance; it is not the elegance and refinement of the items given, but their utility. Such things as straw sandals, face towels, pigs, sheep, chickens, and ducks are all suitable for this purpose.

b. In case there is a lack of goods for material consolation, consolation in the form of honors should be used. For example, one can make flags for presentation, or compose songs in memory of the fallen, or issue an order of the day in their praise.

c. Following a small victory, there should be no large-scale consolation. Consolation should be carried out only if we can devise means for doing it in a place near the battlefield.
6. We should praise examples of combined operations, autonomous actions, and the resolute application of orders. Thus:

a. When there are those who, in the course of a fierce battle, have achieved victory by combined operations, autonomous action, and the resolute execution of orders, the maximum effort should be made to publicize the fact and to praise them. Those who have the misfortune to be defeated in similar circumstances should also be praised.

b. When there is punishment for those who, in order to preserve their own forces, fail to advance, or fail to carry out their tasks energetically, thus bringing about the defeat of another unit of our army, the case should also be the object of large-scale propaganda within the unit. In this way we give a lesson to the officers and soldiers of the whole unit, or of other units, and make them afraid to commit similar offenses.

10. WORK PERTAINING TO CLUBS AND AMUSEMENT ROOMS.

By virtue of the fact that it compensates for a painful and tedious existence in the army, this is also a way of preventing desertion. The essentials regarding the organization and work of clubs are dealt with below.

1. Rules regarding organization.

a. In order to promote entertainment in the army, compensate for a tedious existence, increase interest in our work, and inspire a taste for study, each mess unit within a guerrilla unit should organize an amusement room, This should be divided into a military section, a guerrilla section, and a physical culture section. Each officer and soldier in the mess unit should choose one of these sections, in accordance with his own nature; he can, if he wishes, participate in two or three of the sections.

b. One person from among the company commanders or the particularly energetic and capable platoon commanders should be chosen to be responsible for the amusement room. Each of the three sections should have a section head, chosen at a meeting of the members of the section, for a period of six months with the possibility of being chosen to succeed himself .

c. Each week there should be one meeting of the section heads and one meeting of the members of each section. A meeting of the leaders should be held once a month. It is called separately by the chairman of the section heads.

d. In its work, the amusement room should follow the guidance of the club of the next higher echelon. It is also subject to the supervision and guidance of the commanding officer of the unit. In military affairs, it is absolutely subordinate to the commanding officer of the unit.

e. In order to guide and unify the work of the various amusement rooms, a guerrilla battalion should establish a club. This club should have a chairman and a secretary who are responsible for all its activities.

f. The club should be attached to the political training section, because the work of the amusement rooms constitutes a kind of political training. If there is no political training section, the club is directly subordinated to the commanding of officer.

g. The work of the club consists in guiding and promoting the work of the various amusement rooms. Consequently, each week there should be a meeting of the responsible heads of the various amusement rooms, and each month we should call a meeting of all the officers and soldiers or a meeting of the army and the people together.

All the work of both the clubs and amusement rooms should have as its principle not to interfere with military administration, military training, or military action.

2. The essentials of the work of clubs and amusement rooms.

a. The work of the military section consists in furthering a spirit of independent study among the officers and soldiers, in discussion of military questions, or in the mutual rectification of the actions of the members in order to remedy the lacks and insufficiencies of military training. Its content is as indicated below.

i. Bayonet section (practice, taking a hypothetical enemy dummy as the object).

ii. Grenade section (throwing a wooden hand grenade at a target).

b. Guerrilla section.

i. Taking aim from a fixed support.

ii. Checking one's aim.

iii. Carriage while shooting.

iv. Investigations when setting out.

v. Utilization of obstacles.

vi. Shooting at various types of objectives in the field.

3. Physical culture section. The work of this section lies in strengthening the bodies of the officers and soldiers. It can also remedy insufficiencies in military training. Its contents is as follows:

a. Ball playing (basketball, football, volley ball, tennis, baseball, etc.).

b. Track and field sports (high jump, broad jump, races, obstacle course).

c. Boxing and swordplay.

4. Entertainment section. The work of this section consists in providing amusement for the members of the army, in compensating for a tedious existence, and in increasing the soldiers' interest in their work and their taste for study.

a. Joke section. This section can carry on its activities at any time at all, but attention should be paid to the following points:

i. When jokes are told, we must make them easy to understand. We can take materials from joke books and such, but they should not be too obscene.

ii. When telling stories, we should devote much time to stories about the abundant exploits and great enterprises of the ancients, and to their excellent words and admirable conduct, in order to achieve an inspirational effect.

iii. When reporting on the news, we should devote attention to our own victories and to the atrocities of the enemy.

b. Theatrical section. This section utilizes rest periods, both in the evenings and during the day, to put on all sorts of new-style plays, traditional operas, comedy teams, storytellers with drums, etc.—performances that have political content and are at the same time amusing, in order to improve morale.

c. Song and dance section. In accordance with the circumstances in which the unit finds itself and the nature of its tasks, this section composes all sorts of songs in order to stimulate the interest of the officers and soldiers in singing songs, or it puts on dances in costume, assuming various comical attitudes, in order to make the onlookers laugh until they hold their sides.

d. Music section. This is divided into violin, harmonica, guitar and other groups, which can accompany the plays and dances.

e. The methods of work of all sections should be adapted to the time and circumstances. They should be employed in a lively manner, and on no account in a wooden fashion.

f. The work of all sections should be subject to strict control and supervision. We should also use methods of competition to induce all the officers and soldiers to make spontaneous efforts.

g. All kinds of songs and old and new plays, etc.

h. For the benefit of the work, all groups and sections should have specialized talents.

i. The officers and soldiers who participate in these performances should be excused from their other duties.

ON PRACTICE

On the Relation Between Knowledge and Practice, Between Knowing and
Doing. July 1937

[There used to be a number of comrades in our Party who were dogmatists
and who for a long period rejected the experience of the Chinese
revolution, denying the truth that "Marxism is not a dogma but a guide to
action" and overawing people with words and phrases from Marxist works,
torn out of context. There were also a number of comrades who were
empiricists and who for a long period restricted themselves to their own
fragmentary experience and did not understand the importance of theory
for revolutionary practice or see the revolution as a whole, but worked
blindly though industriously. The erroneous ideas of these two types of
comrades, and particularly of the dogmatists, caused enormous losses to
the Chinese revolution during 1931-34, and yet the dogmatists cloaking
themselves as Marxists, confused a great many comrades. "On Practice"
was written in order to expose the subjectivist errors of dogmatism and
empiricism in the Party, and especially the error of dogmatism, from the
standpoint of the Marxist theory of knowledge. It was entitled "On
Practice" because its stress was on exposing the dogmatist kind of
subjectivism, which belittles practice. The ideas contained in this essay
were presented by Comrade Mao Tse-tung in a lecture at the Anti-
Japanese Military and Political College in Yenan.]

Before Marx, materialism examined the problem of knowledge apart from
the social nature of man and apart from his historical development, and
was therefore incapable of understanding the dependence of knowledge
on social practice, that is, the dependence of knowledge on production
and the class struggle.

Above all, Marxists regard man's activity in production as the most
fundamental practical activity, the determinant of all his other activities.
Man's knowledge depends mainly on his activity in material production,
through which he comes gradually to understand the phenomena, the
properties and the laws of nature, and the relations between himself and
nature; and through his activity in production he also gradually comes to
understand, in varying degrees, certain relations that exist between man
and man. None of this knowledge can be acquired apart from activity in
production. In a classless society every person, as a member of society,
joins in common effort with the other members, enters into definite
relations of production with them and engages in production to meet

man's material needs. In all class societies, the members of the different social classes also enter, in different ways, into definite relations of production and engage in production to meet their material needs. This is the primary source from which human knowledge develops.

Man's social practice is not confined to activity in production, but takes many other forms--class struggle, political life, scientific and artistic pursuits; in short, as a social being, man participates in all spheres of the practical life of society. Thus man, in varying degrees, comes to know the different relations between man and man, not only through his material life but also through his political and cultural life (both of which are intimately bound up with material life). Of these other types of social practice, class struggle in particular, in all its various forms, exerts a profound influence on the development of man's knowledge. In class society everyone lives as a member of a particular class, and every kind of thinking, without exception, is stamped with the brand of a class.

Marxists hold that in human society activity in production develops step by step from a lower to a higher level and that consequently man's knowledge, whether of nature or of society, also develops step by step from a lower to a higher level, that is, from the shallower to the deeper, from the one-sided to the many-sided. For a very long period in history, men were necessarily confined to a one-sided understanding of the history of society because, for one thing, the bias of the exploiting classes always distorted history and, for another, the small scale of production limited man's outlook. It was not until the modern proletariat emerged along with immense forces of production (large-scale industry) that man was able to acquire a comprehensive, historical understanding of the development of society and turn this knowledge into a science, the science of Marxism.

Marxists hold that man's social practice alone is the criterion of the truth of his knowledge of the external world. What actually happens is that man's knowledge is verified only when he achieves the anticipated results in the process of social practice (material production, class struggle or scientific experiment). If a man wants to succeed in his work, that is, to achieve the anticipated results, he must bring his ideas into correspondence with the laws of the objective external world; if they do not correspond, he will fail in his practice. After he fails, he draws his lessons, corrects his ideas to make them correspond to the laws of the external world, and can thus turn failure into success; this is what is meant by "failure is the mother of success" and "a fall into the pit, a gain in your wit". The dialectical-materialist theory of knowledge places practice in the primary position, holding that human knowledge can in no way be

170

separated from practice and repudiating all the erroneous theories which deny the importance of practice or separate knowledge from practice. Thus Lenin said, "Practice is higher than (theoretical) knowledge, for it has not only the dignity of universality, but also of immediate actuality." [1] The Marxist philosophy of dialectical materialism has two outstanding characteristics. One is its class nature: it openly avows that dialectical materialism is in the service of the proletariat. The other is its practicality: it emphasizes the dependence of theory on practice, emphasizes that theory is based on practice and in turn serves practice. The truth of any knowledge or theory is determined not by subjective feelings, but by objective results in social practice. Only social practice can be the criterion of truth. The standpoint of practice is the primary and basic standpoint in the dialectical materialist theory of knowledge. [2]

But how then does human knowledge arise from practice and in turn serve practice? This will become clear if we look at the process of development of knowledge.

knowledge → Practice
Practice ← knowledge

In the process of practice, man at first sees only the phenomenal side, the separate aspects, the external relations of things. For instance, some people from outside come to Yenan on a tour of observation. In the first day or two, they see its topography, streets and houses; they meet many people, attend banquets, evening parties and mass meetings, hear talk of various kinds and read various documents, all these being the phenomena, the separate aspects and the external relations of things. This is called the perceptual stage of cognition, namely, the stage of sense perceptions and impressions. That is, these particular things in Yenan act on the sense organs of the members of the observation group, evoke sense perceptions and give rise in their brains to many impressions together with a rough sketch of the external relations among these impressions: this is the first stage of cognition. At this stage, man cannot as yet form concepts, which are deeper, or draw logical conclusions.

Perceptual Stage →
Conceptual Stage

As social practice continues, things that give rise to man's sense perceptions and impressions in the course of his practice are repeated many times; then a sudden change (leap) takes place in the brain in the process of cognition, and concepts are formed. Concepts are no longer the phenomena, the separate aspects and the external relations of things; they grasp the essence, the totality and the internal relations of things. Between concepts and sense perceptions there is not only a quantitative but also a qualitative difference. Proceeding further, by means of judgement and inference one is able to draw logical conclusions. The expression in San Kuo Yen Yi, [3] "knit the brows and a stratagem comes to

171

mind", or in everyday language, "let me think it over", refers to man's use of concepts in the brain to form judgements and inferences. This is the second stage of cognition. When the members of the observation group have collected various data and, what is more, have "thought them over", they are able to arrive at the judgement that "the Communist Party's policy of the National United Front Against Japan is thorough, sincere and genuine". Having made this judgement, they can, if they too are genuine about uniting to save the nation, go a step further and draw the following conclusion, "The National United Front Against Japan can succeed." This stage of conception, judgement and inference is the more important stage in the entire process of knowing a thing; it is the stage of rational knowledge. The real task of knowing is, through perception, to arrive at thought, to arrive step by step at the comprehension of the internal contradictions of objective things, of their laws and of the internal relations between one process and another, that is, to arrive at logical knowledge. To repeat, logical knowledge differs from perceptual knowledge in that perceptual knowledge pertains to the separate aspects, the phenomena and the external relations of things, whereas logical knowledge takes a big stride forward to reach the totality, the essence and the internal relations of things and discloses the inner contradictions in the surrounding world. Therefore, logical knowledge is capable of grasping the development of the surrounding world in its totality, in the internal relations of all its aspects.

Perceptual Knowledge v. Logical Knowledge

This dialectical-materialist theory of the process of development of knowledge, basing itself on practice and proceeding from the shallower to the deeper, was never worked out by anybody before the rise of Marxism. Marxist materialism solved this problem correctly for the first time, pointing out both materialistically and dialectically the deepening movement of cognition, the movement by which man in society progresses from perceptual knowledge to logical knowledge in his complex, constantly recurring practice of production and class struggle. Lenin said, "The abstraction of matter, of a law of nature, the abstraction of value, etc., in short, all scientific (correct, serious, not absurd) abstractions reflect nature more deeply, truly and completely." [4] Marxism-Leninism holds that each of the two stages in the process of cognition has its own characteristics, with knowledge manifesting itself as perceptual at the lower stage and logical at the higher stage, but that both are stages in an integrated process of cognition. The perceptual and the rational are qualitatively different, but are not divorced from each other; they are unified on the basis of practice. Our practice proves that what is perceived cannot at once be comprehended and that only what is comprehended can be more deeply perceived. Perception only solves the problem of phenomena;

theory alone can solve the problem of essence. The solving of both these problems is not separable in the slightest degree from practice. Whoever wants to know a thing has no way of doing so except by coming into contact with it, that is, by living (practicing) in its environment. In feudal society it was impossible to know the laws of capitalist society in advance because capitalism had not yet emerged, the relevant practice was lacking. Marxism could be the product only of capitalist society. Marx, in the era of laissez-faire capitalism, could not concretely know certain laws peculiar to the era of imperialism beforehand, because imperialism, the last stage of capitalism, had not yet emerged and the relevant practice was lacking; only Lenin and Stalin could undertake this task. Leaving aside their genius, the reason why Marx, Engels, Lenin and Stalin could work out their theories was mainly that they personally took part in the practice of the class struggle and the scientific experimentation of their time; lacking this condition, no genius could have succeeded. The saying, "without stepping outside his gate the scholar knows all the wide world's affairs", was mere empty talk in past times when technology was undeveloped. Even though this saying can be valid in the present age of developed technology, the people with real personal knowledge are those engaged in practice the wide world over. And it is only when these people have come to "know" through their practice and when their knowledge has reached him through writing and technical media that the "scholar" can indirectly "know all the wide world's affairs". If you want to know a certain thing or a certain class of things directly, you must personally participate in the practical struggle to change reality, to change that thing or class of things, for only thus can you come into contact with them as phenomena; only through personal participation in the practical struggle to change reality can you uncover the essence of that thing or class of things and comprehend them. This is the path to knowledge which every man actually travels, though some people, deliberately distorting matters, argue to the contrary. The most ridiculous person in the world is the "know all" who picks up a smattering of hearsay knowledge and proclaims himself "the world's Number One authority"; this merely shows that he has not taken a proper measure of himself. Knowledge is a matter of science, and no dishonesty or conceit whatsoever is permissible. What is required is definitely the reverse--honesty and modesty. If you want knowledge, you must take part in the practice of changing reality. If you want to know the taste of a pear, you must change the pear by eating it yourself. If you want to know the structure and properties of the atom, you must make physical and chemical experiments to change the state of the atom. If you want to know the theory and methods of revolution, you must take part in revolution. All genuine knowledge originates in direct experience. But one cannot have direct experience of everything; as a matter of fact, most of our knowledge

173

comes from indirect experience, for example, all knowledge from past times and foreign lands. To our ancestors and to foreigners, such knowledge was--or is--a matter of direct experience, and this knowledge is reliable if in the course of their direct experience the requirement of "scientific abstraction", spoken of by Lenin, was--or is--fulfilled and objective reality scientifically reflected, otherwise it is not reliable. Hence a man's knowledge consists only of two parts, that which comes from direct experience and that which comes from indirect experience. Moreover, what is indirect experience for me is direct experience for other people. Consequently, considered as a whole, knowledge of any kind is inseparable from direct experience. All knowledge originates in perception of the objective external world through man's physical sense organs. Anyone who denies such perception, denies direct experience, or denies personal participation in the practice that changes reality, is not a materialist. That is why the "know-all" is ridiculous. There is an old Chinese saying, "How can you catch tiger cubs without entering the tiger's lair?" This saying holds true for man's practice and it also holds true for the theory of knowledge. There can be no knowledge apart from practice.

To make clear the dialectical-materialist movement of cognition arising on the basis of the practice which changes reality--to make clear the gradually deepening movement of cognition--a few additional concrete examples are given below.

In its knowledge of capitalist society, the proletariat was only in the perceptual stage of cognition in the first period of its practice, the period of machine-smashing and spontaneous struggle; it knew only some of the aspects and the external relations of the phenomena of capitalism. The proletariat was then still a "class-in-itself". But when it reached the second period of its practice, the period of conscious and organized economic and political struggles, the proletariat was able to comprehend the essence of capitalist society, the relations of exploitation between social classes and its own historical task; and it was able to do so because of its own practice and because of its experience of prolonged struggle, which Marx and Engels scientifically summed up in all its variety to create the theory of Marxism for the education of the proletariat. It was then that the proletariat became a "class-for-itself".

Similarly with the Chinese people's knowledge of imperialism. The first stage was one of superficial, perceptual knowledge, as shown in the indiscriminate anti-foreign struggles of the Movement of the Taiping Heavenly Kingdom, the Yi Ho Tuan Movement, and so on. It was only in the second stage that the Chinese people reached the stage of rational knowledge, saw the internal and external contradictions of imperialism and saw the essential truth that imperialism had allied itself with China's comprador and feudal classes to oppress and exploit the great masses of the Chinese people. This knowledge began about the time of the May 4th Movement of 1919.

Next, let us consider war. If those who lead a war lack experience of war, then at the initial stage they will not understand the profound laws pertaining to the directing of a specific war (such as our Agrarian Revolutionary War of the past decade). At the initial stage they will merely experience a good deal of fighting and, what is more, suffer many defeats. But this experience (the experience of battles won and especially of battles lost) enables them to comprehend the inner thread of the whole war, namely, the laws of that specific war, to understand its strategy and tactics, and consequently to direct the war with confidence. If, at such a moment, the command is turned over to an inexperienced person, then he too will have to suffer a number of defeats (gain experience) before he can comprehend the true laws of the war.

"I am not sure I can handle it." We often hear this remark when a comrade hesitates to accept an assignment. Why is he unsure of himself? Because he has no systematic understanding of the content and circumstances of the assignment, or because he has had little or no contact with such work, and so the laws governing it are beyond him. After a detailed analysis of the nature and circumstances of the assignment, he will feel more sure of himself and do it willingly. If he spends some time at the job and gains experience and if he is a person who is willing to look into matters with an open mind and not one who approaches problems subjectively, one-sidedly and superficially, then he can draw conclusions for himself as to how to go about the job and do it with much more courage. Only those who are subjective, one-sided and superficial in their approach to problems will smugly issue orders or directives the moment they arrive on the scene, without considering the circumstances, without viewing things in their totality (their history and their present state as a whole) and without getting to the essence of things (their nature and the internal relations between one thing and another). Such people are bound to trip and fall.

Thus it can be seen that the first step in the process of cognition is contact with the objects of the external world; this belongs to the stage of perception. The second step is to synthesize the data of perception by arranging and reconstructing them; this belongs to the stage of conception, judgement and inference. It is only when the data of

175

perception are very rich (not fragmentary) and correspond to reality (are not illusory) that they can be the basis for forming correct concepts and theories.

Here two important points must be emphasized. The first, which has been stated before but should be repeated here, is the dependence of rational knowledge upon perceptual knowledge. Anyone who thinks that rational knowledge need not be derived from perceptual knowledge is an idealist. In the history of philosophy there is the "rationalist" school that admits the reality only of reason and not of experience, believing that reason alone is reliable while perceptual experience is not; this school errs by turning things upside down. The rational is reliable precisely because it has its source in sense perceptions, other wise it would be like water without a source, a tree without roots, subjective, self-engendered and unreliable. As to the sequence in the process of cognition, perceptual experience comes first; we stress the significance of social practice in the process of cognition precisely because social practice alone can give rise to human knowledge and it alone can start man on the acquisition of perceptual experience from the objective world. For a person who shuts his eyes, stops his ears and totally cuts himself off from the objective world there can be no such thing as knowledge. Knowledge begins with experience--this is the materialism of the theory of knowledge.

The second point is that knowledge needs to be deepened, that the perceptual stage of knowledge needs to be developed to the rational stage--this is the dialectics of the theory of knowledge. [5] To think that knowledge can stop at the lower, perceptual stage and that perceptual knowledge alone is reliable while rational knowledge is not, would be to repeat the historical error of "empiricism". This theory errs in failing to understand that, although the data of perception reflect certain realities in the objective world (I am not speaking here of idealist empiricism which confines experience to so-called introspection), they are merely one-sided and superficial, reflecting things incompletely and not reflecting their essence. Fully to reflect a thing in its totality, to reflect its essence, to reflect its inherent laws, it is necessary through the exercise of thought to reconstruct the rich data of sense perception, discarding the dross and selecting the essential, eliminating the false and retaining the true, proceeding from the one to the other and from the outside to the inside, in order to form a system of concepts and theories--it is necessary to make a leap from perceptual to rational knowledge. Such reconstructed knowledge is not more empty or more unreliable; on the contrary, whatever has been scientifically reconstructed in the process of cognition, on the basis of practice, reflects objective reality, as Lenin said, more

176

deeply, more truly, more fully. As against this, vulgar "practical men" respect experience but despise theory, and therefore cannot have a comprehensive view of an entire objective process, lack clear direction and long-range perspective, and are complacent over occasional successes and glimpses of the truth. If such persons direct a revolution, they will lead it up a blind alley.

Rational knowledge depends upon perceptual knowledge and perceptual knowledge remains to be developed into rational knowledge-- this is the dialectical-materialist theory of knowledge. In philosophy, neither "rationalism" nor "empiricism" understands the historical or the dialectical nature of knowledge, and although each of these schools contains one aspect of the truth (here I am referring to materialist, not to idealist, rationalism and empiricism), both are wrong on the theory of knowledge as a whole. The dialectical-materialist movement of knowledge from the perceptual to the rational holds true for a minor process of cognition (for instance, knowing a single thing or task) as well as for a major process of cognition (for instance, knowing a whole society or a revolution).

But the movement of knowledge does not end here. If the dialectical-materialist movement of knowledge were to stop at rational knowledge, only half the problem would be dealt with. And as far as Marxist philosophy is concerned, only the less important half at that. Marxist philosophy holds that the most important problem does not lie in understanding the laws of the objective world and thus being able to explain it, but in applying the knowledge of these laws actively to change the world. From the Marxist viewpoint, theory is important, and its importance is fully expressed in Lenin's statement, "Without revolutionary theory there can be no revolutionary movement." [6] But Marxism emphasizes the importance of theory precisely and only because it can guide action. If we have a correct theory but merely prate about it, pigeonhole it and do not put it into practice, then that theory, however good, is of no significance. Knowledge begins with practice, and theoretical knowledge is acquired through practice and must then return to practice. The active function of knowledge manifests itself not only in the active leap from perceptual to rational knowledge, but--and this is more important--it must manifest itself in the leap from rational knowledge to revolutionary practice. The knowledge which grasps the laws of the world, must be redirected to the practice of changing the world, must be applied anew in the practice of production, in the practice of revolutionary class struggle and revolutionary national struggle and in the practice of scientific experiment. This is the process of testing and developing theory, the continuation of the whole process of cognition. The problem of whether theory corresponds to objective reality is not, and cannot be, completely solved in the movement of knowledge from the perceptual to the rational, mentioned above. The only way to solve this problem completely is to redirect rational knowledge to social practice, apply theory to practice and see whether it can achieve the objectives one has in mind. Many theories of natural science are held to be true not only because they were so considered when natural scientists originated them, but because they have been verified in subsequent scientific practice. Similarly, Marxism-Leninism is held to be true not only because it was so considered when it was scientifically formulated by Marx, Engels, Lenin and Stalin but because it has been verified in the subsequent practice of revolutionary class struggle and revolutionary national struggle. Dialectical materialism is universally true because it is impossible for anyone to escape from its domain in his practice. The history of human knowledge tells us that the truth of many theories is incomplete and that this incompleteness is remedied through the test of practice. Many theories are erroneous and it is through the test of practice that their errors are corrected. That is why practice is the criterion of truth and why "the standpoint of life, of practice, should be first and fundamental in the theory of knowledge". [7] Stalin has well said, "Theory becomes purposeless if it is not connected with revolutionary practice, just as practice gropes in the dark if its path is not illumined by revolutionary theory." [8]

When we get to this point, is the movement of knowledge completed? Our answer is: it is and yet it is not. When men in society throw themselves into the practice of changing a certain objective process (whether natural or social) at a certain stage of its development, they can, as a result of the reflection of the objective process in their brains and the exercise of their subjective activity, advance their knowledge from the perceptual to the rational, and create ideas, theories, plans or programmes which correspond in general to the laws of that objective process. They then apply these ideas, theories, plans or programmes in practice in the same objective process. And if they can realize the aims they have in mind, that is, if in that same process of practice they can translate, or on the whole translate, those previously formulated ideas, theories, plans or programmes into fact, then the movement of knowledge may be considered completed with regard to this particular process. In the process of changing nature, take for example the fulfilment of an engineering plan, the verification of a scientific hypothesis, the manufacture of an implement or the reaping of a crop; or in the process of changing society, take for example the victory of a strike, victory in a war or the fulfilment of an educational plan. All these may be considered the realization of aims one has in mind. But generally speaking, whether in the practice of

178

changing nature or of changing society, men's original ideas, theories, plans or programmes are seldom realized without any alteration.

This is because people engaged in changing reality are usually subject to numerous limitations; they are limited not only by existing scientific and technological conditions but also by the development of the objective process itself and the degree to which this process has become manifest (the aspects and the essence of the objective process have not yet been fully revealed). In such a situation, ideas, theories, plans or programmes are usually altered partially and sometimes even wholly, because of the discovery of unforeseen circumstances in the course of practice. That is to say, it does happen that the original ideas, theories, plans or programmes fail to correspond with reality either in whole or in part and are wholly or partially incorrect. In many instances, failures have to be repeated many times before errors In knowledge can be corrected and correspondence with the laws of the objective process achieved, and consequently before the subjective can be transformed into the objective, or in other words, before the anticipated results can be achieved in practice. But when that point is reached, no matter how, the movement of human knowledge regarding a certain objective process at a certain stage of its development may be considered completed.

However, so far as the progression of the process is concerned, the movement of human knowledge is not completed. Every process, whether in the realm of nature or of society, progresses and develops by reason of its internal contradiction and struggle, and the movement of human knowledge should also progress and develop along with it. As far as social movements are concerned, true revolutionary leaders must not only be good at correcting their ideas, theories, plans or programmes when errors are discovered, as has been indicated above; but when a certain objective process has already progressed and changed from one stage of development to another, they must also be good at making themselves and all their fellow-revolutionaries progress and change in their subjective knowledge along with it, that IS to say, they must ensure that the proposed new revolutionary tasks and new working programmes correspond to the new changes in the situation. In a revolutionary period the situation changes very rapidly; if the knowledge of revolutionaries does not change rapidly in accordance with the changed situation, they will be unable to lead the revolution to victory.

It often happens, however, that thinking lags behind reality; this is because man's cognition is limited by numerous social conditions. We are opposed to die-herds in the revolutionary ranks whose thinking fails to advance with changing objective circumstances and has manifested itself historically as Right opportunism. These people fail to see that the struggle of opposites has already pushed the objective process forward while their knowledge has stopped at the old stage. This is characteristic of the thinking of all die-herds. Their thinking is divorced from social practice, and they cannot march ahead to guide the chariot of society; they simply trail behind, grumbling that it goes too fast and trying to drag it back or turn it in the opposite direction.

We are also opposed to "Left" phrase-mongering. The thinking of "Leftists" outstrips a given stage of development of the objective process; some regard their fantasies as truth, while others strain to realize in the present an ideal which can only be realized in the future. They alienate themselves from the current practice of the majority of the people and from the realities of the day, and show themselves adventurist in their actions.

Idealism and mechanical materialism, opportunism and adventurism, are all characterized by the breach between the subjective and the objective, by the separation of knowledge from practice. The Marxist-Leninist theory of knowledge, characterized as it is by scientific social practice, cannot but resolutely oppose these wrong ideologies. Marxists recognize that in the absolute and general process of development of the universe, the development of each particular process is relative, and that hence, in the endless flow of absolute truth, man's knowledge of a particular process at any given stage of development is only relative truth. The sum total of innumerable relative truths constitutes absolute truth. [9] The development of an objective process is full of contradictions and struggles, and so is the development of the movement of human knowledge. All the dialectical movements of the objective world can sooner or later be reflected in human knowledge. In social practice, the process of coming into being, developing and passing away is infinite, and so is the process of coming into being, developing and passing away in human knowledge. As man's practice which changes objective reality in accordance with given ideas, theories, plans or programmes, advances further and further, his knowledge of objective reality likewise becomes deeper and deeper. The movement of change in the world of objective reality is never-ending and so is man's cognition of truth through practice. Marxism-Leninism has in no way exhausted truth but ceaselessly opens up roads to the knowledge of truth in the course of practice. Our conclusion is the concrete, historical unity of the subjective and the objective, of theory and practice, of knowing ant doing, and we are opposed to all erroneous ideologies, whether "Left" or Right, which depart from concrete history.

In the present epoch of the development of society, the responsibility of correctly knowing and changing the world has been placed by history upon the shoulders of the proletariat and its party. This process, the practice of changing the world, which is determined in accordance with scientific knowledge, has already reached a historic moment in the world and in China, a great moment unprecedented in human history, that is, the moment for completely banishing darkness from the world and from China and for changing the world into a world of light such as never previously existed. The struggle of the proletariat and the revolutionary people to change the world comprises the fulfilment of the following tasks: to change the objective world and, at the same time, their own subjective world--to change their cognitive ability and change the relations between the subjective and the objective world. Such a change has already come about in one part of the globe, in the Soviet Union. There the people are pushing forward this process of change. The people of China and the rest of the world either are going through, or will go through, such a process. And the objective world which is to be changed also includes all the opponents of change, who, in order to be changed, must go through a stage of compulsion before they can enter the stage of voluntary, conscious change. The epoch of world communism will be reached when all mankind voluntarily and consciously changes itself and the world.

Discover the truth through practice, and again through practice verify and develop the truth. Start from perceptual knowledge and actively develop it into rational knowledge; then start from rational knowledge and actively guide revolutionary practice to change both the subjective and the objective world. Practice, knowledge, again practice, and again knowledge. This form repeats itself in endless cycles, and with each cycle the content of practice and knowledge rises to a higher level. Such is the whole of the dialectical-materialist theory of knowledge, and such is the dialectical-materialist theory of the unity of knowing and doing.

NOTES   *Endless cycles of Practice/Knowledge etc*

1. V. I. Lenin, "Conspectus of Hegel's The Science of Logic". Collected Works, Russ. ed., Moscow, 1958, Vol. XXXVIII, p. 205.

2. See Karl Marx, "Theses on Feuerbach". Karl Marx and Frederick Engels, Selected Works, in two volumes, Eng. ed., FLPH, Moscow, 1958, Vol. II, p. 403, and V. I. Lenin, Materialism and Empirio-Criticism, ring. ed., FLPH, Moscow, 1952, pp. 136-4.

3. San Kuo Yen Yi (Tales of the Three Kingdoms) is a famous Chinese historical nova by Lo Kuan-chung (late 14th and early 15th century).

4. V. I. Lenin, "Conspectus of Hegel's The Science of Logic", Collected Works, Russ. ed., Moscow, 1958, Vol. XXXVIII, p. 161.

5. "In order to understand, it is necessary empirically to begin understanding, study, to rise from empiricism to the universal." (Ibid., p. 197.)

6. V. I. Lenin, "What Is to Be Done?", Collected Works, Eng. ed., FLPH, Moscow, 1961, Vol. V, p. 369.

7. V. I. Lenin, Materialism and Empirio-Criticism, Eng. ed., FLPH, Moscow, p. 141.

8. J. V. Stalin, "The Foundations of Leninism", Problems of Leninism, Eng. ed., FLPH, Moscow, 1954, p. 31.

9. See V. I. Lenin, Materialism and Empirio-Criticism, Eng. ed., FLPH, Moscow, pp. 129-36.

ON CONTRADICTION
August 1937

[This essay on philosophy was written by Comrade Mao Tse-tung after his essay "On Practice" and with the same object of overcoming the serious error of dogmatist thinking to be found in the Party at the time. Originally delivered as lectures at the Anti-Japanese Military and Political College in Yenan, it was revised by the author on its inclusion in his Selected Works.]

The law of contradiction in things, that is, the law of the unity of opposites, is the basic law of materialist dialectics. Lenin said, "Dialectics in the proper sense is the study of contradiction in the very essence of objects." [1] Lenin often called this law the essence of dialectics; he also called it the kernel of dialectics. [2] In studying this law, therefore, we cannot but touch upon a variety of questions, upon a number of philosophical problems. If we can become clear on all these problems, we shall arrive at a fundamental understanding of materialist dialectics. The problems are: the two world outlooks, the universality of contradiction, the particularity of contradiction, the principal contradiction and the principal aspect of a contradiction, the identity and struggle of the aspects of a contradiction, and the place of antagonism in contradiction.

The criticism to which the idealism of the Deborin school has been subjected in Soviet philosophical circles in recent years has aroused great interest among us. Deborin's idealism has exerted a very bad influence in the Chinese Communist Party, and it cannot be said that the dogmatist thinking in our Party is unrelated to the approach of that school. Our present study of philosophy should therefore have the eradication of dogmatist thinking as its main objective.

I. THE TWO WORLD OUTLOOKS
Throughout the history of human knowledge, there have been two conceptions concerning the law of development of the universe, the metaphysical conception and the dialectical conception, which form two opposing world outlooks. Lenin said:

The two basic (or two possible? or two historically observable?) conceptions of development (evolution) are: development as decrease and increase, as repetition, and development as a unity of opposites (the division of a unity into mutually exclusive opposites and their reciprocal relation). [3]

Here Lenin was referring to these two different world outlooks.

In China another name for metaphysics is hsuan-hsueh. For a long period in history whether in China or in Europe, this way of thinking, which is part and parcel of the idealist world outlook, occupied a dominant position in human thought. In Europe, the materialism of the bourgeoisie in its early days was also metaphysical. As the social economy of many European countries advanced to the stage of highly developed capitalism, as the forces of production, the class struggle and the sciences developed to a level unprecedented in history, and as the industrial proletariat became the greatest motive force in historical development, there arose the Marxist world outlook of materialist dialectics. Then, in addition to open and barefaced reactionary idealism, vulgar evolutionism emerged among the bourgeoisie to oppose materialist dialectics.

The metaphysical or vulgar evolutionist world outlook sees things as isolated, static and one-sided. It regards all things in the universe, their forms and their species, as eternally isolated from one another and immutable. Such change as there is can only be an increase or decrease in quantity or a change of place. Moreover, the cause of such an increase or decrease or change of place is not inside things but outside them, that is, the motive force is external. Metaphysicians hold that all the different kinds of things in the universe and all their characteristics have been the same ever since they first came into being. All subsequent changes have simply been increases or decreases in quantity. They contend that a thing can only keep on repeating itself as the same kind of thing and cannot change into anything different. In their opinion, capitalist exploitation, capitalist competition, the individualist ideology of capitalist society, and so on, can all be found in ancient slave society, or even in primitive society, and will exist for ever unchanged. They ascribe the causes of social development to factors external to society, such as geography and climate. They search in an over-simplified way outside a thing for the causes of its development, and they deny the theory of materialist dialectics which holds that development arises from the contradictions inside a thing. Consequently they can explain neither the qualitative diversity of things, nor the phenomenon of one quality changing into another. In Europe, this mode of thinking existed as mechanical materialism in the 17th and 18th centuries and as vulgar evolutionism at the end of the 19th and the beginning of the 20th centuries. In China, there was the metaphysical thinking exemplified in the saying "Heaven changeth not, likewise the Tao changeth not", [4] and it was supported by the decadent feudal ruling classes for a long time. Mechanical materialism and vulgar evolutionism, which were imported from Europe in the last hundred years, are

184

supported by the bourgeoisie.

As opposed to the metaphysical world outlook, the world outlook of materialist dialectics holds that in order to understand the development of a thing we should study it internally and in its relations with other things; in other words, the development of things should be seen as their internal and necessary self-movement, while each thing in its movement is interrelated with and interacts on the things around it. The fundamental cause of the development of a thing is not external but internal; it lies in the contradictoriness within the thing. There is internal contradiction in every single thing, hence its motion and development. Contradictoriness within a thing is the fundamental cause of its development, while its interrelations and interactions with other things are secondary causes. Thus materialist dialectics effectively combats the theory of external causes, or of an external motive force, advanced by metaphysical mechanical materialism and vulgar evolutionism. It is evident that purely external causes can only give rise to mechanical motion, that is, to changes in scale or quantity, but cannot explain why things differ qualitatively in thousands of ways and why one thing changes into another. As a matter of fact, even mechanical motion under external force occurs through the internal contradictoriness of things. Simple growth in plants and animals, their quantitative development, is likewise chiefly the result of their internal contradictions. Similarly, social development is due chiefly not to external but to internal causes. Countries with almost the same geographical and climatic conditions display great diversity and unevenness in their development. Moreover, great social changes may take place in one and the same country although its geography and climate remain unchanged. Imperialist Russia changed into the socialist Soviet Union, and feudal Japan, which had locked its doors against the world, changed into imperialist Japan, although no change occurred in the geography and climate of either country. Long dominated by feudalism, China has undergone great changes in the last hundred years and is now changing in the direction of a new China, liberated and-free, and yet no change has occurred in her geography and climate. Changes do take place in the geography and climate of the earth as a whole and in every part of it, but they are insignificant when compared with changes in society; geographical and climatic changes manifest themselves in terms of tens of thousands of years, while social changes manifest themselves in thousands, hundreds or tens of years, and even in a few years or months in times of revolution. According to materialist dialectics, changes in nature are due chiefly to the development of the internal contradictions in nature. Changes in society are due chiefly to the development of the internal contradictions in society, that is, the contradiction between the productive forces and the relations of production, the contradiction between classes and the contradiction between the old and the new; it is the development of these contradictions that pushes society forward and gives the impetus for the supersession of the old society by the new. Does materialist dialectics exclude external causes? Not at all. It holds that external causes are the condition of change and internal causes are the basis of change, and that external causes become operative through internal causes. In a suitable temperature an egg changes into a chicken, but no temperature can change a stone into a chicken, because each has a different basis. There is constant interaction between the peoples of different countries. In the era of capitalism, and especially in the era of imperialism and proletarian revolution, the interaction and mutual impact of different countries in the political, economic and cultural spheres are extremely great. The October Socialist Revolution ushered in a new epoch in world history as well as in Russian history. It exerted influence on internal changes in the other countries in the world and, similarly and in a particularly profound way, on internal changes in China. These changes, however, were effected through the inner laws of development of these countries, China included. In battle, one army is victorious and the other is defeated, both the victory and the defeat are determined by internal causes. The one is victorious either because it is strong or because of its competent generalship, the other is vanquished either because it is weak or because of its incompetent generalship; it is through internal causes that external causes become operative. In China in 1927, the defeat of the proletariat by the big bourgeoisie came about through the opportunism then to be found within the Chinese proletariat itself (inside the Chinese Communist Party). When we liquidated this opportunism, the Chinese revolution resumed its advance. Later, the Chinese revolution again suffered severe setbacks at the hands of the enemy, because adventurism had risen within our Party. When we liquidated this adventurism, our cause advanced once again. Thus it can be seen that to lead the revolution to victory, a political party must depend on the correctness of its own political line and the solidity of its own organization.

The dialectical world outlook emerged in ancient times both in China and in Europe. Ancient dialectics, however, had a somewhat spontaneous and naive character; in the social and historical conditions then prevailing, it was not yet able to form a theoretical system, hence it could not fully explain the world and was supplanted by metaphysics. The famous German philosopher Hegel, who lived in the late 18th and early 19th centuries, made most important contributions to dialectics, but his dialectics was idealist. It was not until Marx and Engels, the great protagonists of the proletarian movement, had synthesized the positive achievements in the history of human knowledge and, in particular, critically absorbed the rational elements of Hegelian dialectics and created the great theory of dialectical and historical materialism that an unprecedented revolution occurred in the history of human knowledge. This theory was further developed by Lenin and Stalin. As soon as it spread to China, it wrought tremendous changes in the world of Chinese thought.

This dialectical world outlook teaches us primarily how to observe and analyse the movement of opposites in different things and, on the basis of such analysis, to indicate the methods for resolving contradictions. It is therefore most important for us to understand the law of contradiction in things in a concrete way.

II. THE UNIVERSALITY OF CONTRADICTION

For convenience of exposition, I shall deal first with the universality of contradiction and then proceed to the particularity of contradiction. The reason is that the universality of contradiction can be explained more briefly, for it has been widely recognized ever since the materialist-dialectical world outlook was discovered and materialist dialectics applied with outstanding success to analysing many aspects of human history and natural history and to changing many aspects of society and nature (as in the Soviet Union) by the great creators and continuers of Marxism--Marx, Engels, Lenin and Stalin; whereas the particularity of contradiction is still not dearly understood by many comrades, and especially by the dogmatists. They do not understand that it is precisely in the particularity of contradiction that the universality of contradiction resides. Nor do they understand how important is the study of the particularity of contradiction in the concrete things confronting us for guiding the course of revolutionary practice. Therefore, it is necessary to stress the study of the particularity of contradiction and to explain it at adequate length. For this reason, in our analysis of the law of contradiction in things, we shall first analyse the universality of contradiction, then place special stress on analysing the particularity of contradiction, and finally return to the universality of contradiction.

(haversality)

The universality or absoluteness of contradiction has a twofold meaning. One is that contradiction exists in the process of development of all things, and the other is that in the process of development of each thing a movement of opposites exists from beginning to end.

Engels said, "Motion itself is a contradiction." [5] Lenin defined the law of the unity of opposites as "the recognition (discovery) of the contradictory, mutually exclusive, opposite tendencies in all phenomena and processes of nature (including mind and society)". [6] Are these ideas correct? Yes, they are. The interdependence of the contradictory aspects present in all things and the struggle between these aspects determine the life of all things and push their development forward. There is nothing that does not contain contradiction; without contradiction nothing would exist.

Contradiction is the basis of the simple forms of motion (for instance, mechanical motion) and still more so of the complex forms of motion.

Engels explained the universality of contradiction as follows:

If simple mechanical change of place contains a contradiction, this is even more true of the higher forms of motion of matter, and especially of organic life and its development. ... life consists precisely and primarily in this--that a being is at each moment itself and yet something else. Life is therefore also a contradiction which is present in things and processes themselves, and which constantly originates and resolves itself; and as soon as the contradiction ceases, life, too, comes to an end, and death steps in. We likewise saw that also in the sphere of thought we could not escape contradictions, and that for example the contradiction between man's inherently unlimited capacity for knowledge and its actual presence only in men who are externally limited and possess limited cognition finds its solution in what is--at least practically, for us--an endless succession of generations, in infinite progress.

... one of the basic principles of higher mathematics is the contradiction that in certain circumstances straight lines and curves may be the same....

But even lower mathematics teems with contradictions. [7]

Lenin illustrated the universality of contradiction as follows:

In mathematics: + and - . Differential and integral.

In mechanics: action and reaction.

In physics: positive and negative electricity.

In chemistry: the combination and dissociation of atoms.

In social science: the class struggle. [8]

In war, offence and defence, advance and retreat, victory and defeat are

188

all mutually contradictory phenomena. One cannot exist without the other. The two aspects are at once in conflict and in interdependence, and this constitutes the totality of a war, pushes its development forward and solves its problems.

Every difference in men's concepts should be regarded as reflecting an objective contradiction. Objective contradictions are reflected in subjective thinking, and this process constitutes the contradictory movement of concepts, pushes forward the development of thought, and ceaselessly solves problems in man's thinking.

Opposition and struggle between ideas of different kinds constantly occur within the Party; this is a reflection within the Party of contradictions between classes and between the new and the old in society. If there were no contradictions in the Party and no ideological struggles to resolve them, the Party's life would come to an end.

Thus it is already clear that contradiction exists universally and in all processes, whether in the simple or in the complex forms of motion, whether in objective phenomena or ideological phenomena. But does contradiction also exist at the initial stage of each process?

Is there a movement of opposites from beginning to end in the process of development of every single thing? *Yes.*

As can be seen from the articles written by Soviet philosophers criticizing it, the Deborin school maintains that contradiction appears not at the inception of a process but only when it has developed to a certain stage. If this were the case, then the cause of the development of the process before that stage would be external and not internal. Deborin thus reverts to the metaphysical theories of external causality and of mechanism. Applying this view in the analysis of concrete problems, the Deborin school sees only differences but not contradictions between the kulaks and the peasants in general under existing conditions in the Soviet Union, thus entirely agreeing with Bukharin. In analysing the French Revolution, it holds that before the Revolution there were likewise only differences but not contradictions within the Third Estate, which was composed of the workers, the peasants and the bourgeoisie. These views of the Deborin school are anti-Marxist. This school does not understand that each and every difference already contains contradiction and that difference itself is contradiction. Labour and capital have been in contradiction ever since the two classes came into being, only at first the contradiction had not yet become intense. Even under the social conditions existing in the Soviet

189

Union, there is a difference between workers and peasants and this very difference is a contradiction, although, unlike the contradiction between labour and capital, it will not become intensified into antagonism or assume the form of class struggle; the workers and the peasants have established a firm alliance in the course of socialist construction and are gradually resolving this contradiction in the course of the advance from socialism to communism. The question is one of different kinds of contradiction, not of the presence or absence of contradiction. Contradiction is universal and absolute, it is present in the process of development of all things and permeates every process from beginning to end.

What is meant by the emergence of a new process? The old unity with its constituent opposites yields to a new unity with its constituent opposites, whereupon a new process emerges to replace the old. The old process ends and the new one begins. The new process contains new contradictions and begins its own history of the development of contradictions.

As Lenin pointed out, Marx in his Capital gave a model analysis of this movement of opposites which runs through the process of development of things from beginning to end. This is the method that must be employed in studying the development of all things. Lenin, too, employed this method correctly and adhered to it in all his writings.

In his Capital, Marx first analyses the simplest, most ordinary and fundamental, most common and everyday relation of bourgeois (commodity) society, a relation encountered billions of times, viz. the exchange of commodities. In this very simple phenomenon (in this "cell" of bourgeois society) analysis reveals all the contradictions (or the germs of all the contradictions) of modern society. The subsequent exposition shows us the development (both growth and movement) of these contradictions and of this society in the [summation] of its individual parts, from its beginning to its end.

Lenin added, "Such must also be the method of exposition (or study) of dialectics in general." [9]

Chinese Communists must learn this method; only then will they be able correctly to analyse the history and the present state of the Chinese revolution and infer its future.

III. THE PARTICULARITY OF CONTRADICTION

Contradiction is present in the process of development of all things; it permeates the process of development of each thing from beginning to end. This is the universality and absoluteness of contradiction which we have discussed above. Now let us discuss the particularity and relativity of contradiction.

This problem should be studied on several levels.

First, the contradiction in each form of motion of matter has its particularity. Man's knowledge of matter is knowledge of its forms of motion, because there is nothing in this world except matter in motion and this motion must assume certain forms. In considering each form of motion of matter, we must observe the points which it has in common with other forms of motion. But what is especially important and necessary, constituting as it does the foundation of our knowledge of a thing, is to observe what is particular to this form of motion of matter, namely, to observe the qualitative difference between this form of motion and other forms. Only when we have done so can we distinguish between things. Every form of motion contains within itself its own particular contradiction. This particular contradiction constitutes the particular essence which distinguishes one thing from another. It is the internal cause or, as it may be called, the basis for the immense variety of things in the world. There are many forms of motion in nature, mechanical motion, sound, light, heat, electricity, dissociation, combination, and so on. All these forms are interdependent, but in its essence each is different from the others. The particular essence of each form of motion is determined by its own particular contradiction. This holds true not only for nature but also for social and ideological phenomena. Every form of society, every form of ideology, has its own particular contradiction and particular essence.

The sciences are differentiated precisely on the basis of the particular contradictions inherent in their respective objects of study. Thus the contradiction peculiar to a certain field of phenomena constitutes the object of study for a specific branch of science. For example, positive and negative numbers in mathematics; action and reaction in mechanics; positive and negative electricity in physics; dissociation and combination in chemistry; forces of production and relations of production, classes and class struggle, in social science; offence and defence in military science; idealism and materialism, the metaphysical outlook and the dialectical outlook, in philosophy; and so on--all these are the objects of study of different branches of science precisely because each branch has its own particular contradiction and particular essence. Of course, unless we

191

understand the universality of contradiction, we have no way of discovering the universal cause or universal basis for the movement or development of things; however, unless we study the particularity of contradiction, we have no way of determining the particular essence of a thing which differentiates it from other things, no way of discovering the particular cause or particular basis for the movement or development of a thing, and no way of distinguishing one thing from another or of demarcating the fields of science.

As regards the sequence in the movement of man's knowledge, there is always a gradual growth from the knowledge of individual and particular things to the knowledge of things in general. Only after man knows the particular essence of many different things can he proceed to generalization and know the common essence of things.

When man attains the knowledge of this common essence, he uses it as a guide and proceeds to study various concrete things which have not yet been studied, or studied thoroughly, and to discover the particular essence of each; only thus is he able to supplement, enrich and develop his knowledge of their common essence and prevent such knowledge from withering or petrifying. These are the two processes of cognition: one, from the particular to the general, and the other, from the general to the particular. Thus cognition always moves in cycles and (so long as scientific method is strictly adhered to) each cycle advances human knowledge a step higher and so makes it more and more profound. Where our dogmatists err on this question is that, on the one hand, they do not understand that we have to study the particularity of contradiction and know the particular essence of individual things before we can adequately know the universality of contradiction and the common essence of things, and that, on the other hand, they do not understand that after knowing the common essence of things, we must go further and study the concrete things that have not yet been thoroughly studied or have only just emerged. Our dogmatists are lazy-bones. They refuse to undertake any painstaking study of concrete things, they regard general truths as emerging out of the void, they turn them into purely abstract unfathomable formulas, and thereby completely deny and reverse the normal sequence by which man comes to know truth. Nor do they understand the interconnection of the two processes in cognition-- from the particular to the general and then from the general to the particular. They understand nothing of the Marxist theory of knowledge.

It is necessary not only to study the particular contradiction and the essence determined thereby of every great system of the forms of motion of matter, but also to study the particular contradiction and the essence of each process in the long course of development of each form of motion of matter. In every form of motion, each process of development which is real (and not imaginary) is qualitatively different. Our study must emphasize and start from this point.

Qualitatively different contradictions can only be resolved by qualitatively different methods. For instance, the contradiction between the proletariat and the bourgeoisie is resolved by the method of socialist revolution; the contradiction between the great masses of the people and the feudal system is resolved by the method of democratic revolution; the contradiction between the colonies and imperialism is resolved by the method of national revolutionary war; the contradiction between the working class and the peasant class in socialist society is resolved by the method of collectivization and mechanization in agriculture; contradiction within the Communist Party is resolved by the method of criticism and self-criticism; the contradiction between society and nature is resolved by the method of developing the productive forces. Processes change, old processes and old contradictions disappear, new processes and new contradictions emerge, and the methods of resolving contradictions differ accordingly. In Russia, there was a fundamental difference between the contradiction resolved by the February Revolution and the contradiction resolved by the October Revolution, as well as between the methods used to resolve them. The principle of using different methods to resolve different contradictions is one which Marxist-Leninists must strictly observe. The dogmatists do not observe this principle; they do not understand that conditions differ in different kinds of revolution and so do not understand that different methods should be used to resolve different contradictions; on the contrary, they invariably adopt what they imagine to be an unalterable formula and arbitrarily apply it everywhere, which only causes setbacks to the revolution or makes a sorry mess of what was originally well done.

In order to reveal the particularity of the contradictions in any process in the development of a thing, in their totality or interconnections, that is, in order to reveal the essence of the process, it is necessary to reveal the particularity of the two aspects of each of the contradictions in that process; otherwise it will be impossible to discover the essence of the process. This likewise requires the utmost attention in our study.

There are many contradictions in the course of development of any major thing. For instance, in the course of China's bourgeois-democratic revolution, where the conditions are exceedingly complex, there exist the

193

contradiction between all the oppressed classes in Chinese society and imperialism, the contradiction between the great masses of the people and feudalism, the contradiction between the proletariat and the bourgeoisie, the contradiction between the peasantry and the urban petty bourgeoisie on the one hand and the bourgeoisie on the other, the contradiction between the various reactionary ruling groups, and so on. These contradictions cannot be treated in the same way since each has its own particularity; moreover, the two aspects of each contradiction cannot be treated in the same way since each aspect has its own characteristics. We who are engages in the Chinese revolution should not only understand the particularity of these contradictions in their totality, that is, in their interconnections, but should also study the two aspects of each contradiction as the only means of understanding the totality. When we speak of understanding each aspect of a contradiction, we mean understanding what specific position each aspect occupies, what concrete forms it assumes in its interdependence and in its contradiction with its opposite, and what concrete methods are employed in the struggle with its opposite, when the two are both interdependent and in contradiction, and also after the interdependence breaks down. It is of great importance to study these problems. Lenin meant just this when he said that the most essential thing in Marxism, the living soul of Marxism, is the concrete analysis of concrete conditions. [10] Our dogmatists have violated Lenin's teachings; they never use their brains to analyse anything concretely, and in their writings and speeches they always use stereotypes devoid of content, thereby creating a very bad style of work in our Party.

In studying a problem, we must shun subjectivity, one-sidedness and superficiality. To be subjective means not to look at problems objectively, that is, not to use the materialist viewpoint in looking at problems. I have discussed this in my essay "On Practice". To be one-sided means not to look at problems all-sidedly, for example, to understand only China but not Japan, only the Communist Party but not the Kuomintang, only the proletariat but not the bourgeoisie, only the peasants but not the landlords, only the favourable conditions but not the difficult ones, only the past but not the future, only individual parts but not the whole, only the defects but not the achievements, only the plaintiff's case but not the defendant's, only underground revolutionary work but not open revolutionary work, and so on. In a word, it means not to understand the characteristics of both aspects of a contradiction. This is what we mean by looking at a problem one-sidedly. Or it may be called seeing the part but not the whole, seeing the trees but not the forest. That way it is impossible to kind the method for resolving a contradiction, it is impossible to accomplish the tasks of the revolution, to carry out assignments well or to develop inner-Party ideological struggle correctly. When Sun Wu Tzu said in discussing military science, "Know the enemy and know yourself, and you can fight a hundred battles with no danger of defeat", [11] he was referring to the two sides in a battle. Wei Chengi [12] of the Tang Dynasty also understood the error of one- sidedness when he said, "Listen to both sides and you will be enlightened, heed only one side and you will be benighted." But our comrades often look at problems one-sidedly, and so they often run into snags. In the novel Shui Hu Chuan, Sung Chiang thrice attacked Chu Village. [13] Twice he was defeated because he was ignorant of the local conditions and used the wrong method. Later he changed his method; first he investigated the situation, and he familiarized himself with the maze of roads, then he broke up the alliance between the Li, Hu and Chu Villages and sent his men in disguise into the enemy camp to lie in wait, using a stratagem similar to that of the Trojan Horse in the foreign story. And on the third occasion he won. There are many examples of materialist dialectics in Shui Hu Chuan, of which the episode of the three attacks on Chu Village is one of the best. Lenin said:

... in order really to know an object we must embrace, study, all its sides, all connections and "mediations". We shall never achieve this completely, but the demand for all-sidedness is a safeguard against mistakes and rigidity.[14]

We should remember his words. To be superficial means to consider neither the characteristics of a contradiction in its totality nor the characteristics of each of its aspects; it means to deny the necessity for probing deeply into a thing and minutely studying the characteristics of its contradiction, but instead merely to look from afar and, after glimpsing the rough outline, immediately to try to resolve the contradiction (to answer a question, settle a dispute, handle work, or direct a military operation). This way of doing things is bound to lead to trouble. The reason the dogmatist and empiricist comrades in China have made mistakes lies precisely in their subjectivist, one-sided and superficial way of looking at things. To be one-sided and superficial is at the same time to be subjective. For all objective things are actually interconnected and are governed by inner laws, but instead of undertaking the task of reflecting things as they really are some people only look at things one-sidedly or superficially and who know neither their interconnections nor their inner laws, and so their method is subjectivist.

Not only does the whole process of the movement of opposites in the development of a thing, both in their interconnections and in each of the aspects, have particular features to which we must give attention, but each stage in the process has its particular features to which we must give attention too.

The fundamental contradiction in the process of development of a thing and the essence of the process determined by this fundamental contradiction will not disappear until the process is completed; but in a lengthy process the conditions usually differ at each stage. The reason is that, although the nature of the fundamental contradiction in the process of development of a thing and the essence of the process remain unchanged, the fundamental contradiction becomes more and more intensified as it passes from one stage to another in the lengthy process. In addition, among the numerous major and minor contradictions which are determined or influenced by the fundamental contradiction, some become intensified, some are temporarily or partially resolved or mitigated, and some new ones emerge; hence the process is marked by stages. If people do not pay attention to the stages in the process of development of a thing, they cannot deal with its contradictions properly.

For instance, when the capitalism of the era of free competition developed into imperialism, there was no change in the class nature of the two classes in fundamental contradiction, namely, the proletariat and the bourgeoisie, or in the capitalist essence of society; however, the contradiction between these two classes became intensified, the contradiction between monopoly and non-monopoly capital emerged, the contradiction between the colonial powers and the colonies became intensified, the contradiction among the capitalist countries resulting from their uneven development manifested itself with particular sharpness, and thus there arose the special stage of capitalism, the stage of imperialism. Leninism is the Marxism of the era of imperialism and proletarian revolution precisely because Lenin and Stalin have correctly explained these contradictions and correctly formulated the theory and tactics of the proletarian revolution for their resolution.

Take the process of China's bourgeois-democratic revolution, which began with the Revolution of 1911; it, too, has several distinct stages. In particular, the revolution in its period of bourgeois leadership and the revolution in its period of proletarian leadership represent two vastly different historical stages. In other words, proletarian leadership has fundamentally changed the whole face of the revolution, has brought about a new alignment of classes, given rise to a tremendous upsurge in the peasant revolution, imparted thoroughness to the revolution against imperialism and feudalism, created the possibility of the transition from the democratic revolution to the socialist revolution, and so on. None of these was possible in the period when the revolution was under bourgeois leadership. Although no change has taken place in the nature of the fundamental contradiction in the process as a whole, i.e., in the anti-imperialist, anti- feudal, democratic-revolutionary nature of the process (the opposite of which is its semi-colonial and semi-feudal nature), nonetheless this process has passed through several stages of development in the course of more than twenty years; during this time many great events have taken place-- the failure of the Revolution of 1911 and the establishment of the regime of the Northern warlords, the formation of the first national united front and the revolution of 1924-27, the break-up of the united front and the desertion of the bourgeoisie to the side of the counterrevolution, the wars among the new warlords, the Agrarian Revolutionary War, the establishment of the second national united front and the War of Resistance Against Japan. These stages are marked by particular features such as the intensification of certain contradictions (e.g., the Agrarian Revolutionary War and the Japanese invasion of the four northeastern provinces), the partial or temporary resolution of other contradictions (e.g., the destruction of the Northern warlords and our confiscation of the land of the landlords), and the emergence of yet other contradictions (e.g., the conflicts among the new warlords, and the landlords' recapture of the land after the loss of our revolutionary base areas in the south).

In studying the particularities of the contradictions at each stage in the process of development of a thing, we must not only observe them in their interconnections or their totality, we must also examine the two aspects of each contradiction.

For instance, consider the Kuomintang and the Communist Party. Take one aspect, the Kuomintang. In the period of the first united front, the Kuomintang carried out Sun Yat-sen's Three Great Policies of alliance with Russia, co-operation with the Communist Party, and assistance to the peasants and workers; hence it was revolutionary and vigorous, it was an alliance of various classes for the democratic revolution. After 1927, however, the Kuomintang changed into its opposite and became a reactionary bloc of the landlords and big bourgeoisie. After the Sian Incident in December 1936, it began another change in the direction of ending the civil war and co-operating with the Communist Party for joint opposition to Japanese imperialism. Such have been the particular features of the Kuomintang in the three stages. Of course, these features have arisen from a variety of causes. Now take the other aspect, the Chinese Communist Party. In the period of the first united front, the Chinese Communist Party was in its infancy; it courageously led the revolution of

1924-27 but revealed its immaturity in its understanding of the character, the tasks and the methods of the revolution, and consequently it became possible for Chen Tu-hsiuism, which appeared during the latter part of this revolution, to assert itself and bring about the defeat of the revolution. After 1927, the Communist Party courageously led the Agrarian Revolutionary War and created the revolutionary army and revolutionary base areas; however, it committed adventurist errors which brought about very great losses both to the army and to the base areas. Since 1935 the Party has corrected these errors and has been leading the new united front for resistance to Japan; this great struggle is now developing. At the present stage, the Communist Party is a Party that has gone through the test of two revolutions and acquired a wealth of experience. Such have been the particular features of the Chinese Communist Party in the three stages. These features, too, have arisen from a variety of causes. Without studying both these sets of features we cannot understand the particular relations between the two parties during the various stages of their development, namely, the establishment of a united front, the break-up of the united front, and the establishment of another united front. What is even more fundamental for the study of the particular features of the two parties is the examination of the class basis of the two parties and the resultant contradictions which have arisen between each party and other forces at different periods. For instance, in the period of its first cooperation with the Communist Party, the Kuomintang stood in contradiction to foreign imperialism and was therefore anti-imperialist; on the other hand, it stood in contradiction to the great masses of the people within the country--although in words it promised many benefits to the working people, in fact it gave them little or nothing. In the period when it carried on the anti-Communist war, the Kuomintang collaborated with imperialism and feudalism against the great masses of the people and wiped out all the gains they had won in the revolution, and thereby intensified its contradictions with them. In the present period of the anti-Japanese war, the Kuomintang stands in contradiction to Japanese imperialism and wants co-operation with the Communist Party, without however relaxing its struggle against the Communist Party and the people or its oppression of them. As for the Communist Party, it has always, in every period, stood with the great masses of the people against imperialism and feudalism, but in the present period of the anti-Japanese war, it has adopted a moderate policy towards the Kuomintang and the domestic feudal forces because the Kuomintang has pressed itself in favour of resisting Japan. The above circumstances have resulted now in alliance between the two parties and now in struggle between them, and even during the periods of alliance there has been a complicated state of simultaneous alliance and struggle. If we do not study the particular features of both aspects of the contradiction, we shall fail to understand not only the relations of each party with the other forces, but also the relations between the two parties.

It can thus be seen that in studying the particularity of any kind of contradiction--the contradiction in each form of motion of matter, the contradiction in each of its processes of development, the two aspects of the contradiction in each process, the contradiction at each stage of a process, and the two aspects of the contradiction at each stage--in studying the particularity of all these contradictions, we must not be subjective and arbitrary but must analyse it concretely. Without concrete analysis there can be no knowledge of the particularity of any contradiction. We must always remember Lenin's words, the concrete analysis of concrete conditions.

Marx and Engels were the first to provide us with excellent models of such concrete analysis.

When Marx and Engels applied the law of contradiction in things to the study of the socio-historical process, they discovered the contradiction between the productive forces and the relations of production, they discovered the contradiction between the exploiting and exploited classes and also the resultant contradiction between the economic base and its superstructure (politics, ideology, etc.), and they discovered how these contradictions inevitably lead to different kinds of social revolution in different kinds of class society.

When Marx applied this law to the study of the economic structure of capitalist society, he discovered that the basic contradiction of this society is the contradiction between the social character of production and the private character of ownership. This contradiction manifests itself in the contradiction between the organized character of production in individual enterprises and the anarchic character of production in society as a whole. In terms of class relations, it manifests itself in the contradiction between the bourgeoisie and the proletariat.

Because the range of things is vast and there is no limit to their development, what is universal in one context becomes particular in another. Conversely, what is particular in one context becomes universal in another. The contradiction in the capitalist system between the social character of production and the private ownership of the means of production is common to all countries where capitalism exists and develops; as far as capitalism is concerned, this constitutes the universality

199

Universal — Particular) hence,
Particular — Universal) managed
curr. in
Relatable

of contradiction. But this contradiction of capitalism belongs only to a certain historical stage in the general development of class society; as far as the contradiction between the productive forces and the relations of production in class society as a whole is concerned, it constitutes the particularity of contradiction. However, in the course of dissecting the particularity of all these contradictions in capitalist society, Marx gave a still more profound, more adequate and more complete elucidation of the universality of the contradiction between the productive forces and the relations of production in class society in general.

Since the particular is united with the universal and since the universality as well as the particularity of contradiction is inherent in everything, universality residing in particularity, we should, when studying an object, try to discover both the particular and the universal and their interconnection, to discover both particularity and universality and also their interconnection within the object itself, and to discover the interconnections of this object with the many objects outside it. When Stalin explained the historical roots of Leninism in his famous work, The Foundations of Leninism, he analysed the international situation in which Leninism arose, analysed those contradictions of capitalism which reached their culmination under imperialism, and showed how these contradictions made proletarian revolution a matter for immediate action and created favourable conditions for a direct onslaught on capitalism. What is more, he analysed the reasons why Russia became the cradle of Leninism, why tsarist Russia became the focus of all the contradictions of imperialism, and why it was possible for the Russian proletariat to become the vanguard of the international revolutionary proletariat. Thus, Stalin analysed the universality of contradiction in imperialism, showing why Leninism is the Marxism of the era of imperialism and proletarian revolution, and at the same time analysed the particularity of tsarist Russian imperialism within this general contradiction, showing why Russia became the birthplace of the theory and tactics of proletarian revolution and how the universality of contradiction is contained in this particularity. Stalin's analysis provides us with a model for understanding the particularity and the universality of contradiction and their interconnection.

On the question of using dialectics in the study of objective phenomena, Marx and Engels, and likewise Lenin and Stalin, always enjoin people not to be in any way subjective and arbitrary but, from the concrete conditions in the actual objective movement of these phenomena, to discover their concrete contradictions, the concrete position of each aspect of every contradiction and the concrete interrelations of the contradictions. Our dogmatists do not have this attitude in study and therefore can never get anything right. We must take warning from their failure and learn to acquire this attitude, which is the only correct one in study.

The relationship between the universality and the particularity of contradiction is the relationship between the general character and the individual character of contradiction. By the former we mean that contradiction exists in and runs through all processes from beginning to end; motion, things, processes, thinking--all are contradictions. To deny contradiction is to deny everything. This is a universal truth for all times and all countries, which admits of no exception. Hence the general character, the absoluteness of contradiction. But this general character is contained in every individual character; without individual character there can be no general character. If all individual character were removed, what general character would remain? It is because each contradiction is particular that individual character arises. All individual character exists conditionally and temporarily, and hence is relative.

This truth concerning general and individual character, concerning absoluteness and relativity, is the quintessence of the problem of contradiction in things; failure to understand it is tantamount to abandoning dialectics.

IV. THE PRINCIPAL CONTRADICTION AND THE PRINCIPAL ASPECT OF A CONTRADICTION

There are still two points in the problem of the particularity of contradiction which must be singled out for analysis, namely, the principal contradiction and the principal aspect of a contradiction.

There are many contradictions in the process of development of a complex thing, and one of them is necessarily the principal contradiction whose existence and development determine or influence the existence and development of the other contradictions.

For instance, in capitalist society the two forces in contradiction, the proletariat and the bourgeoisie, form the principal contradiction. The other contradictions, such as those between the remnant feudal class and the bourgeoisie, between the peasant petty bourgeoisie ant the bourgeoisie, between the proletariat and the peasant petty bourgeoisie, between the non-monopoly capitalists and the monopoly capitalists, between bourgeois democracy and bourgeois fascism, among the capitalist countries and between imperialism and the colonies, are all determined or influenced by this principal contradiction.

In a semi-colonial country such as China, the relationship between the principal contradiction and the non-principal contradictions presents a complicated picture.

When imperialism launches a war of aggression against such a country, all its various classes, except for some traitors, can temporarily unite in a national war against imperialism. At such a time, the contradiction between imperialism and the country concerned becomes the principal contradiction, while all the contradictions among the various classes within the country (including what was the principal contradiction, between the feudal system and the great masses of the people) are temporarily relegated to a secondary and subordinate position. So it was in China in the Opium War of 1840, the Sino-Japanese War of 1894 and the Yi Ho Tuan War of 1900, and so it is now in the present Sino-Japanese War.

But in another situation, the contradictions change position. When imperialism carries on its oppression not by war, but by milder means-- political, economic and cultural--the ruling classes in semi-colonial countries capitulate to imperialism, and the two form an alliance for the joint oppression of the masses of the people. At such a time, the masses often resort to civil war against the alliance of imperialism and the feudal classes, while imperialism often employs indirect methods rather than direct action in helping the reactionaries in the semi-colonial countries to oppress the people, and thus the internal contradictions become particularly sharp. This is what happened in China in the Revolutionary War of 1911, the Revolutionary War of 1924-27, and the ten years of Agrarian Revolutionary War after 1927. Wars among the various reactionary ruling groups in the semi-colonial countries, e.g., the wars among the warlords in China, fall into the same category.

When a revolutionary civil war develops to the point of threatening the very existence of imperialism and its running dogs, the domestic reactionaries, imperialism often adopts other methods in order to maintain its rule; it either tries to split the revolutionary front from within or sends armed forces to help the domestic reactionaries directly. At such a time, foreign imperialism and domestic reaction stand quite openly at one pole while the masses of the people stand at the other pole, thus forming the principal contradiction which determines or influences the development of the other contradictions. The assistance given by various capitalist countries to the Russian reactionaries after the October Revolution is an example of armed intervention. Chiang Kai-shek's betrayal in 1927 is an example of splitting the revolutionary front.

But whatever happens, there is no doubt at all that at every stage in the development of a process, there is only one principal contradiction which plays the leading role.

Hence, if in any process there are a number of contradictions, one of them must be the principal contradiction playing the leading and decisive role, while the rest occupy a secondary and subordinate position. Therefore, in studying any complex process in which there are two or more contradictions, we must devote every effort to funding its principal contradiction. Once this principal contradiction is grasped, all problems can be readily solved. This is the method Marx taught us in his study of capitalist society. Likewise Lenin and Stalin taught us this method when they studied imperialism and the general crisis of capitalism and when they studied the Soviet economy. There are thousands of scholars and men of action who do not understand it, and the result is that, lost in a fog, they are unable to get to the heart of a problem and naturally cannot find a way to resolve its contradictions.

As we have said, one must not treat all the contradictions in a process as being equal but must distinguish between the principal and the secondary contradictions, and pay special attention to grasping the principal one. But, in any given contradiction, whether principal or secondary, should the two contradictory aspects be treated as equal? Again, no. In any contradiction the development of the contradictory aspects is uneven. Sometimes they seem to be in equilibrium, which is however only temporary and relative, while unevenness is basic. Of the two contradictory aspects, one must be principal and the other secondary. The principal aspect is the one playing the leading role in the contradiction. The nature of a thing is determined mainly by the principal aspect of a contradiction, the aspect which has gained the dominant position.

But this situation is not static; the principal and the non-principal aspects of a contradiction transform themselves into each other and the nature of the thing changes accordingly. In a given process or at a given stage in the development of a contradiction, A is the principal aspect and B is the non-principal aspect; at another stage or in another process the roles are reversed--a change determined by the extent of the increase or decrease in the force of each aspect in its struggle against the other in the course of the development of a thing.

We often speak of "the new superseding the old". The supersession of the old by the new is a general, eternal and inviolable law of the universe. The transformation of one thing into another, through leaps of different forms in accordance with its essence and external conditions--this is the process of the new superseding the old. In each thing there is contradiction between its new and its old aspects, and this gives rise to a series of struggles with many twists and turns. As a result of these struggles, the new aspect changes from being minor to being major and rises to predominance, while the old aspect changes from being major to being minor and gradually dies out. And the moment the new aspect gains dominance over the old, the old thing changes qualitatively into a new thing. It can thus be seen that the nature of a thing is mainly determined by the principal aspect of the contradiction, the aspect which has gained predominance. When the principal aspect which has gained predominance changes, the nature of a thing changes accordingly.

In capitalist society, capitalism has changed its position from being a subordinate force in the old feudal era to being the dominant force, and the nature of society has accordingly changed from feudal to capitalist. In the new, capitalist era, the feudal forces changed from their former dominant position to a subordinate one, gradually dying out. Such was the case, for example, in Britain and France. With the development of the productive forces, the bourgeoisie changes from being a new class playing a progressive role to being an old class playing a reactionary role, until it is finally overthrown by the proletariat and becomes a class deprived of privately owned means of production and stripped of power, when it, too, gradually dies out. The proletariat, which is much more numerous than the bourgeoisie and grows simultaneously with it but under its rule, is a new force which, initially subordinate to the bourgeoisie, gradually gains strength, becomes an independent class playing the leading role in history, and finally seizes political power and becomes the ruling class. Thereupon the nature of society changes and the old capitalist society becomes the new socialist society. This is the path already taken by the Soviet Union, a path that all other countries will inevitably take.

Look at China, for instance. Imperialism occupies the principal position in the contradiction in which China has been reduced to a semi-colony, it oppresses the Chinese people, and China has been changed from an independent country into a semi-colonial one. But this state of affairs will inevitably change; in the struggle between the two sides, the power of the Chinese people which is growing under the leadership of the proletariat will inevitably change China from a semi-colony into an independent country, whereas imperialism will be overthrown and old China will inevitably change into New China.

204

The change of old China into New China also involves a change in the relation between the old feudal forces and the new popular forces within the country. The old feudal landlord class will be overthrown, and from being the ruler it will change into being the ruled; and this class, too, will gradually die out. From being the ruled the people, led by the proletariat, will become the rulers. Thereupon, the nature of Chinese society will change and the old, semi-colonial and semi-feudal society will change into a new democratic society.

Instances of such reciprocal transformation are found in our past experience. The Ching Dynasty which ruled China for nearly three hundred years was overthrown in the Revolution of 1911, and the revolutionary Tung Meng Hui under Sun Yat-sen's leadership was victorious for a time. In the Revolutionary War of 1924-27, the revolutionary forces of the Communist-Kuomintang alliance in the south changed from being weak to being strong and won victory in the Northern Expedition, while the Northern warlords who once ruled the roost were overthrown. In 1927, the people's forces led by the Communist Party were greatly reduced numerically under the attacks of Kuomintang reaction, but with the elimination of opportunism within their ranks they gradually grew again. In the revolutionary base areas under Communist leadership, the peasants have been transformed from being the ruled to being the rulers, while the landlords have undergone a reverse transformation. It is always so in the world, the new displacing the old, the old being superseded by the new, the old being eliminated to make way for the new, and the new emerging out of the old.

At certain times in the revolutionary struggle, the difficulties outweigh the favourable conditions and so constitute the principal aspect of the contradiction and the favourable conditions constitute the secondary aspect. But through their efforts the revolutionaries can overcome the difficulties step by step and open up a favourable new situation; thus a difficult situation yields place to a favourable one. This- is what happened after the failure of the revolution in China in 1927 and during the Long March of the Chinese Red Army. In the present Sino-Japanese War, China is again in a difficult position, but we can change this and fundamentally transform the situation as between China and Japan. Conversely, favourable conditions can be transformed into difficulty if the revolutionaries make mistakes. Thus the victory of the revolution of 1924-27 turned into defeat. The revolutionary base areas which grew up in the southern provinces after 1927 had all suffered defeat by 1934.

When we engage in study, the same holds good for the contradiction in the passage from ignorance to knowledge. At the very beginning of our study of Marxism, our ignorance of or scanty acquaintance with Marxism stands in contradiction to knowledge of Marxism. But by assiduous study, ignorance can be transformed into knowledge, scanty knowledge into substantial knowledge, and blindness in the application of Marxism into mastery of its application.

Some people think that this is not true of certain contradictions. For instance, in the contradiction between the productive forces and the relations of production, the productive forces are the principal aspect; in the contradiction between theory and practice, practice is the principal aspect; in the contradiction between the economic base and the superstructure, the economic base is the principal aspect; and there is no change in their respective positions. This is the mechanical materialist conception, not the dialectical materialist conception. True, the productive forces, practice and the economic base generally play the principal and decisive role; whoever denies this is not a materialist. But it must also be admitted that in certain conditions, such aspects as the relations of production, theory and the superstructure in turn manifest themselves in the principal and decisive role. When it is impossible for the productive forces to develop without a change in the relations of production, then the change in the relations of production plays the principal and decisive role. The creation and advocacy of revolutionary theory plays the principal and decisive role in those times of which Lenin said, "Without revolutionary theory there can be no revolutionary movement." [15] When a task, no matter which, has to be performed, but there is as yet no guiding line, method, plan or policy, the principal and decisive thing is to decide on a guiding line, method, plan or policy. When the superstructure (politics, culture, etc.) obstructs the development of the economic base, political and cultural changes become principal and decisive. Are we going against materialism when we say this? No. The reason is that while we recognize that in the general development of history the material determines the mental and social being determines social consciousness, we also--and indeed must--recognize the reaction of mental on material things, of social consciousness on social being and of the superstructure on the economic base. This does not go against materialism; on the contrary, it avoids mechanical materialism and firmly upholds dialectical materialism.

In studying the particularity of contradiction, unless we examine these two facets--the principal and the non-principal contradictions in a process, and the principal and the non-principal aspects of a contradiction--that is, unless we examine the distinctive character of these two facets of contradiction, we shall get bogged down in abstractions, be unable to

206

understand contradiction concretely and consequently be unable to find the correct method of resolving it. The distinctive character or particularity of these two facets of contradiction represents the unevenness of the forces that are in contradiction. Nothing in this world develops absolutely evenly; we must oppose the theory of even development or the theory of equilibrium. Moreover, it is these concrete features of a contradiction and the changes in the principal and non-principal aspects of a contradiction in the course of its development that manifest the force of the new superseding the old. The study of the various states of unevenness in contradictions, of the principal and non-principal contradictions and of the principal and the non-principal aspects of a contradiction constitutes an essential method by which a revolutionary political party correctly determines its strategic and tactical policies both in political and in military affairs. All Communists must give it attention.

V. THE IDENTITY AND STRUGGLE OF THE ASPECTS OF A CONTRADICTION
When we understand the universality and the particularity of contradiction, we must proceed to study the problem of the identity and struggle of the aspects of a contradiction.

Identity, unity, coincidence, interpenetration, interpermeation, interdependence (or mutual dependence for existence), interconnection or mutual co-operation--all these different terms mean the same thing and refer to the following two points: first, the existence of each of the two aspects of a contradiction in the process of the development of a thing presupposes the existence of the other aspect, and both aspects coexist in a single entity; second, in given conditions, each of the two contradictory aspects transforms itself into its opposite. This is the meaning of identity.

Lenin said:

Dialectics is the teaching which shows how opposites can be and how they happen to be (how they become) identical--under what conditions they are identical, transforming themselves into one another,--why the human mind should take these opposites not as dead, rigid, but as living, conditional, mobile, transforming themselves into one another. [16]

What does this passage mean?

The contradictory aspects in every process exclude each other, struggle with each other and are in opposition to each other. Without exception, they are contained in the process of development of all things and in all human thought. A simple process contains only a single pair of opposites,

207

while a complex process contains more. And in turn, the pairs of opposites are in contradiction to one another.

That is how all things in the objective world and all human thought are constituted and how they are set in motion.

This being so, there is an utter lack of identity or unity. How then can one speak of identity or unity?

The fact is that no contradictory aspect can exist in isolation. Without its opposite aspect, each loses the condition for its existence. Just think, can any one contradictory aspect of a thing or of a concept in the human mind exist independently? Without life, there would be no death; without death, there would be no life. Without "above", there would be no "below" without "below", there would be no "above". Without misfortune, there would be no good fortune; without good fortune, these would be no misfortune. Without facility, there would be no difficulty without difficulty, there would be no facility. Without landlords, there would be no tenant-peasants; without tenant-peasants, there would be no landlords. Without the bourgeoisie, there would be no proletariat; without the proletariat, there would be no bourgeoisie. Without imperialist oppression of nations, there would be no colonies or semi-colonies; without colonies or semicolonies, there would be no imperialist oppression of nations. It is so with all opposites; in given conditions, on the one hand they are opposed to each other, and on the other they are interconnected, interpenetrating, interpermeating and interdependent, and this character is described as identity. In given conditions, all contradictory aspects possess the character of non-identity and hence are described as being in contradiction. But they also possess the character of identity and hence are interconnected. This is what Lenin means when he says that dialectics studies "how opposites can be ... identical". How then can they be identical? Because each is the condition for the other's existence. This is the first meaning of identity.

But is it enough to say merely that each of the contradictory aspects is the condition for the other's existence, that there is identity between them and that consequently they can coexist in a single entity? No, it is not. The matter does not end with their dependence on each other for their existence; what is more important is their transformation into each other. That is to say, in given conditions, each of the contradictory aspects within a thing transforms itself into its opposite, changes its position to that of its opposite. This is the second meaning of the identity of contradiction.

208 Transformation into each other

Why is there identity here, too? You see, by means of revolution the proletariat, at one time the ruled, is transformed into the ruler, while the bourgeoisie, the erstwhile ruler, is transformed into the ruled and changes its position to that originally occupied by its opposite. This has already taken place in the Soviet Union, as it will take place throughout the world. If there were no interconnection and identity of opposites in given conditions, how could such a change take place?

The Kuomintang, which played a certain positive role at a certain stage in modern Chinese history, became a counter-revolutionary party after 1927 because of its inherent class nature and because of imperialist blandishments (these being the conditions); but it has been compelled to agree to resist Japan because of the sharpening of the contradiction between China and Japan and because of the Communist Party's policy of the united front (these being the conditions). Things in contradiction change into one another, and herein lies a definite identity.

Our agrarian revolution has been a process in which the landlord class owning the land is transformed into a class that has lost its land, while the peasants who once lost their land are transformed into small holders who have acquired land, and it will be such a process once again. In given conditions having and not having, acquiring and losing, are interconnected; there is identity of the two sides. Under socialism, private peasant ownership is transformed into the public ownership of socialist agriculture; this has already taken place in the Soviet Union, as it will take place everywhere else. There is a bridge leading from private property to public property, which in philosophy is called identity, or transformation into each other, or interpenetration.

To consolidate the dictatorship of the proletariat or the dictatorship of the people is in fact to prepare the conditions for abolishing this dictatorship and advancing to the higher stage when all state systems are eliminated. To establish and build the Communist Party is in fact to prepare the conditions for the elimination of the Communist Party and all political parties. To build a revolutionary army under the leadership of the Communist Party and to carry on revolutionary war is in fact to prepare the conditions for the permanent elimination of war. These opposites are at the same time complementary.

War and peace, as everybody knows, transform themselves into each other. War is transformed into peace; for instance, the First World War was transformed into the post-war peace, and the civil war in China has now stopped, giving place to internal peace. Peace is transformed into war; for instance, the Kuomintang-Communist co-operation was transformed into war in 1927, and today's situation of world peace may be transformed into a second world war. Why is this so? Because in class society such contradictory things as war and peace have an identity in given conditions.

All contradictory things are interconnected; not only do they coexist in a single entity in given conditions, but in other given conditions, they also transform themselves into each other. This is the full meaning of the identity of opposites. This is what Lenin meant when he discussed "how they happen to be (how they become) identical--under what conditions they are identical, transforming themselves into one another".

Why is it that "the human mind should take these opposites not as dead, rigid, but as living, conditional, mobile, transforming themselves into one another"? Because that is just how things are in objective reality. The fact is that the unity or identity of opposites in objective things is not dead or rigid, but is living, conditional, mobile, temporary and relative; in given conditions, every contradictory aspect transforms itself into its opposite. Reflected in man's thinking, this becomes the Marxist world outlook of materialist dialectics. It is only the reactionary ruling classes of the past and present and the metaphysicians in their service who regard opposites not as living, conditional, mobile and transforming themselves into one another, but as dead and rigid, and they propagate this fallacy everywhere to delude the masses of the people, thus seeking to perpetuate their rule. The task of Communists is to expose the fallacies of the reactionaries and metaphysicians, to propagate the dialectics inherent in things, and so accelerate the transformation of things and achieve the goal of revolution.

In speaking of the identity of opposites in given conditions, what we are referring to is real and concrete opposites and the real and concrete transformations of opposites into one another. There are innumerable transformations in mythology, for instance, Kua Fu's race with the sun in Shan Hai Ching, [17] Yi's shooting down of nine suns in Huai Nan Tzu, [18] the Monkey King's seventy-two metamorphoses in Hsi Yu Chi, [19] the numerous episodes of ghosts and foxes metamorphosed into human beings in the Strange Tales of Liao Chai, [20] etc. But these legendary transformations of opposites are not concrete changes reflecting concrete contradictions. They are naive, imaginary, subjectively conceived transformations conjured up in men's minds by innumerable real and complex transformations of opposites into one another. Marx said, "All mythology masters and dominates and shapes the forces of nature in and through the imagination; hence it disappears as soon as man gains mastery

210

over the forces of nature." [21] The myriads of changes in mythology (and also in nursery tales) delight people because they imaginatively picture man's conquest of the forces of nature, and the best myths possess "eternal charm", as Marx put it; but myths are not built out of the concrete contradictions existing in given conditions and therefore are not a scientific reflection of reality. That is to say, in myths or nursery tales the aspects constituting a contradiction have only an imaginary identity, not a concrete identity. The scientific reflection of the identity in real transformations is Marxist dialectics.

Why can an egg but not a stone be transformed into a chicken? Why is there identity between war and peace and none between war and a stone? Why can human beings give birth only to human beings and not to anything else? The sole reason is that the identity of opposites exists only in necessary given conditions. Without these necessary given conditions there can be no identity whatsoever.

Why is it that in Russia in 1917 the bourgeois-democratic February Revolution was directly linked with the proletarian socialist October Revolution, while in France the bourgeois revolution was not directly linked with a socialist revolution and the Paris Commune of 1871 ended in failure? Why is it, on the other hand, that the nomadic system of Mongolia and Central Asia has been directly linked with socialism? Why is it that the Chinese revolution can avoid a capitalist future and be directly linked with socialism without taking the old historical road of the Western countries, without passing through a period of bourgeois dictatorship? The sole reason is the concrete conditions of the time. When certain necessary conditions are present, certain contradictions arise in the process of development of things and, moreover, the opposites contained in them are interdependent and become transformed into one another; otherwise none of this would be possible.

Such is the problem of identity. What then is struggle? And what is the relation between identity and struggle?

Lenin said:

The unity (coincidence, identity, equal action) of opposites is conditional, temporary, transitory, relative. The struggle of mutually exclusive opposites is absolute, just as development and motion are absolute. [22]

What does this passage mean?

All processes have a beginning and an end, all processes transform themselves into their opposites. The constancy of all processes is relative, but the mutability manifested in the transformation of one process into another is absolute.

There are two states of motion in all things, that of relative rest and that of conspicuous change. Both are caused by the struggle between the two contradictory elements contained in a thing. When the thing is in the first state of motion, it is undergoing only quantitative and not qualitative change and consequently presents the outward appearance of being at rest. When the thing is in the second state of motion, the quantitative change of the first state has already reached a culminating point and gives rise to the dissolution of the thing as an entity and thereupon a qualitative change ensues, hence the appearance of a conspicuous change. Such unity, solidarity, combination, harmony, balance, stalemate, deadlock, rest, constancy, equilibrium, solidity, attraction, etc., as we see in daily life, are all the appearances of things in the state of quantitative change. On the other hand, the dissolution of unity, that is, the destruction of this solidarity, combination, harmony, balance, stalemate, deadlock, rest, constancy, equilibrium, solidity and attraction, and the change of each into its opposite are all the appearances of things in the state of qualitative change, the transformation of one process into another. Things are constantly transforming themselves from the first into the second state of motion; the struggle of opposites goes on in both states but the contradiction is resolved through the second state. That is why we say that the unity of opposites is conditional, temporary and relative, while the struggle of mutually exclusive opposites is absolute.

When we said above that two opposite things can coexist in a single entity and can transform themselves into each other because there is identity between them, we were speaking of conditionality, that is to say, in given conditions two contradictory things can be united and can transform themselves into each other, but in the absence of these conditions, they cannot constitute a contradiction, cannot coexist in the same entity and cannot transform themselves into one another. It is because the identity of opposites obtains only in given conditions that we have said identity is conditional and relative. We may add that the struggle between opposites permeates a process from beginning to end and makes one process transform itself into another, that it is ubiquitous, and that struggle is therefore unconditional and absolute.

The combination of conditional, relative identity and unconditional, absolute struggle constitutes the movement of opposites in all things.

We Chinese often say, "Things that oppose each other also complement each other." [23] That is, things opposed to each other have identity. This saying is dialectical and contrary to metaphysics. "Oppose each other" refers to the mutual exclusion or the struggle of two contradictory aspects. "Complement each other" means that in given conditions the two contradictory aspects unite and achieve identity. Yet struggle is inherent in identity and without struggle there can be no identity.

In identity there is struggle, in particularity there is universality, and in individuality there is generality. To quote Lenin, ". . . there is an absolute in the relative." [24]

VI. THE PLACE OF ANTAGONISM IN CONTRADICTION

The question of the struggle of opposites includes the question of what is antagonism. Our answer is that antagonism is one form, but not the only form, of the struggle of opposites.

In human history, antagonism between classes exists as a particular manifestation of the struggle of opposites. Consider the contradiction between the exploiting and the exploited classes. Such contradictory classes coexist for a long time in the same society, be it slave society, feudal society or capitalist society, and they struggle with each other; but it is not until the contradiction between the two classes develops to a certain stage that it assumes the form of open antagonism and develops into revolution. The same holds for the transformation of peace into war in class society.

Before it explodes, a bomb is a single entity in which opposites coexist in given conditions. The explosion takes place only when a new condition, ignition, is present. An analogous situation arises in all those natural phenomena which finally assume the form of open conflict to resolve old contradictions and produce new things.

It is highly important to grasp this fact. It enables us to understand that revolutions and revolutionary wars are inevitable in class society and that without them, it is impossible to accomplish any leap in social development and to overthrow the reactionary ruling classes and therefore impossible for the people to win political power. Communists must expose the deceitful propaganda of the reactionaries, such as the assertion that social revolution is unnecessary and impossible. They must firmly uphold the Marxist-Leninist theory of social revolution and enable the people to understand that social revolution is not only entirely

213

necessary but also entirely practicable, and that the whole history of mankind and the triumph of the Soviet Union have confirmed this scientific truth.

However, we must make a concrete study of the circumstances of each specific struggle of opposites and should not arbitrarily apply the formula discussed above to everything. Contradiction and struggle are universal and absolute, but the methods of resolving contradictions, that is, the forms of struggle, differ according to the differences in the nature of the contradictions. Some contradictions are characterized by open antagonism, others are not. In accordance with the concrete development of things, some contradictions which were originally non-antagonistic develop into antagonistic ones, while others which were originally antagonistic develop into non-antagonistic ones.

As already mentioned, so long as classes exist, contradictions between correct and incorrect ideas in the Communist Party are reflections within the Party of class contradictions. At first, with regard to certain issues, such contradictions may not manifest themselves as antagonistic. But with the development of the class struggle, they may grow and become antagonistic. The history of the Communist Party of the Soviet Union shows us that the contradictions between the correct thinking of Lenin and Stalin and the fallacious thinking of Trotsky, Bukharin and others did not at first manifest themselves in an antagonistic form, but that later they did develop into antagonism. There are similar cases in the history of the Chinese Communist Party. At first the contradictions between the correct thinking of many of our Party comrades and the fallacious thinking of Chen Tu-hsiu, Chang Kuo-tao and others also did not manifest themselves in an antagonistic form, but later they did develop into antagonism. At present the contradiction between correct and incorrect thinking in our Party does not manifest itself in an antagonistic form, and if comrades who have committed mistakes can correct them, it will not develop into antagonism. Therefore, the Party must on the one hand wage a serious struggle against erroneous thinking, and on the other give the comrades who have committed errors ample opportunity to wake up. This being the case, excessive struggle is obviously inappropriate. But if the people who have committed errors persist in them and aggravate them, there is the possibility that this contradiction will develop into antagonism.

Economically, the contradiction between town and country is an extremely antagonistic one both in capitalist society, where under the rule of the bourgeoisie the towns ruthlessly plunder the countryside, and in the Kuomintang areas in China, where under the rule of foreign imperialism

214

and the Chinese big comprador bourgeoisie the towns most rapaciously plunder the countryside. But in a socialist country and in our revolutionary base areas, this antagonistic contradiction has changed into one that is non-antagonistic; and when communist society is reached it will be abolished.

— hence conditions in China today — non-antagonistic contradictions

Lenin said, "Antagonism and contradiction are not at all one and the same. Under socialism, the first will disappear, the second will remain." [25] That is to say, antagonism is one form, but not the only form, of the struggle of opposites; the formula of antagonism cannot be arbitrarily applied everywhere.

VII. CONCLUSION

We may now say a few words to sum up. The law of contradiction in things, that is, the law of the unity of opposites, is the fundamental law of nature and of society and therefore also the fundamental law of thought. It stands opposed to the metaphysical world outlook. It represents a great revolution in the history of human knowledge. According to dialectical materialism, contradiction is present in all processes of objectively existing things and of subjective thought and permeates all these processes from beginning to end; this is the universality and absoluteness of contradiction. Each contradiction and each of its aspects have their respective characteristics; this is the particularity and relativity of contradiction. In given conditions, opposites possess identity, and consequently can coexist in a single entity and can transform themselves into each other; this again is the particularity and relativity of contradiction. But the struggle of opposites is ceaseless, it goes on both when the opposites are coexisting and when they are transforming themselves into each other, and becomes especially conspicuous when they are transforming themselves into one another; this again is the universality and absoluteness of contradiction. In studying the particularity and relativity of contradiction, we must give attention to the distinction between the principal contradiction and the non-principal contradictions and to the distinction between the principal aspect and the non-principal aspect of a contradiction; in studying the universality of contradiction and the struggle of opposites in contradiction, we must give attention to the distinction between the different forms of struggle. Otherwise we shall make mistakes. If, through study, we achieve a real understanding of the essentials explained above, we shall be able to demolish dogmatist ideas which are contrary to the basic principles of Marxism-Leninism and detrimental to our revolutionary cause, and our comrades with practical experience will be able to organize their experience into principles and avoid repeating empiricist errors. These are a few simple conclusions from our study of the law of contradiction.

215

NOTES

1. V. I. Lenin, "Conspectus of Hegel's Lectures on the History of Philosophy" Collected Works, Russ. ed., Moscow, 1958, Vol. XXXVIII, p. 249.

2. In his essay "On the Question of Dialectics", Lenin said, "The splitting in two of a single whole and the cognition of its contradictory parts (see the quotation from Philo on Heraclitus at the beginning of Section 3 'On Cognition' in Lassalle's book on Heraclitus) is the essence (one of the 'essentials', one of the principal, if not the principal, characteristics or features) of dialectics." (Collected Works, Russ. ed., Moscow, 1958, Vol. XXXVIII, p. 357.) In his "Conspectus of Hegel's The Science of Logic", he said, "In brief, dialectics can be defined as the doctrine of the unity of opposites. This grasps the kernel of dialectics, but it requires explanations and development." (Ibid., p. 215.)

3. V. I. Lenin, "On the Question of Dialectics", Collected Works, Russ. ed., Moscow, 1958, Vol. XXXVIII, p. 358.

4. A saying of Tung Chung-shu (179-104 B.C.), a well-known exponent of Confucianism in the Han Dynasty.

5. Frederick Engels, "Dialectics. Quantity and Quality", Anti-Duhring, Eng. ed., FLPH, Moscow, 1959, p. 166.

6. V. I. Lenin, "On the Question of Dialectics", Collected Works, Russ. ed., Moscow, 1958, Vol. XXXVIII, pp. 357-58.

7. Frederick Engels, op. cit., pp. 166-67.

8. V. I. Lenin, "On the Question of Dialectics", Collected Works, Russ. ed., Moscow, 1958, Vol. XXXVIII, p. 357.

9. Ibid., pp. 358-59.

10. See "Problems of Strategy in China's Revolutionary War", Note 10, p. 251 of this volume.

11. See ibid., Note :, p. 249 of this volume.

12. Wei Cheng (A.D. 580-643) was a statesman and historian of the Tang Dynasty.

13. Shui Hu Chuan (Heroes of the Marshes), a famous 14th century Chinese novel, describes a peasant war towards the end of the Northern Sung Dynasty. Chu Village was in the vicinity of Liangshanpo, where Sung Chiang, leader of the peasant uprising and hero of the novel, established his base. Chu Chao-feng, the head of this village, was a despotic landlord.

14. V. I. Lenin, "Once Again on the Trade Unions, the Present Situation and the Mistakes of Trotsky and Bukharin", Selected Works, Eng. ed., International Publishers, New York, 1943, Vol. IX, p. 66.

15. V. I. Lenin, "What Is to Be Done?", Collected Works, Eng. ed., FLPH, Moscow, 1961, Vol. V, p. 369.

16. V. I. Lenin, "Conspectus of Hegel's The Science of Logic", Collected Works, Russ. ed., Moscow, 1958, Vol. XXXVIII, pp. 97-98.

17. Shan Hai Chug (Book of Mountains and Seas) was written in the era of the Warring States (403-221 B.C.). In one of its fables Kua Fu, a superman, pursued and overtook the sun. But he died of thirst, whereupon his staff was transformed into the forest of Teng.

18. Yi is one of the legendary heroes of ancient China, famous for his archery. According to a legend in Huai Nan Tzu, compiled in the 2nd century B.C., there were ten suns in the sky in the days of Emperor Yao. To put an end to the damage to vegetation caused by these scorching suns, Emperor Yao ordered Yi to shoot them down. In another legend recorded by Wang Yi (2nd century A.D.), the archer is said to have shot down nine of the ten suns.

19. Hsi Yu Chi (Pilgrimage to the West) is a 16th century novel, the hero of which is the monkey god Sun Wu-kung. He could miraculously change at will into seventy-two different shapes, such as a bird, a tree and a stone.

20. The Strange Tales of Liao Chai, written by Pu Sung-ling in the 17th century, is a well-known collection of 431 tales, mostly about ghosts and fox spirits.

21. Karl Marx, "Introduction to the Critique of Political Economy", A Contribution to the Critique of Political Economy, Eng. ed., Chicago, 1904, pp. 310-11.

22. V. I. Lenin, "On the Question of Dialectics", Collected Works, Russ. ed., Moscow, 1958, Vol. XXXVIII, p. 358.

23. The saying "Things that oppose each other also complement each other" first appeared in the History of the Earlier Han Dynasty by Pan Ku, a celebrated historian in the 1st century A.D. It has long been a popular saying.

24. V. I. Lenin, "On the Question of Dialectics", Collected Works, Russ. ed., Moscow, 1958, Vol. XXXVIII, p. 358.

25. V. I. Lenin, "Remarks on N. I. Bukharin's Economics of the Transitional Period" Selected Works, Russ. ed., Moscow-Leningrad, 1931, Vol. XI, p. 357.

THE PERIOD OF THE WAR OF RESISTANCE AGAINST JAPAN

POLICIES, MEASURES AND PERSPECTIVES FOR RESISTING THE JAPANESE INVASION

July 23, 1937

[On July 7, 1937, the Japanese imperialists staged the Lukouchiao Incident in their attempt to annex the whole of China by armed force. The Chinese people unanimously demanded war against Japan. Ten days elapsed before Chiang Kai-shek tardily made a public statement at Lushan announcing armed resistance to Japan. He did so under nation-wide popular pressure and as a result of the serious blow the Japanese invasion had dealt to the interests both of the British and U.S. imperialists in China and of the big landlords and the big bourgeoisie whom Chiang Kai-shek directly represented. But at the same time the Chiang Kai-shek government continued to parley with the Japanese aggressors and even accepted the so-called peaceful settlements they concluded with local authorities. It was not until August 13, 1937, when the Japanese aggressors launched a major attack on Shanghai and thus made it impossible for Chiang Kai-shek to maintain his rule in southeastern China, that he was compelled to embark on armed resistance; but Chiang never ceased his clandestine attempts to make peace with Japan right up to 1944. Throughout the War of Resistance Chiang Kai-shek opposed all-out people's war in which the entire people are mobilized, and pursued the reactionary policy of passively resisting Japan but actively opposing the Communist Party and the people; thus his actions completely violated his own Lushan statement that "once war breaks out, every person, young or old, in the north or in the south, must take up the responsibility of resisting Japan and defending our homeland". The two policies, two sets of measures and two perspectives discussed by Comrade Mao Tse-tung in this article reflect the struggle between the line of the Communist Party and Chiang Kai-shek's line in the War of Resistance.]

I. TWO POLICIES

On July 8, the day after the Lukouchiao Incident, [1] the Central Committee of the Communist Party of China issued a manifesto to the whole nation calling for a war of resistance. The manifesto reads in part:

Fellow-countrymen! Peiping and Tientsin are in peril! Northern China is in peril! The Chinese nation is in peril! A war of resistance by the whole nation is the only way out. We demand immediate and resolute resistance to the invading Japanese armies and immediate preparations to meet all emergencies. From top to bottom the whole nation must at once abandon any idea of being able to live in submissive peace with the Japanese aggressors. Fellow-countrymen! We should acclaim and support the heroic resistance of Feng Chih-an's troops. We should acclaim and support the declaration of the local authorities of northern China that they will defend the homeland to the death. We demand that General Sung Cheh-yuan immediately mobilize the entire 29th Army [2] and send it into action at the front. Of the Central Government in Nanking we demand the following: Give effective aid to the 29th Army. Immediately lift the ban on patriotic movements among the masses and let the people give full play to their enthusiasm for armed resistance. Immediately mobilize all the country's land, sea and air forces for action. Immediately weed out all the hidden traitors and Japanese agents in China and so consolidate our rear. We call on the people of the whole country to throw all their strength behind the sacred war of self-defence against Japan. Our slogans are: Armed defence of Peiping, Tientsin and northern China ! Defend our homeland to the last drop of our blood ! Let the people of the whole country, the government, and the armed forces unite and build up the national united front as our solid Great Wall of resistance to Japanese aggression! Let the Kuomintang and the Communist Party closely co-operate and resist the new attacks of the Japanese aggressors! Drive the Japanese aggressors out of China !

This is a declaration of policy.

On July 17, Mr. Chiang Kai-shek made a statement at Lushan. Setting out as it did a policy of preparing for a war of resistance, the statement was the Kuomintang's first correct declaration on foreign affairs for many years and it has consequently been welcomed by all our countrymen as well as by ourselves. The statement listed four conditions for the settlement of the Lukouchiao Incident:

(1) Any settlement must not infringe China's sovereignty and territorial integrity; (2) there must be no unlawful change in the administrative structure of Hopei and Chahar Provinces; (3) there must be no dismissal and replacement, at the demand of others, of local officials appointed by the Central Government; (4) the 29th Army must not be confined to the area in which it is now stationed.

The concluding remarks of the statement read:

Concerning the Lukouchiao Incident, the government has decided on a policy and a stand to which it will always adhere. We realize that when the whole nation goes to war, sacrifices to the bitter end will be called for, and we should not cherish the faintest hope of an easy way out. Once war breaks out, every person, young or old, in the north or in the south, must take up the responsibility of resisting Japan and defending our homeland.

This, too, is a declaration of policy.

221

Here we have two historic political declarations on the Lukouchiao Incident, one by the Communist Party and the other by the Kuomintang. They have this point in common: both stand for a resolute war of resistance and oppose compromise and concessions.

This is one kind of policy for meeting Japanese invasion, the correct policy.

But there is the possibility of the adoption of another kind of policy. In recent months the traitors and the pro-Japanese elements in Peiping and Tientsin have been very active, they have been trying to get the local authorities to acquiesce in Japan's demands, they have been undermining the policy of resolute armed resistance and advocating compromise and concessions. These are extremely dangerous signs.

The policy of compromise and concessions is the diametrical opposite of the policy of resolute armed resistance. If it is not speedily reversed, Peiping, Tientsin and the whole of northern China will fall into the hands of the enemy, and the entire nation will be seriously imperilled. Everyone must be on the alert.

Patriotic officers and men of the 29th Army, unite! Oppose compromise and concessions and conduct resolute armed resistance!

Fellow patriots of Peiping, Tientsin and northern China, unite! Oppose compromise and concessions and support resolute armed resistance!

Fellow patriots throughout the country, unite! Oppose compromise and concessions and support resolute armed resistance!

Mr. Chiang Kai-shek and all patriotic members of the Kuomintang! We hope that you will firmly adhere to your policy, fulfil your promises, oppose compromise and concessions, conduct resolute armed resistance, and thus answer the outrages of the enemy with deeds.

Let all the armed forces in the country, including the Red Army, support Mr. Chiang Kai-shek's declaration, oppose compromise and concessions and conduct resolute armed resistance!

We Communists are whole-heartedly and faithfully carrying out our own manifesto, and at the same time we resolutely support Mr. Chiang Kai-shek's declaration; together with the members of the Kuomintang and all our fellow-countrymen, we are ready to defend the homeland to the last drop of our blood; we oppose any hesitation, vacillation, compromise or concessions, and will conduct resolute armed resistance.

II. TWO SETS OF MEASURES

To achieve its purpose the policy of resolute armed resistance calls for a whole set of measures.

What are they? The principal ones are the following:

1. Mobilize all the armed forces of the whole country. Mobilize our standing armed forces of well over two million men, including the land, sea and air forces, the Central Army, the local troops and the Red Army, and immediately send the main forces to the national defence lines, while keeping some forces in the rear to maintain order. Entrust the command on the various fronts to generals loyal to the national interests. Call a national defence conference to decide on strategy and to achieve unity of purpose in military operations. Overhaul the political work in the army in order to achieve unity between officers and men and between the army and the people. Establish the principle that guerrilla warfare should carry the responsibility for one aspect of the strategic task, and ensure proper co-ordination between guerrilla and regular warfare. Weed out traitors from the army. Call up an adequate number of reserves and train them for service at the front. Adequately replenish the equipment and supplies of the armed forces. Military plans on these lines must be made, in keeping with the general policy of resolute armed resistance. China's troops are far from few, but unless these plans are executed, they will not be able to defeat the enemy. However, if the political and material factors are combined, our armed forces will become unmatched in East Asia.

2. Mobilize the whole people. Lift the ban on patriotic movements, release political prisoners, annul the "Emergency Decree for Dealing with Actions Endangering the Republic" [3] and the "Press Censorship Regulations", [4] grant legal status to existing patriotic organizations, extend these organizations among the workers, peasants, businessmen and intellectuals, arm the people for self-defence and for operations in support of the army. In a word, give the people freedom to express their patriotism. By their combined strength the people and the army will deal a death-blow to Japanese imperialism. Beyond doubt, there can be no victory in a national war without reliance on the great masses of the people. Let us take warning from the fall of Abyssinia. [5] No one who is sincere about waging a resolute war of resistance can afford to ignore this point.

3. Reform the government apparatus. Bring representatives of all political parties and groups and public leaders into the government for joint management of the affairs of the state and weed out the hidden pro-Japanese elements and traitors in the government, so that the government can become one with the people. Resistance to Japan is a gigantic task which cannot be performed by a few individuals alone. If they insist on keeping it in their own hands, they will only bungle it. If the government is to be a real government of national defence, it must rely on the people and practice democratic centralism. It must be at once democratic and centralized; it is this kind of government which is the most powerful. The national assembly must be truly representative of the people; it must be the supreme organ of authority, determine the major policies of the state and decide on the policies and plans for resisting Japan and saving the nation.

4. Adopt an anti-Japanese foreign policy. Accord the Japanese imperialists no advantages or facilities, but on the contrary confiscate their property, repudiate their loans, weed out their lackeys and expel their spies. Immediately conclude a military and political alliance with the Soviet Union and closely unite with the Soviet Union, the country which is most reliable, most powerful and most capable of helping China to resist Japan. Enlist the sympathy of Britain, the United States and France for our resistance to Japan, and secure their help provided that it entails no loss of our territory or our sovereign rights. We should rely mainly on our own strength to defeat the Japanese aggressors; but foreign aid cannot be dispensed with, and an isolationist policy will only play into the enemy's hands.

5. Proclaim a programme for improving the livelihood of the people and immediately begin to put it into effect. Start with the following minimum points: Abolish exorbitant taxes and miscellaneous levies, reduce land rent, restrict usury, increase the workers' pay, improve the livelihood of the soldiers and junior officers, improve the livelihood of office workers, and provide relief for victims of natural calamities. Far from making a mess of the country's finances as some people argue, these new measures will increase the people's purchasing power and lead to thriving commercial and financial conditions. They will add immeasurably to our strength for resisting Japan and consolidate the government's foundations.

6. Institute education for national defence. Radically reform the existing educational policy and system. All projects that are not urgent and all measures that are not rational must be discarded. Newspapers, books and magazines, films, plays, literature and art should all serve national defence. Traitorous propaganda must be prohibited.

7. Adopt financial and economic policies for resisting Japan. Financial policy should be based on the principle that those with money should contribute money and that the property of the Japanese imperialists and Chinese traitors should be confiscated, and economic policy should be based on the principle of boycotting Japanese goods and promoting home products--everything for the sake of resistance to Japan. Financial strain is the product of wrong measures and can surely be overcome after the adoption of new policies such as these, which serve the interests of the people. It is sheer nonsense to say that a country with so vast a territory and so huge a population is financially and economically helpless.

8. Unite the entire Chinese people, the government and the armed forces to build up the national united front as our solid Great Wall. The application of the policy of armed resistance and of the above measures depends on this united front. Here the key is close cooperation between the Kuomintang and the Communist Party. Let the government, the troops, all the political parties and the whole people unite on the basis of such co-operation between the two parties. The slogan "Unity in good faith to meet the national crisis" must not be limited to fine words but must be demonstrated in fine deeds. Unity must be genuine, deception will not do. There must be more large-mindedness and a broader sweep in the conduct of state affairs. Petty niggling, mean tricks, bureaucracy, and Ah Q-ism [6] are of no use at all. They are of no avail against the enemy and simply ridiculous if practiced on one's own countrymen. There are major and minor principles in everything, and the minor principles are all subordinate to the major. Our compatriots must think things over carefully in the light of the major principles, for only then will they be able to orientate their own ideas and actions properly. Today, anyone who has not begun to have some genuine desire for unity ought to examine his conscience in the stillness of the night and feel some shame, even if no one else censures him.

The set of measures for resolute armed resistance described above may be called the Eight-Point Programme.

The policy of resolute armed resistance must be accompanied by this set of measures, or otherwise victory will never be achieved and Japanese aggression against China will never be ended, while China will be helpless against Japan and hardly be able to escape the fate of Abyssinia.

Whoever is sincere about the policy of resolute armed resistance must put this set of measures into practice. And the test of whether or not he is sincere about resolute armed resistance is whether or not he accepts and carries out this set of measures.

There is another set of measures which is contrary to this set in every respect.

Not the total mobilization of the armed forces, but their immobilization or withdrawal.

Not freedom for the people, but oppression.

Not a government of national defence based on democratic centralism, but an autocratic government of bureaucrats, compradors and big landlords.

Not a foreign policy of resisting Japan, but one of fawning on her.

Not the improvement of the people's livelihood, but continued extortions so that they groan under their sufferings and are powerless to resist Japan.

Not education for national defence, but education for national subjugation.

Not financial and economic policies for resisting Japan, but the same old, or even worse, financial and economic policies benefiting the enemy rather than our own country.

Not building up the Anti-Japanese National United Front as our Great Wall, but tearing it down, or talking glibly about unity while never doing anything to advance it.

Measures stem from policy. If the policy is one of non-resistance, all measures will reflect non-resistance; we have been taught this lesson over the last six years. If the policy is one of resolute armed resistance, then it is imperative to apply the appropriate measures-- the Eight-Point Programme.

III. TWO PERSPECTIVES

What are the perspectives? This is what everyone is anxious about. Pursue the first policy and adopt the first set of measures, and the perspective will definitely be the expulsion of Japanese imperialism and the attainment of China's liberation. Can there still be any doubt about it? I think not.

Pursue the second policy and adopt the second set of measures, and the perspective will definitely be the occupation of China by the Japanese imperialists, with the Chinese people being turned into slaves and beasts of burden. Can there still be any doubt about it? Again, I think not.

IV. CONCLUSION

It is imperative to carry out the first policy, to adopt the first set of measures and to strive for the first perspective.

It is imperative to oppose the second policy, to reject the second set of measures and to avert the second perspective.

Let all patriotic members of the Kuomintang and all members of the Communist Party unite and steadfastly carry out the first policy, adopt the first set of measures and strive for the first perspective; let them steadfastly oppose the second policy, reject the second set of measures and avert the second perspective.

Let all patriotic people, patriotic troops and patriotic parties and groups unite as one and steadfastly carry out the first policy, adopt the first set of measures and strive for the first perspective, let them steadfastly oppose the second policy, reject the second set of measures and avert the second perspective.

Long live the national revolutionary war!

Long live the liberation of the Chinese nation!

NOTES
1. On July 7, 1937, the Japanese invading forces attacked the Chinese garrison at Lukouchiao, some ten kilometres southwest of Peking. Under the influence of the ardent nation-wide anti-Japanese movement, the Chinese troops put up resistance. This incident marked the beginning of the Chinese people's heroic War of Resistance Against Japan which lasted for eight years.

2. The 28th Army, which was originally part of the Kuomintang's Northwestern Army under Feng Yu-hsiang, was then stationed in Hopei and Chahar Provinces. Sung Cheh-yuan was its commander and Feng Chih-an one of its divisional commanders.

3. The Kuomintang government promulgated the so-called "Emergency Decree for Dealing with Actions Endangering the Republic" on January 31, 1931, using the trumped-up charge of "endangering the Republic" to persecute and slaughter patriots and revolutionaries. This decree imposed extremely brutal measures of persecution.

4. "Press Censorship Regulations" was another name for the "General Measures for Press Censorship" issued by the Kuomintang government in August 1934 to stifle the voice of the people. They laid down that "all news copy must be submitted to censorship".

5. See "The Tasks of the Chinese Communist Party in the Period of Resistance to Japan", Selected Works of Mao Tse-tung, Eng. ed., Foreign Languages Press, Peking, 1965, Vol. I, p. ,67.

6. Ah Q is the leading character in The True Story of Ah Q, the famous work by the great Chinese writer Lu Hsun. Ah Q typifies all those who compensate themselves for their failures and setbacks in real life by regarding them as moral or spiritual victories.

FOR THE MOBILIZATION OF ALL THE NATION'S FORCES FOR VICTORY IN THE WAR OF RESISTANCE

August 25, 1937

[This was an outline for propaganda and agitation written by Comrade Mao Tse-tung in August 1937 for the propaganda organs of the Central Committee of the Chinese Communist Party. It was approved by the enlarged meeting of the Political Bureau of the Central Committee at Lochuan, northern Shensi.]

A. The Lukouchiao Incident of July 7 marked the beginning of the Japanese imperialist all-out invasion of China south of the Great Wall. The fight put up by the Chinese troops at Lukouchiao marked the beginning of China's nation-wide War of Resistance. The ceaseless Japanese attacks, the people's resolute struggle, the national bourgeoisie's tendency towards resistance, the Communist Party's vigorous advocacy and firm application of a national united front policy and the nation-wide support this policy has won--all these have compelled the Chinese authorities to begin changing their policy of nonresistance, as pursued ever since the September 18th Incident of 1931, to a policy of resistance since the Lukouchiao Incident, and have caused the Chinese revolution to develop beyond the stage reached after the December 9th Movement, [1] i.e., the stage of ending the civil war and preparing for resistance, into the stage of actual resistance. The initial changes in the Kuomintang's policy with the Sian Incident and the Third Plenary Session of its Central Executive Committee as their starting point, Mr. Chiang Kai-shek's Lushan statement of July on the question of resistance to Japan, and many of his measures of national defence, all deserve commendation. The troops at the front, whether the land and air forces or the local armed units, have all fought courageously and demonstrated the heroic spirit of the Chinese nation. In the name of the national revolution, the Chinese Communist Party ardently salutes our patriotic troops and fellow-countrymen throughout China.

B. But on the other hand, even after the Lukouchiao Incident of July 7, the Kuomintang authorities are continuing to pursue the wrong policy they have pursued ever since the September 18th Incident, making compromises and concessions, [2] suppressing the zeal of the patriotic troops and clamping down on the patriotic people's national salvation movement. There is no doubt that, having seized Peiping and Tientsin, Japanese imperialism will press ahead with its policy of large-scale offensives, take the second and third steps in its premeditated war plan and launch fierce attacks on the whole of northern China and other areas, relying on its own brute military strength while at the same time drawing support from German and Italian imperialism and exploiting the vacillations of British imperialism and the estrangement of the Kuomintang from the broad masses of the working people. The flames of war are already raging in Chahar and in Shanghai. To save our motherland, to resist the attacks of the powerful invaders, to defend northern China and the seacoast and recover Peiping, Tientsin and northeastern China, the Kuomintang authorities and the whole people must thoroughly learn the lesson of the loss of northeastern China, Peiping and Tientsin, learn and take warning from the fall of Abyssinia, learn from the Soviet Union's past victories over its foreign enemies, [3] learn from Spain's present experience in successfully defending Madrid, [4] and firmly unite to fight to the end in defence of the motherland. Henceforth the task is: "Mobilize all the nation's forces for victory in the War of Resistance", and the key to its accomplishment is a complete and thorough change in Kuomintang policy. The step forward taken by the Kuomintang on the question of resistance is to be commended; it is what the Chinese Communist Party and the people of the whole country have for years been hoping for, and we welcome it. But the Kuomintang has not changed its policies on such matters as the mobilization of the masses and the introduction of political reforms. It is still basically unwilling to lift the ban on the people's anti-Japanese movement or make fundamental changes in the government apparatus, it still has no policy for improving the people's livelihood, and is still not sufficiently sincere in its co-operation with the Communist Party. If, at this critical juncture of life or death for our nation, the Kuomintang continues in the same old groove and does not quickly change its policy, it will bring disaster to the War of Resistance. Some Kuomintang members say, "Let political reforms be instituted after victory." They think the Japanese aggressors can be defeated by the government's efforts alone, but they are wrong. A few battles may be won in a war of resistance fought by the government alone, but it will be impossible to defeat the Japanese aggressors thoroughly. This can be done only by a war of total resistance by the whole nation. Such a war, however, requires a complete and drastic change in Kuomintang policy and the joint efforts of the whole nation from top to bottom to carry out a thoroughgoing programme of resistance to Japan, that is, a national salvation programme formulated in the spirit of the revolutionary Three People's Principles and the Three Great Policies [5] drawn up personally by Dr. Sun Yat-sen during the Best period of Kuomintang Communist co-operation.

230

C. In all earnestness the Chinese Communist Party proposes to the Kuomintang, to the people of the whole country, to all political parties and groups, to people in all walks of life and to all the armed forces a Ten-Point National Salvation Programme for the purpose of completely defeating the Japanese aggressors. It firmly believes that only by carrying out this programme fully, sincerely and resolutely will it be possible to defend the motherland and defeat the Japanese aggressors. Otherwise, the responsibility will fall on those who procrastinate and allow the situation to deteriorate; once the country's doom is sealed, it will be too late for regrets and lamentations. The ten points are as follows:

1. Overthrow Japanese imperialism.

Sever diplomatic relations with Japan, expel Japanese officials, arrest Japanese agents, confiscate Japanese property in China, repudiate debts to Japan, abrogate treaties signed with Japan and take back all Japanese Concessions.

Fight to the finish in defence of northern China and the seacoast.

Fight to the finish for the recovery of Peiping, Tientsin and northeastern China.

Drive the Japanese imperialists out of China.

Oppose all vacillation and compromise.

2. Mobilize the military strength of the whole nation.

Mobilize all land, sea and air forces for a nation-wide war of resistance.

Oppose a passive, purely defensive strategy and adopt an active, independent strategy.

Set up a permanent council of national defence to deliberate and decide on national defence plans and strategy.

Arm the people and develop anti-Japanese guerrilla warfare in co-ordination with the operations of the main forces.

Reform the political work in the armed forces to achieve unity between officers and men.

Achieve unity between the army and the people and bring the army's militant spirit into play.

Support the Northeast Anti-Japanese United Army and disrupt the enemy's rear.

Give equal treatment to all troops fighting in the War of Resistance.

Establish military zones in all parts of the country, mobilize the whole nation to join in the war and thus effect a gradual change from the mercenary system to one of general military service.

3. Mobilize the people of the whole country.

Let all the people of the country (with the exception of the traitors) have freedom of speech, the press, assembly and association in resisting Japan and saving the nation, and the right to take up arms against the enemy.

Annul all old laws and decrees which restrict the people's patriotic movements and promulgate new, revolutionary laws and decrees.

Release all patriotic and revolutionary political prisoners and lift the ban on political parties.

Let the people of the whole country mobilize, take up arms and join the War of Resistance. Let those with strength contribute strength, those with money contribute money, those with guns contribute guns, and those with knowledge contribute knowledge.

Mobilize the Mongolian, the Hui and all other minority nationalities, in accordance with the principle of national self-determination and autonomy, in the common fight against Japan.

4. Reform the government apparatus.

Call a national assembly which is genuinely representative of the people to adopt a genuinely democratic constitution, to decide on policies for resisting Japan and saving the nation, and to elect a government of national defence.

The government of national defence must draw in the revolutionaries of all parties and mass organizations, and expel the pro-Japanese elements.

The government of national defence shall practice democratic centralism, and shall be at once democratic and centralized.

The government of national defence shall pursue revolutionary policies for resisting Japan and saving the nation.

Institute local self-government, throw out corrupt officials and establish clean government.

5. Adopt an anti-Japanese foreign policy.

Conclude anti-aggression alliances and anti-Japanese pacts for mutual military aid with all countries that are opposed to Japanese aggression, provided that this entails no loss of our territory or of our sovereign rights.

Support the international peace front and oppose the front of aggression of Germany, Japan and Italy.

Unite with the worker and peasant masses of Korea and Japan against Japanese imperialism.

6. Adopt wartime financial and economic policies.

Financial policy should be based on the principle that those with money should contribute money and that the property of the traitors should be confiscated in order to meet war expenditures. Economic policy should consist in readjusting and expanding defence production, developing the rural economy and assuring self-sufficiency in wartime commodities. Encourage the use of Chinese goods and improve local products. Completely prohibit Japanese goods. Suppress profiteering merchants and ban speculation and manipulation of the market.

7. Improve the people's livelihood.

Improve the conditions of workers, office employees and teachers, and of soldiers fighting the Japanese.

Give preferential treatment to the families of the soldiers fighting the Japanese.

Abolish exorbitant taxes and miscellaneous levies.

Reduce rent and interest.

Give relief to the unemployed.

Regulate grain supplies.

Aid the victims of natural calamities.

8. Adopt an anti-Japanese educational policy.

Change the existing educational system and curriculum and put into effect a new system and curriculum aimed at resisting Japan and saving the nation.

9. Weed out traitors and pro-Japanese elements and consolidate the rear.

10. Achieve national unity against Japan.

Build up the Anti-Japanese National United Front of all political parties and groups, people in all walks of life and all armed forces on the basis of Kuomintang-Communist co-operation in order to lead the War of Resistance, unite in good faith and meet the national crisis.

D. It is imperative to discard the policy of resistance by the government alone and to enforce the policy of total resistance by the whole nation. The government must unite with the people, fully restore the revolutionary spirit of Dr. Sun Yat-sen, put the above Ten-Point Programme into effect and strive for complete victory. Together with the masses of the people and the armed forces under its leadership, the Chinese Communist Party will firmly adhere to this programme and stand in the forefront of the War of Resistance, defending the motherland to the last drop of its blood. In keeping with its consistent policy, the Chinese Communist Party is ready to stand side by side with the Kuomintang and the other political parties and groups and unite with them in building the solid Great Wall of the national united front to defeat the infamous Japanese aggressors and strive for a new China which is independent, happy and free. To achieve this goal, we must firmly repudiate the traitors' theories of compromise and capitulation, and combat national defeatism according to which it is impossible to defeat the Japanese aggressors. The Chinese Communist Party firmly believes that the Japanese aggressors can definitely be defeated provided the above Ten-Point Programme is carried out. If our 450 million countrymen all exert themselves, the Chinese nation will certainly achieve final victory!

Down with Japanese imperialism!

Long live the national revolutionary war!

Long live New China, independent, happy and free!

NOTES

1. The year 1935 witnessed a new upsurge in the popular patriotic movement throughout the country. Students in Peking, under the leadership of the Communist Party of China, held a patriotic demonstration on December 9, putting forward such slogans as "Stop the civil war and unite to resist foreign aggression" and "Down with Japanese imperialism". This movement broke through the long reign of terror imposed by the Kuomintang government in league with the Japanese invaders and very quickly won the people's support throughout the country. It is known as the "December 8th Movement". The outcome was that new changes manifested themselves in the relations among the various classes in the country, and the Anti-Japanese National United Front proposed by the Communist Party of China became the openly advocated policy of all patriotic people. The Chiang Kai-shek government with its traitorous policy became very isolated.

2. See the introductory note to "Policies, Measures and Perspectives for Resisting the Japanese Invasion", pp. 13-14 of this volume.

3. See History of the Communist Party of the Soviet Union (Bolsheviks), Short Course, Eng. ed., FLPH, Moscow, 1951, pp. 347-81.

4. The defence of Madrid, starting in October 1936, lasted for two years and five months. In 1936, fascist Germany and Italy made use of the Spanish fascist warlord Franco to launch a war of aggression against Spain. The Spanish people, led by the Popular Front Government, heroically defended democracy against aggression. The battle of Madrid, the capital of Spain, was the bitterest in the whole war. Madrid fell in March 1939 because Britain, France and other imperialist countries assisted the aggressors by their hypocritical policy of "non-intervention" and because divisions arose within the Popular Front.

5. The Three People's Principles were the principles and the programme put forward by Sun Yat-sen on the questions of nationalism, democracy and people's livelihood in China's bourgeois-democratic revolution. In the manifesto adopted by the Kuomintang at its First National Congress in

1924 Sun Yat-sen restated the Three People's Principles. Nationalism was interpreted as opposition to imperialism and active support was expressed for the movements of the workers and peasants. Thus the old Three People's Principles were transformed into the new Three People's Principles characterized by the Three Great Policies, that is, alliance with Russia, co-operation with the Communist Party, and assistance to the peasants and workers. The new Three People's Principles provided the political basis for the co-operation between the Communist Party of China and the Kuomintang during the First Revolutionary Civil War period.

COMBAT LIBERALISM

September 7, 1937

We stand for active ideological struggle because it is the weapon for ensuring unity within the Party and the revolutionary organizations in the interest of our fight. Every Communist and revolutionary should take up this weapon.

But liberalism rejects ideological struggle and stands for unprincipled peace, thus giving rise to a decadent, Philistine attitude and bringing about political degeneration in certain units and individuals in the Party and the revolutionary organizations.

Liberalism manifests itself in various ways.

To let things slide for the sake of peace and friendship when a person has clearly gone wrong, and refrain from principled argument because he is an old acquaintance, a fellow townsman, a schoolmate, a close friend, a loved one, an old colleague or old subordinate. Or to touch on the matter lightly instead of going into it thoroughly, so as to keep on good terms. The result is that both the organization and the individual are harmed. This is one type of liberalism.

To indulge in irresponsible criticism in private instead of actively putting forward one's suggestions to the organization. To say nothing to people to their faces but to gossip behind their backs, or to say nothing at a meeting but to gossip afterwards. To show no regard at all for the principles of collective life but to follow one's own inclination. This is a second type.

To let things drift if they do not affect one personally; to say as little as possible while knowing perfectly well what is wrong, to be worldly wise and play safe and seek only to avoid blame. This is a third type.

Not to obey orders but to give pride of place to one's own opinions. To demand special consideration from the organization but to reject its discipline. This is a fourth type.

To indulge in personal attacks, pick quarrels, vent personal spite or seek revenge instead of entering into an argument and struggling against incorrect views for the sake of unity or progress or getting the work done properly. This is a fifth type.

237

To hear incorrect views without rebutting them and even to hear counter-revolutionary remarks without reporting them, but instead to take them calmly as if nothing had happened. This is a sixth type.

To be among the masses and fail to conduct propaganda and agitation or speak at meetings or conduct investigations and inquiries among them, and instead to be indifferent to them and show no concern for their well-being, forgetting that one is a Communist and behaving as if one were an ordinary non-Communist. This is a seventh type.

Remember that you are a Communist

To see someone harming the interests of the masses and yet not feel indignant, or dissuade or stop him or reason with him, but to allow him to continue. This is an eighth type.

To work half-heartedly without a definite plan or direction; to work perfunctorily and muddle along--"So long as one remains a monk, one goes on tolling the bell." This is a ninth type. *- In my personal work life, this could be said to be true*

To regard oneself as having rendered great service to the revolution, to pride oneself on being a veteran, to disdain minor assignments while being quite unequal to major tasks, to be slipshod in work and slack in study. This is a tenth type.

To be aware of one's own mistakes and yet make no attempt to correct them, taking a liberal attitude towards oneself. This is an eleventh type.

Self-Criticism to be followed by rectification

We could name more. But these eleven are the principal types.

They are all manifestations of liberalism.

Liberalism is extremely harmful in a revolutionary collective. It is a corrosive which eats away unity, undermines cohesion, causes apathy and creates dissension. It robs the revolutionary ranks of compact organization and strict discipline, prevents policies from being carried through and alienates the Party organizations from the masses which the Party leads. It is an extremely bad tendency.

Liberalism stems from petty-bourgeois selfishness, it places personal interests first and the interests of the revolution second, and this gives rise to ideological, political and organizational liberalism.

People who are liberals look upon the principles of Marxism as abstract dogma. They approve of Marxism, but are not prepared to practice it or to

Remember that Marxism is not Abstraction.

practice it in full; they are not prepared to replace their liberalism by Marxism. These people have their Marxism, but they have their liberalism as well--they talk Marxism but practice liberalism; they apply Marxism to others but liberalism to themselves. They keep both kinds of goods in stock and find a use for each. This is how the minds of certain people work.

Liberalism is a manifestation of opportunism and conflicts fundamentally with Marxism. It is negative and objectively has the effect of helping the enemy; that is why the enemy welcomes its preservation in our midst. Such being its nature, there should be no place for it in the ranks of the revolution.

We must use Marxism, which is positive in spirit, to overcome liberalism, which is negative. A Communist should have largeness of mind and he should be staunch and active, looking upon the interests of the revolution as his very life and subordinating his personal interests to those of the revolution; always and everywhere he should adhere to principle and wage a tireless struggle against all incorrect ideas and actions, so as to consolidate the collective life of the Party and strengthen the ties between the Party and the masses; he should be more concerned about the Party and the masses than about any private person, and more concerned about others than about himself. Only thus can he be considered a Communist.

All loyal, honest, active and upright Communists must unite to oppose the liberal tendencies shown by certain people among us, and set them on the right path. This is one of the tasks on our ideological front.

URGENT TASKS FOLLOWING THE ESTABLISHMENT OF KUOMINTANG-COMMUNIST CO-OPERATION

September 29, 1937

As far back as 1933, the Chinese Communist Party issued a declaration stating that it was ready to conclude an agreement for resisting Japan with any section of the Kuomintang army on three conditions, namely, that attacks on the Red Army be stopped, that democratic freedoms be granted to the people and that the people be armed. This declaration was made because after the September 18th Incident in 1931, resistance to the Japanese imperialist invasion became the primary task of the Chinese people. But we did not succeed in our objective.

In August 1935, the Chinese Communist Party and the Chinese Red Army called upon all political parties and groups and the people throughout the country to organize an anti-Japanese united army and a government of national defence for a common fight against Japanese imperialism.[1] In December of that year, the Chinese Communist Party adopted a resolution [2] on the formation of an anti-Japanese national united front with the national bourgeoisie. In May 1936, the Red Army published an open telegram [3] demanding that the Nanking government stop the civil war and make common cause against Japan. In August of that year, the Central Committee of the Chinese Communist Party sent a letter [4] to the Central Executive Committee of the Kuomintang demanding that the Kuomintang stop the civil war and form a united front of the two parties to fight jointly against Japanese imperialism. In September of the same year, the Communist Party passed a resolution [5] on the establishment of a unified democratic republic in China. Besides the declaration, the open telegram, the letter and the resolutions, we sent representatives to hold discussions with people from the Kuomintang side on many occasions, and yet all in vain. It was only towards the end of 1936 after the Sian Incident that the plenipotentiary of the Chinese Communist Party and the responsible chief of the Kuomintang reached an agreement on a contemporary issue of vital political importance, namely, cessation of the civil war between the two parties, and brought about the peaceful settlement of the Sian Incident. This was a great event in Chinese history and provided a prerequisite for the renewal of cooperation between the two parties.

On February 10 this year, the Central Committee of the Chinese Communist Party sent a telegram [6] to the Third Plenary Session of the Kuomintang Central Executive Committee on the eve of its meeting, making comprehensive proposals for concrete co-operation between the two parties. In that telegram we demanded that the Kuomintang give the Communist Party guarantees on the following five points: the ending of the civil war, the realization of democratic freedoms, the convening of a national assembly, speedy preparations for resisting Japan, and improvement of the people's livelihood. At the same time the Communist Party offered guarantees to the Kuomintang on the following four points: the elimination of the state of antagonism between the two regimes, the redesignation of the Red Army, the application of the new-democratic system in the revolutionary base areas, and the discontinuance of the confiscation of the land of the landlords. This was likewise an important political step, for without it the establishment of co-operation between the two parties would have been retarded, which would have been wholly detrimental to speedy preparations for resisting Japan.

Since then the two parties have moved a step closer to each other in their negotiations. The Communist Party has made more specific proposals on the question of a common political programme for the two parties, on the question of lifting the ban on the mass movements and releasing political prisoners, and on the question of redesignating the Red Army. So far the common programme has not yet been promulgated, nor has the ban on the mass movements been lifted, nor has the new system in the revolutionary base areas been recognized; however, about a month after the fall of Peiping and Tientsin an order was issued to the effect that the Red Army was to be redesignated as the Eighth Route Army of the National Revolutionary Army (also called the Eighteenth Group Army in the anti-Japanese battle order). The declaration of the Central Committee of our Party on the establishment of bi-partisan co-operation, which had been conveyed to the Kuomintang as early as July 15, and Chiang Kai-shek's statement recognizing the legal status of the Communist Party of China, which should have been published as agreed simultaneously with the declaration, were finally released to the public (alas after a long delay) by the Kuomintang Central News Agency on September 22 and 23 respectively, when the situation at the front had become critical. The Communist Party's declaration and Chiang Kai-shek's statement announced the establishment of co-operation between the two parties and laid the necessary foundation for the great cause of alliance between the two parties to save the nation. The declaration of the Communist Party not only embodies the principle of unity between the two parties but also embodies the basic principle of the great unity of the people throughout the country. It is good that Chiang Kai-shek, in his statement, recognized the legal status of the Communist Party throughout China and spoke of the necessity of unity to save the nation; however, he has not abandoned his Kuomintang arrogance or made any necessary self-criticism, and we can hardly be satisfied with that. Nevertheless, the united front between the two parties has been proclaimed as established. This has ushered in a new epoch in the history of the Chinese revolution. It will exert a widespread and profound influence on the Chinese revolution and play a decisive role in defeating Japanese imperialism.

Ever since 1924, the relationship between the Kuomintang and the Chinese Communist Party has played a decisive role in the Chinese revolution. The revolution of 1924-27 took place as a result of the co-operation of the two parties on the basis of a definite programme. In a mere two or three years, tremendous successes were achieved in the national revolution to which Dr. Sun Yat-sen had devoted forty years and which he had left unaccomplished; these successes were the establishment of the revolutionary base in Kwangtung and the victory of the Northern Expedition. They were the products of the formation of the united front of the two parties. But at the very moment when the revolution was nearing its triumph, some people who failed to uphold the revolutionary cause disrupted the two-party united front and so brought about the failure of the revolution, and the door was left open for foreign aggression. These were the products of the disruption of the united front of the two parties. Now the newly formed united front between the two parties has ushered in a new period in the Chinese revolution. There are still people who do not understand the historical role of the united front and its great future and regard it as a mere temporary makeshift devised under the pressure of circumstances; nevertheless, through this united front, the wheel of history will propel the Chinese revolution forward to a completely new stage. Whether China can extricate herself from the national and social crisis which is now so grave depends on how this united front will develop. There is already fresh evidence that the prospects are favourable. First, as soon as the policy of the united front was put forward by the Chinese Communist Party, it won the approval of the people everywhere. This is a clear expression of the will of the people. Second, immediately after the Sian Incident was settled peacefully and the two parties ended the civil war, all political parties and groups, people in all walks of life and all armed forces in the country achieved unprecedented unity. This unity, however, still falls far short of meeting the needs of resisting Japan, especially as the problem of unity between the government and the people remains basically unsolved. Third, and most striking of all, is the fact that the nation-wide War of Resistance has started. We are not satisfied with the War of Resistance in its present state because, though national in character, it is still confined to the government and the armed forces. As we pointed out earlier, Japanese imperialism cannot be defeated through a war of resistance of this kind. Nevertheless, for the first time in a hundred years, China is definitely putting up nation-wide resistance to a foreign invader, and this could never have come about without internal peace and without co-operation between the two parties. If the Japanese aggressors were able to take the four northeastern provinces without firing a single shot during the time when the two-party united front was broken up, then today, when the united front has been re-established, they will not be able to occupy more Chinese territory without paying a price in bloody battles. Fourth, there is the effect abroad. The proposal for the anti-Japanese united front put forward by the Chinese Communist Party has won the support of the workers and peasants and the Communist Parties all over the world. With the establishment of co-operation between the Kuomintang and the Communist Party, the people of various countries, and particularly of the Soviet Union, will help China more actively. China and the Soviet Union have concluded a treaty of non-aggression [7] and the relations between the two countries can be expected to improve still further. From all this evidence we can state with certainty that the growth of the united front will carry China towards a bright and great future, namely, the defeat of Japanese imperialism and the establishment of a unified democratic republic.

However, the united front cannot accomplish this great task if it remains in its present state. The united front of the two parties must be developed

243

further. For in its present state it is not yet broadly based or consolidated.

Should the Anti-Japanese National United Front be confined to the Kuomintang and the Communist Party? No, it should be a united front of the whole nation, with the two parties forming only a part of it. It should be a united front of all parties and groups, people in all walks of life and all armed forces, a united front of all patriots-- the workers, peasants, soldiers, intellectuals and businessmen. So far, the united front has in fact been confined to the two parties, while the masses of the workers, peasants, soldiers and urban petty bourgeoisie and a large number of other patriots have not yet been aroused, called into action, organized or armed. This is the most serious problem at present. It is serious because it makes victories at the front impossible. It is no longer possible to conceal the critical situation at the front both in northern China and in Kiangsu and Chekiang Provinces, nor is there any need to do so; the question is how to save the situation. And the only way to save it is to put Dr. Sun Yat-sen's Testament into practice, to "arouse the masses of the people". In his deathbed Testament, Dr. Sun declared he was deeply convinced, from the experience accumulated over forty years, that only thus could the goal of revolution be achieved. What reason is there for obstinately refusing to put this testament into practice? What reason is there for failing to do so at a moment when the fate of the nation is at stake? Everybody knows that autocracy and suppression run counter to the principle of "arousing the masses of the people". Resistance by the government and the army alone can never defeat Japanese imperialism. Early in May this year we warned the ruling Kuomintang in all seriousness that unless the masses of the people were aroused to resist, China would follow the same path to disaster as Abyssinia. This point has been made not only by the Chinese Communists but by progressives throughout the country and by many intelligent members of the Kuomintang itself. Yet the policy of autocratic rule remains unchanged. As a result the government has estranged itself from the people, the army from the masses, and the military command from the rank and file. Unless the united front is reinforced by the participation of the masses, the crisis on the war fronts will inevitably be aggravated, not mitigated.

The present anti-Japanese united front still lacks a political programme to replace the Kuomintang's policy of autocratic rule, a programme accepted by both parties and formally promulgated. In relation to the masses the Kuomintang is continuing the same practices it has followed for the last ten years; there has been no change and on the whole everything has remained the same for the last ten years, from the government apparatus, the army system and the policy towards civilians to financial, economic and educational policies. Changes there are and very great ones too--cessation of civil war and unity against Japan. The two parties have ended the civil war and the nation-wide War of Resistance Against Japan has started, which mean a tremendous change in the Chinese political scene since the Sian Incident. But so far there has been no change in the practices enumerated above, and there is thus a disharmony between the things that have not changed and those that have. The old practices are suited only to compromise abroad and suppression of the revolution at home, and they prove ill-suited in every respect and reveal all their inadequacies when it comes to coping with the Japanese imperialist invasion. It would be another story if we did not want to resist Japan, but since we do and resistance has actually begun, and since a serious crisis has already revealed itself, refusal to change over to new ways will lead to the gravest dangers imaginable. Resistance to Japan requires a broadly based united front, and hence all the people should be mobilized to join it. Resistance to Japan requires a consolidated united front, and this calls for a common programme. The common programme will be the united front's guide to action and will serve also as the tie which, like a cord, closely binds together all the organizations and individuals in the united front, all political parties and groups, people in all walks of life and all armed forces. Only in this way will we be able to speak of firm unity. We are opposed to the old binding rules, because they are unsuited to the national revolutionary war. We look forward to the introduction of new binding rules to replace the old, that is, to the promulgation of a common programme and the establishment of revolutionary order. Nothing else will suit the War of Resistance.

What should the common programme be? It should be the Three People's Principles of Dr. Sun Yat-sen and the Ten-Point Programme for Resisting Japan and Saving the Nation [8] proposed by the Communist Party on August 25 this year.

In its declaration announcing Kuomintang-Communist cooperation, the Chinese Communist Party stated that "the Three People's Principles of Dr. Sun Yat-sen being what China needs today, our Party is ready to fight for their complete realization". Some people find it strange that the Communist Party should be ready to put the Three People's Principles of the Kuomintang into practice; Chu Ching-lai [9] of Shanghai, for instance, has expressed doubts in a local periodical. These people think that communism and the Three People's Principles are incompatible. This is a purely formal approach. Communism will be put into practice at a future stage of the development of the revolution; at the present stage the communists harbour no illusions about being able to realize it but will carry out the national and democratic revolution as required by history. This is the basic reason why the Communist Party has proposed an anti-Japanese national united front and a unified democratic republic. As for the Three People's Principles, at the Kuomintang's First National Congress the Communist Party and the Kuomintang jointly decided to put them into practice during the first two-party united front over ten years ago, and they were put into practice from 1924 to 1927 in large areas of the country through the efforts of all loyal Communists and all loyal members of the Kuomintang. Unfortunately that united front broke up in 1927, and in the subsequent ten years the Kuomintang opposed the application of the Three People's Principles. But as far as the Communist Party is concerned, all its policies in these ten years have been fundamentally in line with the revolutionary spirit of Dr. Sun's Three People's Principles and Three Great Policies. Not a day has passed without the Communist Party's conducting a struggle against imperialism, which means the thoroughgoing application of the Principle of Nationalism; the worker-peasant democratic dictatorship is nothing but the thoroughgoing application of the Principle of Democracy; the Agrarian Revolution is the thoroughgoing application of the Principle of People's Livelihood. Why, then, has the Communist Party announced the abolition of the worker-peasant democratic dictatorship and the discontinuance of confiscating the land of landlords? The reason, as we explained some time ago, is not that there is anything at all wrong with these things, but that the Japanese imperialist armed aggression has led to a change in class relations in the country, and has thereby not only made it necessary to unite all classes of the nation against Japanese imperialism, but also created the possibility of doing so. An anti-fascist united front for the sake of the common struggle against fascism is both necessary and possible not only in China but throughout the world. Therefore we stand for the establishment of a national and democratic united front in China. It is on these grounds that we have proposed a democratic republic based on the alliance of all classes in place of a worker-peasant democratic dictatorship. The Agrarian Revolution put into effect the principle of "land to the tiller", which is precisely what Dr. Sun Yat-sen proposed. We have now discontinued it for the sake of uniting greater numbers of people against Japanese imperialism, but that does not mean China does not need to solve her land problem. We have unequivocally explained our position on the causes of these changes in policy and their timing. It is precisely because the Chinese Communist Party, basing itself on Marxist principles, has constantly adhered to and developed the revolutionary Three People's Principles--the common programme of the first Kuomintang-Communist united front--that, in this hour of national crisis when our country is invaded by a powerful aggressor, the Party has been able to put forward the timely proposal for a national and democratic united front, which is the only policy capable of saving the nation, and to apply this policy with unremitting effort. The question now is not whether it is the Communist Party which believes in or carries out the revolutionary Three People's Principles, but whether it is the Kuomintang which does so. The present task is to restore the revolutionary spirit of Dr. Sun's Three People's Principles throughout the country, and on this basis to work out a definite programme and policy and put them into practice sincerely and not half-heartedly, conscientiously and not perfunctorily, promptly and not tardily; the Chinese Communist Party has been earnestly praying day and night for this to happen. For this very reason, it put forward the Ten-Point Programme for Resisting Japan and Saving the Nation after the Lukouchiao Incident. The Ten-Point Programme is in line both with Marxism and with the genuine revolutionary Three People's Principles. It is an initial programme, the programme for the Chinese revolution at the present stage, which is the stage of the anti-Japanese national revolutionary war; China can be saved only if this programme is put into effect. History will punish those who persist in any course conflicting with this programme.

It is impossible to put this programme into practice throughout the country without the consent of the Kuomintang, because the Kuomintang today is still the biggest party in China and the party in power. We believe that the day will come when intelligent members of the Kuomintang will agree to this programme. For if they do not, the Three People's Principles will for ever remain an empty phrase, and it will be impossible to restore the revolutionary spirit of Dr. Sun Yat-sen, impossible to defeat Japanese imperialism and impossible for the Chinese people to escape becoming the slaves of a foreign power. No really intelligent member of the Kuomintang can possibly want this to happen, and our people will never allow themselves to be turned into slaves. Moreover, in his statement of September 23 Mr. Chiang Kai-shek declared:

I hold that we who stand for the revolution should put aside personal grudges and prejudices and devote ourselves to the realization of the Three People's Principles. At this critical juncture of life and death, we should all the more let bygones be bygones and together with the whole nation make a completely fresh start, and work strenuously for unity in order to preserve the very life and existence of our country.

This is most true. The urgent task at present is to strive for the realization of the Three People's Principles, to discard personal and factional prejudices, to change the old set of practices, to carry out a revolutionary programme in line with the Three People's Principles immediately and to make a completely fresh start together with the whole nation. Today this is the only course. With further delay it will be too late to repent.

But there must be instruments for carrying out the Three People's Principles and the Ten-Point Programme, and this raises the question of reforming the government and the army. The present government is still a one-party dictatorship of the Kuomintang and not a government of the national democratic united front. In the absence of a government of the national democratic united front, it is impossible to carry out the Three People's Principles and the Ten-Point Programme. The present army system of the Kuomintang is still the old one, and it is impossible to defeat Japanese imperialism with troops organized under this system. The troops are now engaged in resistance and we have great admiration and respect for them all, and especially for those fighting at the front. But the lessons of the War of Resistance in the last three months demonstrate that the Kuomintang army system must be changed, as it is unsuited to the task of completely defeating the Japanese aggressors and to the successful application of the Three People's Principles and the revolutionary programme. The change should be based on the principles of unity between officers and men and unity between the army and the people. The present army system of the Kuomintang is fundamentally opposed to both these principles. It prevents the mass of officers and men from giving their best despite their loyalty and courage, and therefore an immediate start must be made to reform it. This does not mean that the fighting has to stop until the system is reformed; it can be reformed while the fighting is going on. Here the central task is to bring about a change in the army's political spirit and its political work. The National Revolutionary Army during the Northern Expedition provides an admirable precedent, for in general it did establish unity between officers and men and between the army and the people; a revival of the spirit of those days is absolutely necessary. China should learn from the war in Spain where the Republican army has been built up under extremely adverse circumstances. China is in a better position than Spain, but she lacks a broadly based and consolidated united front, she lacks a united front government capable of carrying out the whole revolutionary programme and large numbers of troops organized according to a new system. She must remedy these defects. With regard to the war as a whole, the Red Army led by the Chinese Communist Party can at present only play a vanguard role, it cannot yet play a decisive role on a national scale. Nevertheless its political, military and organizational merits are well worth acquiring by friendly armies throughout the country. At its inception the Red Army was not what it is today; it, too, has undergone many reforms, the main ones being the weeding out of feudal practices within the army and the application of the principles of unity between officers and men and unity between the army and the people. Friendly armies throughout the country can draw on this experience.

Anti-Japanese comrades of the ruling Kuomintang party! Today we share with you the responsibility for saving the nation from extinction and ensuring its survival. You have already formed an anti-Japanese united front with us. That is very good. You have started resisting Japan. That is also very good. But we do not approve of your continuing your other policies in the old way. We should all develop and broaden the united front and draw in the masses of the people. It is necessary to consolidate the united front and pursue a common programme. It is essential resolutely to reform the political and army systems. It is absolutely necessary to have a new government, which alone can carry out the revolutionary programme and start to reform the armies on a national scale. This proposal of ours answers the needs of the times. Many people in your party also feel that now is the time to put it into practice. Dr. Sun Yat-sen, in his day, made up his mind and reformed the political and army systems, thereby laying the foundation for the revolution of 1924-27. The responsibility for effecting the same kind of reform now falls on your shoulders. We believe that no loyal and patriotic member of the Kuomintang will consider that our proposal is ill-suited to the needs of the situation. We are firmly convinced that it meets the objective needs.

The fate of our nation is at stake--let the Kuomintang and the Communist Party unite closely! Let all our fellow-countrymen who refuse to become slaves unite closely on the basis of Kuomintang Communist unity! The urgent task in the Chinese revolution today is to make all the reforms necessary to overcome all difficulties. When this task is accomplished, we can surely defeat Japanese imperialism. If we try hard, our future will be bright.

NOTES
1. See "The Tasks of the Chinese Communist Party in the Period of Resistance to Japan", Note 2, Selected Works of Mao Tse-tung, Eng. ed., FLP, Peking, 1965, Vol. I, pp. 276-77.

2. For the resolution see ibid., Note 3, pp. 277-78.

3. For the open telegram see ibid., Note 4, pp. 279-80.

4. For the contents of the letter see "A Statement on Chiang Kai-shek's Statement", Note 7, ibid., pp. 259-61.

5. For the resolution see "The Tasks of the Chinese Communist Party in the Period of Resistance to Japan", Note 6, ibid., pp. 280-81.

6. For the telegram see ibid., Note 7, pp. 281-82.

7. The Treaty of Non-Aggression Between the Republic of China and the Union of Soviet Socialist Republics was concluded on August 21, 1937.

8. For the Ten-Point Programme see "For the Mobilization of All the Nation's Forces for Victory in the War of Resistance", pp. 25-28 of this volume.

9. Chu Ching-lai was a leader of the National Socialist Party (a small clique organized by reactionary landlords, bureaucrats and big bourgeoisie) who later became a member of the traitorous Wang Ching-wei government.

INTERVIEW WITH THE BRITISH JOURNALIST JAMES BERTRAM

October 25, 1937

THE COMMUNIST PARTY OF CHINA AND THE WAR OF RESISTANCE

James Bertram: What specific pronouncements has the Chinese Communist Party made before and since the outbreak of the Sino-Japanese war?

Mao Tse-tung: Before the war broke out, the Chinese Communist Party warned the whole nation time and again that war with Japan was inevitable, and that all the Japanese imperialists' talk of a "peaceful settlement" and all the fine phrases of the Japanese diplomats were only so much camouflage to screen their preparations for war. We repeatedly stressed that a victorious war of national liberation cannot be waged unless the united front is strengthened and a revolutionary policy is adopted. The most important point in this revolutionary policy is that the Chinese government must institute democratic reforms in order to mobilize all the people to join the anti-Japanese front. We repeatedly pointed out the error of those who believed in Japan's "peace pledge" and thought that war might be avoided, or of those who believed in the possibility of resisting the Japanese aggressors without mobilizing the masses. Both the outbreak of the war and its course have proved our views to be correct. The day after the Lukouchiao Incident, the Communist Party issued a manifesto to the whole country, calling upon all political parties and groups and all social strata to make common cause in resisting Japanese aggression and strengthening the national united front. Soon afterwards we announced the Ten-Point Programme for Resisting Japan and Saving the Nation, in which we set out the policies that the Chinese government ought to adopt in the War of Resistance. With the institution of Kuomintang-Communist co-operation we issued another important declaration. All this testifies to our firm adherence to the principle of waging the War of Resistance by strengthening the united front and putting a revolutionary policy into effect. In the present period our basic slogan is "Total resistance by the whole nation".

THE WAR SITUATION AND ITS LESSONS
Question: As you see it, what are the results of the war up to the present?

Answer: There are two main aspects. On the one hand, by capturing our cities, seizing our territory, raping, plundering, burning and massacring, the Japanese imperialists have irrevocably brought the Chinese people face to face with the danger of national subjugation. On the other hand, the majority of the Chinese people have consequently become very much aware that the crisis cannot be overcome without greater unity and without resistance by the whole nation. At the same time, the peace-loving countries of the world are being awakened to the necessity of resisting the Japanese menace. These are the results produced by the war so far.

Question: What do you think are Japan's objectives, and how far have they been achieved?

Answer: Japan's plan is to occupy northern China and Shanghai as the first step and then to occupy other regions of China. As to how far the Japanese aggressors have realized their plan, they seized the three provinces of Hopei, Chahar and Suiyuan within a short space of time, and now they are threatening Shansi; the reason is that China's War of Resistance has hitherto been confined to resistance by the government and the army alone. This crisis can be overcome only if resistance is carried out jointly by the people and the government.

Question: In your opinion, has China scored any achievements in the War of Resistance? If there are any lessons to be drawn, what are they?

Answer: I would like to discuss this question with you in some detail. First of all, there have been achievements, and great achievements too. They are to be seen in the following: (1) Never since imperialist aggression began against China has there been any thing comparable to the present War of Resistance Against Japan. Geographically, it is truly a war involving the whole country. This war is revolutionary in character. (2) The war has changed a disunited country into a relatively united one. The basis of this unity is Kuomintang-communist co-operation. (3) The war has the sympathy of world public opinion. Those who once despised China for her nonresistance now respect her for her resistance. (4) The war has inflicted heavy losses on the Japanese aggressors. The daily drain on their resources is reported to be twenty million yen and their casualties are also undoubtedly very heavy, though figures are not yet available. While the Japanese aggressors took the four northeastern provinces with ease and with hardly any exertion, now they cannot occupy Chinese territory without fighting bloody battles. The aggressors expected to be able to gorge themselves in China, but China's protracted resistance will bring about the collapse of Japanese imperialism. Thus China is fighting not only to save herself but also to discharge her great duty in the world anti-fascist front. Here also the revolutionary character of the War of Resistance is manifest. (5) We have learned some lessons from the war. They have been paid for in territory and blood.

As for the lessons, they are likewise great ones. Several months of fighting have disclosed many of China's weaknesses. They are manifest above all in the political sphere. Although geographically the war involves the whole country, it is not being waged by the whole nation. As in the past, the broad masses are restrained by the government from taking part, and so the war is not yet of a mass character. Unless it has a mass character, the war against Japanese imperialist aggression cannot possibly succeed. Some say, "The war is already an all-embracing war." But this is true only in the sense that vast parts of the country are involved. As regards participation, it is still a partial war because it is being waged only by the government and the army, and not by the people. It is precisely here that the chief reason for the great loss of territory and for the many military setbacks during the last few months is to be found. Therefore, although the present armed resistance is a revolutionary one, its revolutionary character is incomplete because it is not yet a mass war. Here, too, the problem of unity is involved. Although the political parties and groups are relatively united as compared with the past, unity still falls far short of what is needed. Most of the political prisoners have not yet been released, and the ban on political parties has not been completely lifted. Relations are still very bad between the government and the people, between the army and the people, and between officers and men, and here one observes estrangement instead of unity. This is a fundamental problem. Unless it is solved, victory is out of the question. In addition, military blunders are another major reason for our losses in men and territory. The battles fought have been mostly passive, or to put it in military terms, have been battles of "pure defence". We can never win by fighting this way. For the attainment of victory, policies radically different from the present ones are necessary in both the political and the military fields. These are the lessons we have learned.

Question: What, then, are the political and military prerequisites?

Answer: On the political side, first, the present government must be transformed into a united front government in which the representatives of the people play their part. This government must be at once democratic and centralized. It should carry out the necessary revolutionary policies. Secondly, the people must be granted freedom of speech, freedom of the press, and freedom of assembly and association and the right to take up arms against the enemy, so that the war will acquire a mass character. Thirdly, the people's livelihood must be improved through such measures as the abolition of exorbitant taxes and miscellaneous levies, the reduction of rent and interest, better conditions for workers, junior officers and soldiers, preferential treatment for the families of the soldiers fighting the Japanese, and relief for victims of natural calamities and war refugees. Government finance should be based on the principle of equitable distribution of the economic burden, which means that those who have money should contribute money. Fourthly, there should be a positive foreign policy. Fifthly, cultural and educational policy should be changed. Sixthly, traitors must be sternly suppressed. The problem has become extremely serious. The traitors are running wild. At the front they are helping the enemy; in the rear they are creating disturbances, and some of them even put on an anti-Japanese pose and denounce patriotic people as traitors and have them arrested. Effective suppression of the traitors will be possible only when the people are free to co-operate with the government. On the military side, comprehensive reforms are required, the most important of these being to change from pure defence in strategy and tactics to the principle of active attack; to change the armies of the old type into armies of a new type; to change the method of forcible recruitment into one of arousing the people to go to the front; to change the divided command into a unified command, to change the indiscipline which alienates the army from the people into conscious discipline which forbids the slightest violation of the people's interests; to change the present situation in which the regular army is fighting alone into one in which extensive guerrilla warfare by the people is developed in co-ordination with regular army operations; and so on and so forth. All these political and military prerequisites are listed in our published Ten-Point Programme. They all conform to the spirit of Dr. Sun Yat-sen's Three People's Principles, his Three Great Policies and his Testament. The war can be won only when they are carried into effect.

Question: What is the Communist Party doing to carry out this programme?

Answer: We take it as our task tirelessly to explain the situation and to unite with the Kuomintang and all other patriotic parties and groups in the effort to expand and consolidate the Anti-Japanese National United Front, mobilize all forces and achieve victory in the War of Resistance. The Anti-Japanese National United Front is still very limited in scope and it is necessary to broaden it, that is, to "arouse the masses of the people", as called for in Dr. Sun Yat-sen's Testament, by mobilizing the people at the grass roots to join the united front. Consolidation of the united front means carrying out a common programme which will be binding on all political parties and groups in their actions. We agree to accept Dr. Sun's revolutionary Three People's Principles, Three Great Policies and Testament as the common programme of the united front of all political parties and all social classes. But so far this programme has not been accepted by all the parties, and above all the Kuomintang has not agreed to the proclamation of such an over-all programme. Dr. Sun Yat-sen's Principle of Nationalism has been partially put into practice by the Kuomintang, as shown in its resistance to Japan. But neither his Principle of Democracy nor his Principle of People's Livelihood has been applied, and the present serious crisis in the War of Resistance is the result. The war situation having become so critical, it is high time that the Kuomintang applied the Three People's Principles in full, or otherwise it will be too late to repent. It is the duty of the Communist Party to raise its voice and tirelessly and persuasively explain all this to the Kuomintang and the whole nation so that the genuinely revolutionary Three People's Principles, the Three Great Policies and Dr. Sun Yat-sen's Testament are fully and thoroughly applied throughout the country, and the Anti-Japanese National United Front is broadened and consolidated.

THE EIGHTH ROUTE ARMY IN THE WAR OF RESISTANCE
Question: Please tell me about the Eighth Route Army in which so many people are interested--for instance, about its strategy and tactics, its

political work, and so on.

Answer: Indeed a large number of people have become interested in its activities since the Red Army was redesignated as the Eighth Route Army and went to the front. I shall now give you a general account.

First about its field operations. Strategically, the Eighth Route Army is centring them on Shansi. As you know, it has won many victories. Examples are the battle of Pinghsingkuan, the recapture of Chingping, Pinglu and Ningwu, the recovery of Laiyuan and Kuangling, the capture of Tzechingkuan, the cutting of the three main supply routes of the Japanese troops (between Tatung and Yenmenkuan, between Weihsien and Pinghsingkuan, and between Shuohsien and Ningwu), the assault on the rear of the Japanese forces south of Yenmenkuan, the recapture twice over of Pinghsingkuan and Yenmenkuan, and the recent recovery of Chuyang and Tanghsien. The Japanese troops in Shansi are being strategically encircled by the Eighth Route Army and other Chinese troops. We may say with certainty that the Japanese troops will meet with the most stubborn resistance in northern China. If they try to ride roughshod over Shansi, they will certainly encounter greater difficulties than ever.

Next about strategy and tactics. We are doing what the other Chinese troops have not done, i.e., operating chiefly on the enemy's flanks and rear. This way of fighting is vastly different from purely frontal defence. We are not against employing part of the forces in frontal operations, for that is necessary. But the main forces must be used against the enemy's flanks and it is essential to adopt encircling and outflanking tactics in order to attack the enemy independently and with the initiative in our hands, for that is the only way to destroy his forces and preserve our own. Furthermore, the use of some of our armed forces against the enemy's rear is particularly effective, because they can disrupt his supply lines and bases. Even the frontal forces should rely mainly on "counter assault" and not on purely defensive tactics. One important reason for the military setbacks in the last few months has been the use of unsuitable methods of fighting. The methods of fighting employed by the Eighth Route Army are what we call guerrilla and mobile warfare applied independently and with the initiative in our hands. In principle these methods are basically the same as those we used during the civil war, but there are certain differences. For example, at the present stage, in order to facilitate our surprise attacks on the enemy's flanks and rear over an extensive area, we divide our forces more often than we concentrate them. Since the armed forces of the country as a whole are numerically strong, some of them should be used for frontal defence and some dispersed to carry on

256

guerrilla operations, but the main forces should always be concentrated against the enemy's flanks. The first essential in war is to preserve oneself and to destroy the enemy, and for this purpose it is necessary to wage guerrilla and mobile warfare independently and with the initiative in our hands and to avoid all passive and inflexible tactics. If a vast number of troops wage mobile warfare with the Eighth Route Army assisting them by guerrilla warfare, our victory will be certain.

Next about political work. Another highly significant and distinctive feature of the Eighth Route Army is its political work, which is guided by three basic principles. First, the principle of unity between officers and men, which means eradicating feudal practices in the army, prohibiting beating and abuse, building up a conscious discipline, and sharing weal and woe-- as a result of which the entire army is closely united. Second, the principle of unity between the army and the people, which means maintaining a discipline that forbids the slightest violation of the people's interests, conducting propaganda among the masses, organizing and arming them, lightening their financial burdens and suppressing the traitors and collaborators who do harm to the army and the people--as a result of which the army is closely united with the people and welcomed everywhere. Third, the principle of disintegrating the enemy troops and giving lenient treatment to prisoners of war. Our victory depends not only upon our military operations but also upon the disintegration of the enemy troops. Although our measures for disintegrating the enemy troops and for treating prisoners of war leniently have not yielded conspicuous results as yet, they will certainly do so in the future. Moreover, in line with the second of the three principles, the Eighth Route Army replenishes its forces not by coercion but by the much more effective method of arousing the people to volunteer for the front.

Although Hopei, Chahar and Sulyuan and part of Shansi have been lost, we are not at all discouraged but are resolutely calling upon the entire army to co-ordinate with the friendly armies and fight with grim determination to defend Shansi and recover the lost territories. The Eighth Route Army will co-ordinate its actions with those of other Chinese troops in order to maintain the resistance in Shansi; this will be very important for the war as a whole, and especially for the war in northern China.

Question: In your opinion, can these good points of the Eighth Route Army also be acquired by the other Chinese armies?

Answer: Certainly they can. In 1924-27 the spirit of the Kuomintang troops was broadly similar to that of the Eighth Route Army today. The

Communist Party and the Kuomintang were then co-operating in organizing armed forces of a new type which, beginning with only two regiments, rallied round themselves many other troops and won their first victory when they defeated Chen Chiung-ming. These forces later grew into an army corps and still more troops came under its influence; only then did the Northern Expedition take place. A fresh spirit prevailed among these forces; on the whole there was unity between officers and men and between the army and the people, and the army was filled with a revolutionary militancy. The system of Party representatives and of political departments, adopted for the first time in China, entirely changed the complexion of these armed forces. The Red Army, which was founded in 1927, and the Eighth Route Army of today have inherited this system and developed it. In the revolutionary period of 1924-27, the armed forces which were imbued with this new spirit naturally employed methods of fighting consistent with their political outlook, operating not in a passive and inflexible way but with initiative and with an eagerness to take the offensive, and consequently they were victorious in the Northern Expedition. It is troops of this kind we need on the battlefields today. We do not necessarily need them in millions; with a nucleus of a few hundred thousand such men, we can defeat Japanese imperialism. We deeply esteem the armies throughout the country for their heroic sacrifices since the War of Resistance began, but there are lessons to be learned from the bloody battles that have been fought.

Question: Japanese army discipline being what it is, will not your policy of giving lenient treatment to prisoners of war prove ineffective? For instance, the Japanese command may kill the prisoners when you release them and the Japanese army as a whole will not understand the meaning of your policy.

Answer: That is impossible. The more they kill, the more sympathy will be aroused for the Chinese forces among the Japanese soldiers. Such facts cannot be concealed from the rank and file. We will persevere in this policy of ours. For instance, we shall not change it even if the Japanese army carries out its declared intention of using poison-gas against the Eighth Route Army. We shall go on giving lenient treatment to captured Japanese soldiers and to those captured junior officers who have fought us under coercion; we shall not insult or abuse them, but shall set them free after explaining to them the identity of the interests of the people of the two countries. Those who do not want to go back may serve in the Eighth Route Army. If an international brigade appears on the anti-Japanese battle front, they may join it and take up arms against Japanese imperialism.

CAPITULATIONISM IN THE WAR OF RESISTANCE

Question: I understand that while carrying on the war, Japan is spreading peace rumours in Shanghai. What are her real objectives?

Answer: After succeeding in certain of their plans, the Japanese imperialists will once again put up a smokescreen of peace in order to attain three objectives. They are: (1) to consolidate the positions already captured for use as a strategic springboard for further offensives; (2) to split China's anti-Japanese front; and (3) to break up the international front of support for China. The present peace rumours are simply the first smoke-bomb. The danger is that there are certain vacillating elements in China who are ready to succumb to the enemy's wiles and that the traitors and collaborators are manoeuvering among them and spreading all kinds of rumours in their efforts to make China capitulate to the Japanese aggressors.

Question: As you see it, what could this danger lead to?

Answer: There can be only two courses of development: either the Chinese people will overcome capitulationism, or capitulationism will prevail, with the result that the anti-Japanese front will be split and China will be plunged into disorder.

Question: Which of the two is the more likely?

Answer: The whole Chinese people demand that the war be fought to a finish. If a section of the ruling group takes the road of capitulation, the rest who remain firm will certainly oppose it and carry on resistance together with the people. Of course it would be a misfortune for China's anti-Japanese front. But I am sure that the capitulationists cannot win mass support and that the masses will overcome capitulationism, persevere in the war and achieve victory.

Question: May I ask how capitulationism can be overcome?

Answer: Both by words, that is, by exposing the danger of capitulationism, and by deeds, that is, by organizing the masses to stop the capitulationist activities. Capitulationism has its roots in national defeatism or national pessimism, that is, in the idea that having lost some battles, China has no strength left to fight Japan. These pessimists do not realize that failure is the mother of success, that the lessons learned from failures are the basis for future triumphs. They see the defeats but not the successes in the War of Resistance, and in particular they fail to see that our defeats contain the elements of victory, while the enemy's victories contain the elements of defeat. We must show the masses of the people the victorious prospects of the war and help them to understand that our defeats and difficulties are temporary and that, as long as we keep on fighting in spite of all setbacks, the final victory will be ours. Deprived of a mass base, the capitulationists will have no chance to play their tricks, and the anti-Japanese front will be consolidated.

DEMOCRACY AND THE WAR OF RESISTANCE

Question: What is the meaning of "democracy" as put forward by the Communist Party in its programme? Does it not conflict with a "wartime government"?

Answer: Not at all. The Communist Party put forward the slogan of a "democratic republic" as early as August 1936. Politically and organizationally this slogan signifies: (1) The state and government must not belong to a single class but must be based on the alliance of all the anti-Japanese classes to the exclusion of traitors and collaborators, and must include the workers, the peasants and other sections of the petty bourgeoisie. (2) The organizational form of such a government will be democratic centralism, which is at once democratic and centralized, with the two seeming opposites of democracy and centralization united in a definite form. (3) This government will grant the people all the necessary political freedoms, especially the freedom to organize and train and arm themselves for self-defence. In these three respects, it can be seen that a democratic republic in no way conflicts with a wartime government, but is precisely the form of state and government advantageous to the War of Resistance.

Question: Is not "democratic centralism" a self-contradictory term?

Answer: We must look not only at the term but at the reality. There is no impassable gulf between democracy and centralism, both of which are essential for China. On the one hand, the government we want must be truly representative of the popular will; it must have the support of the broad masses throughout the country and the people must be free to support it and have every opportunity of influencing its policies. This is the meaning of democracy. On the other hand, the centralization of administrative power is also necessary, and once the policy measures demanded by the people are transmitted to their own elected government through their representative body, the government will carry them out and will certainly be able to do so smoothly, so long as it does not go against the policy adopted in accordance with the people's will. This is the meaning of centralism. Only by adopting democratic centralism can a government be really strong, and this system must be adopted by China's government of national defence in the anti-Japanese war.

Question: This does not correspond to a war cabinet, does it?

Answer: It does not correspond to some of the war cabinets of the past.

Question: Have there ever been any war cabinets of this kind?

Answer: Yes. Systems of government in wartime may generally be divided into two kinds, as determined by the nature of the war--one kind is democratic centralism and the other absolute centralism. All wars in history may be divided into two kinds according to their nature: just wars and unjust wars. For instance, the Great War in Europe some twenty years ago was an unjust, imperialist war. The governments of the imperialist countries forced the people to fight for the interests of imperialism and thus went against the people's interests, these circumstances necessitating a type of government such as the Lloyd George government in Britain. Lloyd George repressed the British people, forbidding them to speak against the imperialist war and banning organizations or assemblies that expressed popular opinion against the war; even though Parliament remained, it was merely the organ of a group of imperialists, a parliament which rubber-stamped the war budget. The absence of unity between the government and the people in a war gives rise to a government of absolute centralism with all centralism and no democracy. But historically there have also been revolutionary wars, e.g., in France, Russia, and present-day Spain. In such wars the government does not fear popular disapproval, because the people are most willing to wage this kind of war; far from fearing the people, it endeavours to arouse them and encourages them to express their views so that they will actively participate in the war, because the government rests upon the people's voluntary support. China's war of national liberation has the full approval of the people and cannot be won without their participation; therefore democratic centralism becomes a necessity. In the Northern Expedition of 1926-27, too, the victories were achieved through democratic centralism. Thus it can be seen that when the aims of a war directly reflect the interests of the people, the more democratic the government, the more effectively can the war be prosecuted. Such a government need have no fear that the people will oppose the war; rather it should be worried lest the people remain inactive or indifferent to the war. The nature of a war determines the relationship between the government and the people--this is a law of history.

Question: Then what steps are you prepared to take for this system of government to be instituted?

Answer: The key question is co-operation between the Kuomintang and the Communist Party.

Question: Why?

Answer: For the last fifteen years, the relationship between the Kuomintang and the Communist Party has been the decisive political factor in China. The co-operation of the two parties in 1924-27 resulted in the victories of the first revolution. The split between the two parties in 1927 resulted in the unfortunate situation of the last decade. However, the responsibility for the split was not ours; we were compelled to resist the Kuomintang's oppression, and we persisted in holding high the glorious banner of China's liberation. Now the third stage has come, and the two parties must co-operate fully on a definite programme in order to resist Japan and save the nation. Through our ceaseless efforts, the establishment of co-operation has at last been announced, but the point is that both sides must accept a common programme and act upon it. An essential part of such a programme is the setting up of a new system of government.

Question: How can the new system be set up through the cooperation of the two parties?

Answer: We are proposing a reconstruction of the government apparatus and the army system. We propose that a provisional national assembly be convened to meet the present emergency. Delegates to this assembly should be chosen in due proportion from the various anti-Japanese political parties, anti-Japanese armies and anti-Japanese popular and business organizations, as Dr. Sun Yat-sen suggested in 1924. This assembly should function as the supreme organ of state authority to decide on the policies for saving the nation, adopt a constitutional programme and elect the government. We hold that the War of Resistance has reached a critical turning point and that only the immediate convening of such a national assembly vested with authority and representative of the popular will can regenerate China's political life and overcome the present crisis. We are exchanging views with the Kuomintang about this proposal and hope to obtain its agreement.

Question: Has not the National Government announced that the national assembly has been called off?

Answer: It was right to call it off. What has been called off is the national assembly which the Kuomintang was preparing to convene; according to the Kuomintang's stipulations it would not have had the slightest power, and the procedure for its election was entirely in conflict with the popular will. Together with the people of all sections of society, we disapproved of that kind of national assembly. The provisional national assembly we are proposing is radically different from the one that has been called off. The convening of this provisional national assembly will undoubtedly impart a new spirit to the whole country and provide the essential prerequisite for reconstructing the government apparatus and the army and for mobilizing the entire people. On this hinges the favourable turn in the War of Resistance.

THE SITUATION AND TASKS IN THE ANTI-JAPANESE WAR AFTER THE FALL OF SHANGHAI AND TAIYUAN

November 12, 1937

[This was the outline for a report made by Comrade Mao Tse-tung in Yenan, in November 1937 at a meeting of Party activists. It met with immediate opposition from the Right opportunists in the Party, and not until the Sixth Plenary Session of the Sixth Central Committee in October 1938 was the Right deviation basically overcome.]

I. THE PRESENT SITUATION IS ONE OF TRANSITION FROM A WAR OF PARTIAL RESISTANCE TO A WAR OF TOTAL RESISTANCE

1. We support any kind of war of resistance, even though partial, against the invasion of Japanese imperialism. For partial resistance is a step forward from non-resistance, and to a certain extent it is revolutionary in character and is a war in defence of the motherland.

2. However, a war of partial resistance by the government alone without the mass participation of the people will certainly fail, as we have already pointed out (at the meeting of Party activists in Yenan in April of this year, at the Party's National Conference in May, and in the resolution [1] of the Political Bureau of the Central Committee in August). For it is not a national revolutionary war in the full sense, not a people's war.

3. We stand for a national revolutionary war in the full sense, a war in which the entire people are mobilized, in other words, total resistance. For only such resistance constitutes a people's war and can achieve the goal of defending the motherland.

4. Although the war of partial resistance advocated by the Kuomintang also constitutes a national war and is revolutionary in character to a certain extent, its revolutionary character is far from complete. Partial resistance is bound to lead to defeat in the war; it can never successfully defend the motherland.

5. Herein lies the difference in principle between the stand of the Communist Party and the present stand of the Kuomintang with regard to resistance. If Communists forget this difference in principle, they will be unable to guide the War of Resistance correctly, they will be powerless to overcome the Kuomintang's one-sidedness, and they will debase

264

themselves to the point of abandoning their principles and reduce their Party to the level of the Kuomintang. That would be a crime against the sacred cause of the national revolutionary war and the defence of the motherland.

6. In a national revolutionary war in the full sense, in a war of total resistance, it is essential to put into effect the Ten-Point Programme for Resisting Japan and Saving the Nation proposed by the Communist Party, and it is essential to have a government and an army that will enforce this programme in its entirety.

7. The situation after the fall of Shanghai and Taiyuan is as follows:

(1) In northern China, regular warfare in which the Kuomintang played the chief role has ended, and guerrilla warfare in which the Communist Party is playing the chief role has become primary. In Kiangsu and Chekiang Provinces, the Japanese aggressors have broken through the Kuomintang's battle lines and are advancing on Nanking and the Yangtse valley. It is already dear that the Kuomintang's partial resistance cannot last long.

(2) In their own imperialist interests, the governments of Britain, the United States and France have indicated that they will help China, but so far there has been only verbal sympathy and no practical aid whatsoever.

(3) The German and Italian fascists are doing everything to assist Japanese imperialism.

(4) The Kuomintang is still unwilling to make any fundamental change in its one-party dictatorship and autocratic rule over the people, through which it is carrying on partial resistance.

This is one side of the picture. The other side is seen in the following:

(1) The political influence of the Communist Party and the Eighth Route Army is spreading fast and far, and they are being acclaimed throughout the country as "the saviours of the nation". The Communist Party and the Eighth Route Army are determined to keep up the guerrilla warfare in northern China, so as to defend the whole country, tie down the Japanese aggressors and hinder them from attacking the Central Plains and the Northwest.

(2) The mass movement has developed a step further.

(3) The national bourgeoisie is leaning towards the left.

(4) Forces favouring reforms are growing within the Kuomintang.

(5) The movement to oppose Japan and aid China is spreading among the people of the world.

(6) The Soviet Union is preparing to give practical assistance to China.

This is the other side of the picture.

8. Therefore, the present situation is one of transition from partial to total resistance. While partial resistance cannot last long, total resistance has not yet begun. The transition from one to the other, the gap in time, is fraught with danger.

9. In this period, China's partial resistance may develop in one of three directions:

The first is the ending of partial resistance and its replacement by total resistance. This is what the majority of the nation demands, but the Kuomintang is still undecided.

The second is the ending of armed resistance and its replacement by capitulation. This is what the Japanese aggressors, the collaborators and the pro-Japanese elements demand, but the majority of the Chinese people oppose it.

The third is the coexistence of armed resistance and capitulation in China. This could come about as a result of the intrigues of the Japanese aggressors, the collaborators and the pro-Japanese elements to split China's anti-Japanese front when they kind it impossible to attain the second direction. They are now engineering something of this kind. Indeed this danger is very grave.

10. Judging from the present situation, the domestic and international factors which prevent capitulationism from winning out have the upper hand. These factors include: Japan's persistence in its policy of subjugating China, which leaves China no alternative but to fight; the existence of the Communist Party and the Eighth Route Army; the wishes of the Chinese people; the wishes of the majority of the Kuomintang members; the anxiety of Britain, the United States and France lest capitulation by the Kuomintang damage their interests; the existence of the Soviet Union and

its policy of helping China; the high hopes which the Chinese people place (not without foundation) in the Soviet Union. The proper and co-ordinated use of these factors would not only frustrate capitulationism and splitting but also overcome the obstructions to any advance beyond partial resistance.

11. Therefore, the prospect of going over from partial to total resistance does exist. To strive for this prospect is the urgent common task of all Chinese Communists, all progressive members of the Kuomintang, and all the Chinese people.

12. China's anti-Japanese national revolutionary war is now confronting a grave crisis. This crisis may be prolonged, or it may be overcome fairly quickly. Internally, the decisive factors are Kuomintang-Communist co-operation and a change in Kuomintang policy on the basis of this co-operation, and the strength of the worker and peasant masses. Externally, the decisive factor is assistance from the Soviet Union.

13. Political and organizational reform of the Kuomintang is both necessary and possible.[2] The main reasons are Japanese pressure, the Chinese Communist Party's united front policy, the wishes of the Chinese people, and the growth of new forces inside the Kuomintang. Our task is to work for this reform of the Kuomintang as a basis for reforming the government and the army. This reform undoubtedly requires the consent of the Central Executive Committee of the Kuomintang, and we are only in a position to offer suggestions.

14. The government should be reformed. We have proposed the convening of a provisional national assembly, which is likewise both necessary and possible. Undoubtedly this reform also requires the consent of the Kuomintang.

15. The task of reforming the army consists in building up new armies and reforming the old armies. If a new army of '50,000 to 300,000 men imbued with a new political spirit can be built up within six to twelve months, the situation on the anti-Japanese battlefield will begin to mend. Such an army would influence all the old armies and rally them around itself. This would provide the military basis for the turn to the strategic counter-offensive in the War of Resistance. This reform likewise requires the Kuomintang's consent. The Eighth Route Army ought to have an exemplary role to play in the course of this reform. And the Eighth Route Army itself should be expanded.

II. CAPITULATIONISM MUST BE COMBATED BOTH INSIDE THE PARTY AND THROUGHOUT THE COUNTRY

INSIDE THE PARTY, OPPOSE CLASS CAPITULATIONISM

16. In 1927 Chen Tu-hsiu's capitulationism led to the failure of the revolution. No member of our Party should ever forget this historical lesson written in blood.

17. With regard to the Party's line of an anti-Japanese national united front, the main danger inside the Party before the Lukouchiao Incident was "Left" opportunism, that is, closed-doorism, the reason being chiefly that the Kuomintang had not yet begun to resist Japan.

18. Since the Lukouchiao Incident the main danger inside the Party is no longer "Left" closed-doorism but Right opportunism, that is, capitulationism, the reason being chiefly that the Kuomintang has begun to resist Japan.

19. Already in April at the Yenan meeting of Party activists, then again in May at the National Conference of the Party, and especially in August at the meeting of the Political Bureau of the Central Committee (the Lochuan meeting), we posed the following question: Will the proletariat lead the bourgeoisie in the united front, or the bourgeoisie the proletariat? Will the Kuomintang draw over the Communist Party, or the Communist Party the Kuomintang? In relation to the current specific political task this question means: Is the Kuomintang to be raised to the level of the Ten-Point Programme for Resisting Japan and Saving the Nation, to the level of the total resistance advocated by the Communist Party? Or is the Communist Party to sink to the level of the Kuomintang dictatorship of the landlords and bourgeoisie, to the level of partial resistance?

20. Why must we pose the question so sharply? The answer is:

On the one hand, we have the Chinese bourgeoisie's proneness to compromise; the Kuomintang's superiority in material strength; the declaration and the decisions of the Third Plenary Session of the Central Executive Committee of the Kuomintang, which slander and insult the Communist Party and cry out for "an end to the class struggle"; the Kuomintang's yearning for "the capitulation of the Communist Party" and its widespread propaganda to this end; Chiang Kai-shek's attempts to place the Communist Party under his control; the Kuomintang's policy of restricting and weakening the Red Army and the anti-Japanese democratic base areas; the plan concocted during the Kuomintang's Lushan Training Course [3] in July "to reduce the Communist Party's strength by two-fifths in the course of the War of Resistance"; the attempts of the Kuomintang to seduce Communist cadres with offers of fame and fortune and wine and women; the political capitulation of certain petty-bourgeois radicals (represented by Chang Nai-chi [4]); etc.

On the other hand, we have the uneven theoretical level among Communists; the fact that many of our Party members lack the experience of co-operation between the two parties gained during the Northern Expedition; the fact that a large number of Party members are of petty-bourgeois origin; the reluctance of some Party members to continue a life of bitter struggle; the tendency towards unprincipled accommodation with the Kuomintang in the united front; the emergence of a tendency towards a new type of warlordism in the Eighth Route Army; the emergence of the problem of Communist participation in the Kuomintang government; the emergence of a tendency towards excessive accommodation in the anti-Japanese democratic base areas; etc.

We must sharply pose the question of who is to lead and must resolutely combat capitulationism in view of the grave situation described above.

21. For several months now, and especially since the outbreak of the War of Resistance, the Central Committee and Party organizations at all levels have waged a clear-cut and firm struggle against capitulationist tendencies, actual or potential, have taken various necessary precautions against them and have achieved good results.

The Central Committee has issued a draft resolution [5] on the problem of Communist participation in the government.

A struggle has been started against the tendency towards new warlordism in the Eighth Route Army. This tendency is manifest in certain individuals who, since the redesignation of the Red Army, have become unwilling to submit strictly to Communist Party leadership, have developed individualistic heroism, taken pride in being given appointments by the Kuomintang (i.e., in becoming officials), and so forth. The tendency towards this new type of warlordism has the same root (the reduction of the Communist Party to the level of the Kuomintang) and the same result (the alienation of the masses) as the tendency towards the old type of warlordism, which expressed itself in beating and abusing people, violating discipline, etc.; it is particularly dangerous because it is occurring in the period of the Kuomintang-Communist united front, and it therefore calls for special attention and determined opposition. Both the system of political commissars, which was abolished because of Kuomintang intervention, and the system of political departments, which were renamed "political training offices" for the same reason, have now been restored. We have initiated and staunchly carried out the new strategic principle of "independent guerrilla warfare in the mountain regions with the initiative in our own hands", thus basically ensuring the Eighth Route Army's successes in fighting and in its other tasks. We have rejected the Kuomintang's demand that its members should be sent to the Eighth Route Army units as cadres and have upheld the principle of absolute leadership of the Eighth Route Army by the Communist Party. Similarly, we have introduced the principle of "independence and initiative within the united front"in the revolutionary anti-Japanese base areas. We have corrected the tendency towards "parliamentarism" [6] (of course not the parliamentarism of the Second International, which is absent in the Chinese Party); we have also persisted in our struggle against bandits, enemy spies and saboteurs.

In Sian we have corrected the tendency towards unprincipled accommodation in our relations with the Kuomintang and have developed the mass struggle anew.

In eastern Kansu we have on the whole done the same as in Sian.

In Shanghai we have criticized Chang Nai-chi's line of "issuing fewer calls and offering more suggestions" and begun to correct the tendency towards excessive accommodation in the work of the national salvation movement.

In the guerrilla zones in the south--these representing part of the gains of our decade of sanguinary warfare with the Kuomintang, our strategic strongholds for the anti-Japanese national revolutionary war in the southern provinces, and our forces which the Kuomintang tried to wipe out by "encirclement and suppression" even after the Sian Incident, and which it has tried to weaken by the newer method of "luring the tiger out of the mountains" even after the Lukouchiao Incident--we have taken special care (1) to guard against concentrating our forces regardless of circumstances (which would suit the Kuomintang's desire to destroy these strongholds), (2) to reject Kuomintang appointees, and (3) to be on the alert against the danger of another Ho Ming Incident [7] (i.e., the danger of being surrounded and disarmed by the Kuomintang).

Our attitude in the Liberation Weekly [8] has continued to be one of serious and fair criticism.

22. In order to persevere in armed resistance and win final victory as well as to turn partial resistance into total resistance, it is necessary to adhere to the Anti-Japanese National United Front and expand and strengthen it. No views disruptive of the Kuomintang-Communist united front will be tolerated. We must still guard against "Left" closed-doorism. But at the same time we must closely adhere to the principle of independence and initiative in all our united front work. Our united front with the Kuomintang and other parties is based on the execution of a definite programme. Without this basis there can be no united front, and in that case co-operation would become unprincipled and a manifestation of capitulationism. Thus the key to leading the anti-Japanese national revolutionary war to victory is to explain, apply and uphold the principle of "independence and initiative within the united front".

23. What is our purpose in all this? In one respect, it is to hold the ground we have already won, for this ground is our strategic point of departure and its loss would mean the end of everything. But our chief purpose is to extend the ground already won and realize the positive aim of "winning the masses in their millions for the Anti-Japanese National United Front and the overthrow of Japanese imperialism". Holding our ground and extending it are inseparably connected. In the last few months, many more left-wing members of the petty bourgeoisie have become united under our influence, the new forces in the Kuomintang camp have grown, the mass struggle in Shansi has developed, and our Party organizations have expanded in many places.

24. But we must clearly understand that generally speaking the organizational strength of our Party is still quite small in the country as a whole. The strength of the masses in the country as a whole is also very small, because the workers and peasants, the basic sections of the masses, are not yet organized. All this is due to the Kuomintang's policy of control and repression on the one hand and the inadequacy of our own work or even its complete absence on the other. This is the fundamental weakness of our Party in the present anti-Japanese national revolutionary war. Unless we overcome this weakness, Japanese imperialism cannot be defeated. To this end we must apply the principle of "independence and initiative within the united front" and overcome all tendencies towards capitulation or excessive accommodation.

IN THE COUNTRY AS A WHOLE, OPPOSE NATIONAL CAPITULATIONISM
25. The above points deal with class capitulationism. This tendency would lead the proletariat to accommodate itself to bourgeois reformism and bourgeois lack of thoroughness. Unless it is overcome, we cannot succeed

in carrying forward the anti-Japanese national revolutionary war, in turning partial resistance into total resistance and in defending the motherland.

But there is also the other kind of capitulationism, national capitulationism, which would lead China to accommodate herself to the interests of Japanese imperialism, make China a Japanese colony and turn the Chinese people into colonial slaves. This tendency has now appeared in the right wing of the Anti-Japanese National United Front.

26. The left wing of the Anti-Japanese National United Front is composed of the Communist-led masses, which include the proletariat, the peasantry and the urban petty bourgeoisie. Our task is to do our utmost to extend and consolidate this wing. The accomplishment of this task is the basic prerequisite for reforming the Kuomintang, the government and the army, for establishing a unified democratic republic, for turning partial resistance into total resistance and for overthrowing Japanese imperialism.

27. The intermediate section of the Anti-Japanese National United Front is composed of the national bourgeoisie and the upper stratum of the petty bourgeoisie. Those for whom the leading Shanghai newspapers speak are now tending towards the Left, [9] while some members of the Fu Hsing Society have begun to vacillate and some members of the C.C. Clique are also wavering. [10] The armies resisting Japan have learned severe lessons, and some have begun or are preparing to introduce reforms. Our task is to help the intermediate section to move forward and change its stand.

28. The right wing of the Anti-Japanese National United Front consists of the big landlords and big bourgeoisie, and it is the nerve centre of national capitulationism. It is inevitable that these people should tend towards capitulationism, for they fear both the destruction of their property in the war and the rise of the masses. Many of them are already collaborators, many have become or are ready to become pro-Japanese, many are vacillating, and only a few, owing to special circumstances, are firmly anti-Japanese. Some of them have joined the national united front for the time being under compulsion and with reluctance. Generally speaking, it will not be long before they split away. Indeed many of the worst elements among the big landlords and big bourgeoisie are at this very moment engineering a split in the Anti-Japanese National United Front. They are manufacturing rumours, and stories such as "the Communists are engaged in insurrection" and "the Eighth Route Army is in retreat" are sure to multiply daily. Our task is to combat national capitulationism resolutely and, in the course of this struggle, to expand and consolidate the left wing and help the intermediate section to move forward and change its stand.

THE RELATION BETWEEEN CLASS CAPITULATIONISM AND NATIONAL CAPITULATIONISM

29. Class capitulationism is actually the reserve force of national capitulationism in the anti-Japanese national revolutionary war; it is a vile tendency that lends support to the camp of the right wing and leads to defeat in the war. We must fight this tendency inside the Communist Party and the proletariat and extend the fight to all spheres of our work, in order to invigorate the struggle against national capitulationism, and in order to achieve the liberation of the Chinese nation and the emancipation of the toiling masses.

NOTES

1. This refers to the "Resolution on the Present Situation and the Tasks of the Party" adopted by the Political Bureau of the Central Committee of the Chinese Communist Party at its meeting in Lochuan, northern Shensi, on August 25, 1937. The full text reads as follows:

(1) The military provocation by the Japanese aggressors at Lukouchiao and their occupation of Peiping and Tientsin represent only the beginning of their large-scale invasion of China south of the Great Wall. They have already begun their national mobilization for war. Their propaganda that they have "no desire to aggravate the situation"is only a smokescreen for further attacks.

(2) Under the pressure of the Japanese aggressors' attacks and the Chinese people's indignation, the Nanking government is beginning to make up its mind to fight. General defence arrangements and actual resistance in some places have already started. Full-scale war between China and Japan is inevitable. The resistance at Lukouchiao on July 7 marked the starting point of China's national war of resistance.

(3) Thus a new stage has opened in China's political situation, the stage of actual resistance. The stage of preparation for resistance is over. In the present stage the central task is to mobilize all the nation's forces for victory in the War of Resistance. The winning of democracy, which was not accomplished in the previous stage because of the Kuomintang's unwillingness and the inadequate mobilization of the people, is a task that must be fulfilled in the course of the struggle for victory in the War of Resistance.

(4) Our differences and disputes with the Kuomintang and other anti-Japanese groups in this new stage are no longer about whether to wage

273

war of resistance but about how to win victory.

(5) The key to victory in the war now lies in developing the resistance that has already begun into a war of total resistance by the whole nation. Only through such a war of total resistance can final victory be won. The Ten-Point Programme for Resisting Japan and Saving the Nation now proposed by our Party spells out concretely the way to win final victory in the War of Resistance.

(6) A great danger lurks in the present state of resistance. The main reason for this danger is that the Kuomintang is still unwilling to arouse the whole people to take part in the war. Instead, it regards the war as the concern of the government alone, and at every turn fears and restricts the people's participation in the war, prevents the government and the army from forming close ties with the people, denies the people the democratic right to resist Japan and save the nation, and refuses to reform the government apparatus thoroughly and to turn the government into a national defence government of the whole nation. A war of resistance of this kind may achieve partial victories, but never final victory. On the contrary, it may end in grievous failure.

(7) The existence of serious weaknesses in the War of Resistance may lead to many setbacks, retreats, internal splits, betrayals, temporary and partial compromises and other such reverses. Therefore it should be realized that the war will be an arduous and protracted war. But we are confident that, through the efforts of our Party and the whole people, the resistance already started will sweep aside all obstacles and continue to advance and develop. We must overcome all difficulties and firmly fight for the realization of the Ten-Point Programme for victory proposed by our Party. We must firmly oppose all wrong policies which run counter to it and combat national defeatism and the pessimism and despair it engenders.

(8) Together with the people and the armed forces under the leadership of the Party, members of the Communist Party must actively take their stand in the forefront of the struggle, become the core of the nation's resistance and do their utmost to develop the anti-Japanese mass movement. They must never for a moment relax or miss a single opportunity to do propaganda among the masses and to organize and arm them. Victory in the War of Resistance Against Japan will be certain provided the masses in their millions are really organized in the national united front.

2. In the initial period of the War of Resistance, the Kuomintang and Chiang Kai-shek made a number of promises to introduce various reforms

under popular pressure, but very quickly broke them one after another. The possibility that the Kuomintang might introduce the reforms desired by the whole people was not actualized. As Comrade Mao Tse-tung said later in "On Coalition Government":

All the people, including the Communists and other democrats, earnestly hoped that the Kuomintang government would seize the opportunity, at a time when the nation was in peril and the people were filled with enthusiasm, to institute democratic reforms and put Dr. Sun Yat-sen's revolutionary Three People's Principles into practice. But their hopes came to nought. (See Selected Work of Mao Tse-tung, Eng. ed., FLP, Peking, 1965, Vol. III, p. 263.)

3. The Lushan Training Course was set up by Chiang Kai-shek at Lushan, Kiangsi Province, to train high and middle-ranking officials of the Kuomintang party and government to form the core of his reactionary regime.

4. Chang Nai-chi was then advocating "issuing fewer calls and offering more suggestions". But it would have been useless merely to submit "suggestions" to the Kuomintang, since it was following a policy of oppression. Calls had to be made directly to the masses, in order to arouse them to struggle against the Kuomintang. Otherwise, it would have been impossible to keep up the war against Japan or to resist Kuomintang reaction. Chang Nai-chi was wrong on this point, and gradually he realized his mistake.

5. This refers to the "Draft Resolution of the Central Committee of the Communist Party of China Concerning the Communist Party's Participation in the Government" which was drawn up on September 25, 1937. The full text reads as follows:

(1) The present situation in the anti-Japanese war urgently requires a united front government representing the whole nation, for only such a government can effectively lead the anti-Japanese national revolutionary war and defeat Japanese imperialism. The Communist Party is ready to participate in such a government, that is, to undertake administrative responsibilities in the government directly and officially and play an active part in it. But such a government does not yet exist. What exists today is still the government of the Kuomintang one-party dictatorship.

(2) The Communist Party of China can participate in the government only when it is changed from a one-party dictatorship of the Kuomintang into a

275

united front government of the whole nation, that is, when the present Kuomintang government (a) accepts the fundamentals of the Ten-Point Programme for Resisting Japan and Saving the Nation proposed by our Party and promulgates an administrative programme in accordance therewith; (b) begins to show by deeds the sincerity of its efforts to carry out this programme and achieves definite results; and (c) permits the legal existence of Communist Party organizations and guarantees the Communist Party freedom to mobilize, organize and educate the masses.

(3) Before the Central Committee of the Party decides to participate in the Central Government, members of the Communist Party must not as a rule participate in any local government or in any administrative councils or committees attached to the administrative organs of the government, central or local. For such participation would only obscure the distinctive features of the Communist Party, prolong the Kuomintang's dictatorship and hinder rather than help the effort to bring a unified democratic government into being.

(4) However, members of the Communist Party may participate in the local governments of certain particular regions, such as battle areas, where the old authorities find it impossible to rule as before and are on the whole willing to put the Communist Party's policies into effect, where the Communist Party is free to operate openly, and where the present emergency makes Communist participation a necessity in the opinion both of the people and of the government. Still more so in the Japanese-occupied areas, the Communist Party should come forward openly as the organizer of the anti-Japanese united front governments.

(5) Before the Communist Party officially joins the government, it is permissible in principle for Party members to participate in representative bodies, such as an all-China national assembly, for the purpose of discussing a democratic constitution and policies to save the nation. Thus, the Communist Party should strive to get its members elected to such assemblies and use them as a forum for propagating the Party's views, so as to mobilize the people and rally them round the Party and promote the establishment of a unified democratic government.

(6) Given a definite common programme and the principle of absolute equality, the Central Committee of the Communist Party or its local branches may form united front organizations with the Central Executive Committee of the Kuomintang or its local headquarters, such as various joint committees (e.g., national revolutionary leagues, committees for mass movements and committees for mobilization in the war zones), and

through such joint activities the Communist Party should achieve co-operation with the Kuomintang.

(7) With the redesignation of the Red Army as part of the National Revolutionary Army and the change of the organ of Red political power into the Government of the Special Region, their representatives may, by virtue of the legal status they have acquired, join all the military and mass organizations which further the resistance to Japan and the salvation of the nation.

(8) It is most essential to maintain absolutely independent Communist Party leadership in what was originally the Red Army and in all the guerrilla units, and Communists must not show any vacillation on this matter of principle.

6."Parliamentarism" here refers to the proposal of some Party comrades that the system of political power in the revolutionary base areas, the system of people's representative conferences, should be changed into the bourgeois parliamentary system.

7. The Ho Ming Incident took place after the outbreak of the anti-Japanese war. In October 1934, when the Central Red Army moved northward, Red Army guerrilla units stayed behind and maintained guerrilla warfare in extremely difficult circumstances in fourteen areas in the eight southern provinces of Kiangsi, Fukien, Kwangtung, Hunan, Hupeh, Honan, Chekiang and Anhwei. When the anti-Japanese war began, these units, acting on instructions from the Central Committee of the Chinese Communist Party, entered into negotiations with the Kuomintang for the cessation of civil war and organized themselves into a single army (namely, the New Fourth Army which later stubbornly fought the Japanese on the southern and northern banks of the Yangtse River) and moved to the front to resist Japan. But Chiang Kai-shek plotted to exploit these negotiations for the purpose of wiping out the guerrilla units. Ho Ming was one of the guerrilla leaders in the Fukien-Kwangtung border area which was one of the fourteen guerrilla areas. He was not on the alert against Chiang Kai-shek's plot, with the result that more than one thousand of the guerrillas under his command were surrounded and disarmed by the Kuomintang forces after they assembled.

8. Founded in Yenan in 1937, the Liberation Weekly was the organ of the Central Committee of the Communist Party of China. It was superseded by the Liberation Daily in 1941.

9. They were that section of the national bourgeoisie for whom newspapers like the Shanghai Shen Pao served as a vehicle.

10. The Pu Hsing Society and the C.C. Clique, two fascist organizations within the Kuomintang, were headed by Chiang Kai-shek and Chen Li-fu respectively. They served the oligarchic interests of the big landlords and the big bourgeoisie. But many petty-bourgeois elements had joined them under compulsion or had been duped into joining. The text refers to the section of the Fu Hsing Society consisting mainly of lower and middle-ranking officers in the Kuomintang army and to the section of the C.C. Clique consisting mainly of members not in power.

DIALECTICAL MATERIALISM

April - June, 1938

[This text includes about two thirds of the first chapter, and about one fifth of the first six sections of the second chapter of Mao's 'Pien-Cheng-fa wei--wu-lun (chiang-shou t'i-kang)' ('Dialectical materialism-notes of lectures'), as published in K'ang-chan ta-hsueh, nos. 6 to 8, April to June 1938.]

CHAPTER I

IDEALISM AND MATERIALISM

1. THE STRUGGLE BETWEEN TWO ARMIES IN PHILOSOPHY

The whole history of philosophy is the history of the struggle and the development of two mutually opposed schools of philosophy -- idealism and materialism. All philosophical currents and schools are manifestations of these two fundamental schools.

All philosophical theories have been created by men belonging to a definite social class. The ideas of these men have moreover been historically determined by a definite social existence. All philosophical doctrines express the needs of a definite social class and reflect the level of development of the productive forces of society and the historical stage in men's comprehension of nature . . .

Phil. Division emanates from Class Antagonism

The social origins of idealism and materialism lie in a social structure marked by class contradictions. The earliest appearance of idealism was the product of the ignorance and superstition of savage and primitive man. Then, with the development of the productive forces, and the ensuing development of scientific knowledge, it stands to reason that idealism should decline and be replaced by materialism. And yet, from ancient times to the present, idealism not only has not declined, but, on the contrary has developed and carried on a struggle for supremacy with materialism from which neither has emerged the victor. The reason lies in the division of society into classes. On the one hand, in its own interest, the oppressing class must develop and reinforce its idealist doctrines. On the other hand, the oppressed classes, likewise in their own interest, must develop and reinforce their materialist doctrines. Both idealism and materialism are weapons in the class struggle, and the struggle between idealism and materialism cannot disappear so long as classes continue to exist. Idealism, in the process of its historical development, represents the ideology of the exploiting classes and serves reactionary purposes. Materialism, on the other hand, is the world view of the revolutionary class; in a class society, it grows and develops in the midst of an incessant struggle against the reactionary philosophy of idealism. Consequently, the history of the struggle between idealism and materialism in philosophy reflects the struggle of interests between the reactionary class and the revolutionary class.... A given philosophical tendency is in the last analysis a manifestation in a particular guise of the policy of the social class to which the philosophers belong.

The distinguishing characteristic of Marxist philosophy -- i.e., dialectical materialism -- is its effort to explain clearly the class nature of all social consciousness (including philosophy). It publicly declares a resolute struggle between its own proletarian nature and the idealist philosophy of the propertied class. Moreover, it subordinates its own special and independent tasks to such general tasks as overthrowing capitalism, organizing and building a proletarian dictatorship, and edifying a socialist society.

2. THE DIFFERENCE BETWEEN IDEALISM AND MATERIALISM.

[handwritten: Spirit v. Matter]

Wherein lies the basic difference between idealism and materialism? It lies in the opposite answers given by the two to the fundamental question in philosophy, that of the relationship between spirit and matter (that of the relationship between consciousness and existence). Idealism considers spirit (consciousness, concepts, the subject) as the source of all that exists on earth, and matter (nature and society, the object) as secondary and subordinate, Materialism recognizes the independent existence of matter as detached from spirit and considers spirit as secondary and subordinate..

3. THE SOURCE OF THE GROWTH AND THE DEVELOPMENT OF IDEALISM.

Idealism see matter as the product of the spirit. This is turning the real world upside down. Where is the source of the growth and the development of such a philosophy?

[handwritten: Idealism from Ignorance of Primitives]

As mentioned above, the earliest manifestation of idealism was brought about by the superstition and ignorance of primitive, savage man. But with the development of production, the separation between manual labour and intellectual labour was responsible for ranking idealism first among currents of philosophical thought. With the development of the productive forces of society, the division of labour made its appearance; the further development of the division of labour saw the emergence of persons devoting themselves entirely and exclusively to intellectual labour. But when the productive forces are still weak, the division between the two does not reach the stage of complete separation. Only after classes and private property appear and exploitation becomes the foundation of the existence of the ruling class do great changes occur. Intellectual labour then becomes the exclusive privilege of the ruling class. while manual labour becomes the fate of the oppressed classes. The ruling class begins to examine the relationship between themselves and the oppressed classes in an upside-down fashion: It is not the labourers who furnish them with means for existence, but rather they who supply the labourers with these means. Hence, they despise manual labour and develop idealist conceptions. To eliminate the distinction between manual labour and intellectual labour is one of the preconditions for eliminating idealist philosophy.

[handwritten: Distinction between Mental & Manual must be obliterated]

The social root that makes possible the development of idealist philosophy lies principally in the fact that this kind of philosophical consciousness is the manifestation of the interests of the exploiting class ... The final decline of idealism will come with the elimination of classes, after the establishment of a communist society.

[handwritten: No Classes No Idealism]

The source that enables idealism to develop and deepen and gives it the strength to struggle with materialism must be sought in the process of human knowing.. When men think, they must use concepts. This can easily cause our knowledge to be split into two aspects: reality, which is of an individual and particular character; and concepts, which are of a general character... In the nature of things, the particular and the general are inseparably linked; once separated, they depart from objective truth... To separate the general from the particular, and to view the general as objective reality and the particular merely as the form in which the general exists— this is the method adopted by all idealists. All idealists put consciousness, spirit, or concepts in place of objective reality existing independently from human consciousness... They cannot point out the materialist truth according to which consciousness is limited by matter, but believe that only consciousness is active, whereas matter is only an inert composite entity. Urged on moreover by their own class nature, the idealists then use every method to exaggerate the activity of consciousness, developing this aspect unilaterally... Idealism in economics exaggerates beyond measure a nonessential aspect of exchange,, raising the law of supply and demand to the status of the fundamental law of capitalism... Idealist historians regard heroes as the makers of history. Idealist politicians regard politics as omnipotent. Idealist military leaders practice the methods of desperate combat [p'ing-ming-chu-i-ti tso-chan]. Idealist revolutionaries advocate Blanquism. The diehards say that the only way to revive our nation is to restore the old morality. All this results from exaggerating subjective factors beyond measure...

Pre-Marxist materialism (mechanistic materialism) did not stress the thought process in the development of knowledge, but regarded thought merely as the object of action, as the mirror that reflects nature... Only dialectical materialism correctly shows the active role of thought, and at the same time points out the limitation imposed upon thought by matter. It points out that thought arises from social practice and at the same time actively shapes practice. Only this kind of dialectical theory of the unity of knowledge and action can thoroughly vanquish idealism.

Thought is Active, but limited by Matter;

4. THE ORIGIN OF THE INCEPTION AND THE DEVELOPMENT OF MATERIALISM

The recognition that matter exists independently and apart from consciousness in the external world is the foundation of materialism. Man created this foundation through practice... Obliged to submit to natural forces, and capable of using only simple tools, primitive man could not explain the surrounding phenomena and hence sought help from spirits. This is the origin of religion and idealism. But in the long-range process of production, man came into contact with surrounding nature, acted upon nature, changed nature, and created things to eat, to live in, and to use, and adapted nature to the interests of man and caused man to believe that matter has an objective existence. *Via Knowledge production*

In the social existence of humanity, reciprocal relationships and influences arise between individuals. In a class society there is moreover a class struggle. The oppressed class considers the circumstances and estimates its strength, and then makes its plans. When they succeed in the struggle, the members of this class are convinced that their views are not the product of fantasy, but the reflection of the objectively existing material world. Because the oppressed class fails when it adopts the wrong plans and succeeds by correcting its plans it learns to understand that it can achieve its purpose only when its subjective plans rest upon the accurate understanding of the material nature of the objective world and the fact that the objective world is governed by laws. The history of science furnishes man with proof of the material nature of the world and of the fact that it is governed by laws and helps man to see the futility of the illusions of religion and idealism and to arrive at materialist conclusions. In sum, the history of man's practice comprises the history of his struggle with nature, the history of the class struggle, the history of science. Owing to the necessity to live and struggle, men have thought about the reality of matter and its laws, have proved the correctness of materialism, and have found the necessary intellectual tool for their struggle— materialist philosophy. The higher the level to which social production develops, the greater the development of the class struggle, and the more scientific knowledge reveals the 'secretes' of nature, the greater the development and consolidation of materialist philosophy. Thus man can be delivered gradually from the dual and crushing oppression of nature and society. .

CHAPTER II

DIALECTICAL MATERIALISM

1. DIALECTICAL MATERIALISM IS THE REVOLUTIONARY ARM OF THE PROLETARIAT

The Chinese proletariat, having assumed at the present time the historical task of the bourgeois-democratic revolution, must make use of dialectical materialism as its mental-arm... The study of dialectical materialism is even more indispensable for the cadres who lead the revolutionary movement, because the two erroneous theories and methods of work of subjectivism and mechanism frequently subsist among the cadres, and as a result frequently cause the cadres to go against Marxism, and lead the revolutionary movement on to the wrong path. If we wish to avoid or correct such deficiencies, the only solution lies in conscious study and understanding of dialectical materialism, in order to arm one's brain anew.

2. THE RELATION BETWEEN THE OLD PHILOSOPHICAL HERITAGE AND DIALECTICAL MATERIALISM

After the May 4th Movement of 1919, as a consequence of the conscious appearance of the Chinese proletariat on the political stage, and the rise in the scientific level of the country, a Marxist philosophical movement arose and developed in China. In its first period, however, the level of understanding of materialist dialectics within the materialist current of thought was rather weak, and mechanistic materialism influenced by the bourgeoisie, as well as the subjectivism of Deborin, were its principal components. Following the defeat of the revolution in 1927 the level of understanding of Marxism and Leninism progressed, and the thinking of materialist dialectics gradually developed. Just recently, because of the severity of the national and social crisis, and also because of the influence of the movement for liquidating deviations in Soviet philosophy, a broad movement of materialist dialectics has developed in China's intellectual circles.

Because of the backwardness of China's social development the dialectical materialist philosophical currents developing in China today do not result from taking over and reforming our own philosophical heritage, but from the study of Marxism-Leninism. However, if we wish to ensure that dialectical materialist thought shall penetrate profoundly in China and continue to develop, and shall moreover give firm direction to the Chinese revolution and lead it to final victory in the future, then we must struggle with all the old and rotten philosophical theories existing in China on the ideological front throughout the whole country, raise the flag of criticism and in this way liquidate the philosophical heritage of ancient China. Only thus we can attain our goal.

3. THE UNITY OF WORLD VIEW AND METHODOLOGY IN DIALECTICAL MATERIALISM

Dialectical materialism is the world view of the proletariat. At the same time it is the method of the proletariat for taking cognizance of the surrounding world, and the method of revolutionary action of the proletariat. It is the unity of world view and methodology....

4. THE QUESTION OF THE OBJECT OF MATERIALIST DIALECTICS -- WHAT DO MATERIALIST DIALECTICS SERVE TO STUDY?

Marx, Engels and Lenin all explained materialist dialectics as the theory of development...

Under the heading of the object of philosophy we must still solve another problem, namely the problem of the unity of dialectics, logic and epistemology. . .

Materialist dialectics is the only scientific epistemology, and it is also the only scientific logic. Materialist dialectics studies the origin and development of our knowledge of the outside world. It studies the transition from not knowing to knowing and from incomplete knowledge to more complete knowledge; it studies how the laws of the development of nature and society are daily reflected more profoundly and more extensively in the mind of humanity. This is precisely the unity of materialist dialectics with epistemology...

The essence of the concept of development consists in regarding laws as the reflection in and transplanting to our minds (moreover further elaborated in our minds) of the manifestations of the movement of matter...

Only by using materialism to arrive at a solution of the problem of the relations between existence and thought, only by taking one's stand on the theory of the reflection, can one arrive at a thorough solution to the problems of dialectics, logic and epistemology....

5. ON MATTER
The very first condition for belonging to the materialist camp consists in recognizing the independent existence of the material world, separate from human consciousness -- the fact that it existed before the appearance of humanity, and continues to exist since the appearance of humanity, independently and outside of human consciousness. To recognize this point is a fundamental premise of all scientific research.

How shall we demonstrate this? The proofs are extremely numerous. Humanity is constantly in contact with the external world and must, moreover, struggle fiercely against the pressure and resistance of the outside world (nature and society). Moreover, we not only must, but can overcome this pressure and resistance. All of these real circumstances of the social practice of humanity, as manifested in the historical development of human society, are the best proof [of the existence of the material world]. China does not doubt the objective existence of Japanese imperialism which has invaded our country, nor of the Chinese people themselves. The students of the Anti-Japanese Military-Political University also do not doubt the objective existence of this university and of the students themselves...

If we consider this thing known as consciousness in the light of thoroughgoing materialism (that is to say in the light of materialist-dialectics), then what we call consciousness is nothing else but a form of the movement of matter, a particular characteristic of the material brain of humanity; it is that particular characteristic of the material brain which causes the material processes outside consciousness to be reflected in consciousness. From this we see that when we distinguish matter from consciousness and when, moreover we oppose them one to another, this is only conditional that is to say, it has meaning only from the standpoint of epistemology.. ... ...

In a word, matter is everything in the universe. 'All power belongs to Ssu-Ma- I.' We say, 'All power belongs to matter.' This is the source of the unity of the world.

6. ON MOVEMENT (ON DEVELOPMENT)

The first fundamental principle of dialectical materialism lies in its view of matter... This principle of the unity of the world has already been explained above in discussing matter.

The second fundamental principle of dialectical materialism lies in its theory of movement (or theory of development). This means the recognition that movement is the form of the existence of matter, an inherent attribute of matter, a manifestation of the multiplicity of matter. This is the principle of the development of the world. The combination of the principle of the development of the world with the principle of the unity of the world, set forth above, constitutes the whole of the world view of dialectical materialism. The world is nothing else but the material world in a process of unlimited development...

Dialectical materialism's theory of movement is in opposition first of all with philosophical idealism and with the theological concepts of religion. The fundamental nature of all philosophical idealism and religious theology derives from their denial of the unity and material nature of the world; and in imagining that the movement and development of the world takes place apart from matter, or took place at least in the beginning apart from matter, and is the result of the action of spirit, God, or divine forces, The German idealist philosopher, Hegel, held that the present world results from the development of the so-called 'world idea'. In China the philosophy of the Book of Changes, and the metaphysics of the Sung and Ming, all put forward idealist views of the development of the universe. Christianity says that God created the world, Buddhism and all of China's various fetishist religions attribute the movement and development of all the myriad phenomena (Wan Wu) of the universe to spiritual forces. All of these doctrines which think about movement apart from matter are fundamentally incompatible with dialectical materialism...

Dialectical materialism... considers that rest or equilibrium are merely one element of movement, that they are merely one particular circumstance of movement... A sentence popular with the metaphysical thinkers of ancient China, 'Heaven does not change and the Way also does not change,' corresponds to... a theory of the immobility of the universe. . . In their view, the basic nature of the universe and of society was eternally unchanging. The reason why they adopted this attitude is to be found primarily in their class limitations. If the feudal landlord class had recognized that the basic nature of the universe and of society is subject to movement and development, then most certainly they would have been pronouncing in theory a death sentence on their own class. The philosophies of all reactionary forces are theories of immobilism. Revolutionary classes and the popular masses have all perceived the principle of the development of the world, and consequently advocate transforming society and the world; their philosophy is dialectical materialism..

The causes of the transformation of matter is to be found not without, but within. It is not because of the impulsion of external mechanical forces, but because of the existence within the matter in question of two components different in their nature and mutually contradictory which struggle with one another, thus giving an impetus to the movement and development of the matter. As a result of the discovery of the laws of such movement and transformation, dialectical materialism is capable of enlarging the principle of the material unity of the world, extending it to the history of nature and society. Thus, not only it is possible to investigate the world considered as matter in perpetual movement, but the world can also be investigated as matter endlessly in movement from a lower form to a higher form. That is to say, it is possible to investigate the world as development and process.

Dialectical materialism investigate the development of the world as a progressive movement from the inorganic to the organic, and from thence to the highest form of the movement of matter (society).

What we have just discussed is the theory of the movement of the world, or the principle of the development of the world in accordance with dialectical materialism. This doctrine is the essence of Marxist philosophy. If the proletariat and all revolutionaries take up this consistently scientific arm, they will then be able to understand this world, and transform the world.

PROCLAMATION BY THE GOVERNMENT OF THE SHENSI-KANSU-NINGSIA BORDER REGION AND THE REAR HEADQUARTERS OF THE EIGHTH ROUTE ARMY

May 15, 1938

[This proclamation was written by Comrade Mao Tse-tung for the Government of the Shensi-Kansu-Ningsia Border Region and the Rear Headquarters of the Eighth Route Army with a view to countering disruptive activities by the Chiang Kai-shek clique. Shortly after the establishment of Kuomintang-Communist cooperation, the Chiang Kai-shek clique began to plot disruption against the revolutionary forces under Communist leadership. The disruption of the Shensi-Kansu-Ningsia Border Region was part of their plot. Comrade Mao Tse-tung maintained that a firm stand was necessary to defend the interests of the revolution. The proclamation dealt a blow at the opportunist stand of some Party members in the anti-Japanese united front with regard to the intrigues of the Chiang clique.]

Be it hereby proclaimed: Ever since the Lukouchiao Incident, all our patriotic countrymen have been firmly waging the War of Resistance. Officers and men at the front are shedding their blood and sacrificing their lives. All political parties and groups have united in good faith. All sections of the people have joined forces to save the nation. This points to a bright future for the Chinese nation and affords a firm guarantee for victory over Japan. All our fellow-countrymen must continue along this line of advance. The army and the people of out Shensi-Kansu-Ningsia Border Region [1] have followed the Government's leadership and devoted their efforts to the cause of national salvation. Whatever they have done has been just and honourable. Under bitter hardships, they have struggled on tirelessly and uncomplainingly. The people throughout the country are unanimous in praising them. For their part the Border Region Government and the Rear Headquarters will encourage the people of the whole region to continue their efforts to the very end. Nobody will be allowed to neglect his duty and nothing will be allowed to undermine the cause of national salvation. However, recent investigations in the Border Region have disclosed that, disregarding the public interest, some persons are using various means to force the peasants to return land and houses that have been distributed to them, to compel debtors to pay back old cancelled loans, [2] to coerce the people into changing the democratic system that has been built up, or to disrupt the military, economic, cultural and mass organizations that have been established. Some of them are even acting as spies, conspiring with bandits, inciting our soldiers to mutiny, making surveys and maps of our region, secretly collecting information, or openly spreading propaganda against the Border Region Government. Clearly, all these activities are violations of the basic principle of unity for resistance to Japan, run counter to the will of the people of the Border Region, and are intended to foment internal dissension, disrupt the united front, damage the people's interests, undermine the prestige of the Border Region Government and increase the difficulties of mobilization against Japan. The reason is that a handful of die-herds are behaving unscrupulously to the detriment of the national interest. Some are even serving as tools of the Japanese aggressors, using various guises to camouflage their conspiratorial activities. For several months, reports demanding our daily attention have been steadily pouring in from people in the counties requesting us to put a stop to such activities. With a view to strengthening the anti-Japanese forces, consolidating the rear against Japan, and safeguarding the interests of the people, the Government and the Rear Headquarters find it imperative to proscribe the above-mentioned activities. Accordingly, we hereby unequivocally proclaim:

(1) The Government and the Rear Headquarters, in order to protect the rights already secured by the people, forbid any unauthorized change in the distribution of land or houses and in the cancellation of debts made within the areas under the jurisdiction of the Border Region Government before internal peace was established.

(2) The Government and the Rear Headquarters will protect the activities of all the military, political, economic, cultural and mass organizations which were in existence when internal peace was established and which have since advanced and expanded in accordance with the principle of the united front, will promote their progress, and stop all intrigues and disruptive activities against them.

(3) The Government and the Rear Headquarters, resolutely carrying out the Programme of Armed Resistance and National Reconstruction' will gladly initiate and promote any undertaking that serves the cause of resistance to Japan and national salvation. We welcome sincere assistance from people in every quarter. But to guard against impostors and keep out traitors, we prohibit any person, whatever his activities, from entering and staying in the Border Region unless he secures permission and written authorization from the Government and the Rear Headquarters.

(4) In this tense period of armed resistance, it is right and proper for the people to report any person who tries to sabotage, engage in disruption, stir up sedition or ferret out military secrets within the boundaries of the Border Region. Upon valid evidence, persons so charged may be arrested on the spot. If convicted, offenders will be punished with due severity.

These four regulations must be observed by all members of the armed forces and all civilians throughout the Border Region, and no violation whatsoever will be permitted. Henceforward, should any lawless person dare to plot disruption, the Border Region Government and the Rear Headquarters will enforce these regulations to the letter and will accept no plea of ignorance.

This proclamation is hereby issued with the full force of the law.

NOTES

1. The Shensi-Kansu-Ningsia Border Region was the revolutionary base area which was gradually built up after 1931 through revolutionary guerrilla war in northern Shensi. When the Central Red Army arrived in northern Shensi after the Long March, it became the central base area of the revolution and the seat of the Central Committee of the Chinese Communist Party. It was named the Shensi-Kansu-Ningsia Border Region after the formation of the Anti-Japanese National United Front in 1937, and it included twenty-three counties along the common borders of the three provinces.

2. By 1936 most places in the Border Region had carried out the policy of confiscating the land of the landlords and distributing it among the peasants and cancelling the old debts of the peasants. After 1936, in order to facilitate the formation of a broad anti-Japanese national united front, the Chinese Communist Party changed its policy for the country as a whole to one of reduction of rent and interest; at the same time, however, it resolutely protected the gains already secured by the peasants in the land reform.

PROBLEMS OF STRATEGY IN GUERRILLA WAR AGAINST JAPAN

May 1938

[In the early days of the War of Resistance Against Japan, many people inside and outside the Party belittled the important strategic role of guerrilla warfare and pinned their hopes on regular warfare alone, and particularly on the operations of the Kuomintang forces. Comrade Mao Tse-tung refuted this view and wrote this article to show the correct road of development for anti-Japanese guerrilla warfare. As a result, the Eighth Route Army and the New Fourth Army, which had just over 40,000 men when the War of Resistance began in 1937, grew to a great army of one million by the time Japan surrendered in 1945, established many revolutionary base areas, played a great part in the war and thus, throughout this period, made Chiang Kai-shek afraid to capitulate to Japan or launch a nation-wide civil war. In 1946, when Chiang Kai-shek did launch a nation-wide civil war, the People's Liberation Army, formed out of the Eighth Route and New Fourth Armies, was strong enough to deal with his attacks.]

CHAPTER I
WHY RAISE THE QUESTION OF STRATEGY IN GUERRILLA WAR?
In the War of Resistance Against Japan, regular warfare is primary and guerrilla warfare supplementary. This point has already been correctly settled. Thus, it seems there are only tactical problems in guerrilla warfare. Why then raise the question of strategy?

If China were a small country in which the role of guerrilla warfare was only to render direct support over short distances to the campaigns of the regular army, there would, of course, be only tactical problems but no strategic ones. On the other hand, if China were a country as strong as the Soviet Union and the invading enemy could either be quickly expelled, or, even though his expulsion were to take some time, he could not occupy extensive areas, then again guerrilla warfare would simply play a supporting role in campaigns, and would naturally involve only tactical but not strategic problems.

The question of strategy in guerrilla war does arise, however, in the case of China, which is neither small nor like the Soviet Union, but which is both a large and a weak country. This large and weak country is being attacked by a small and strong country, but the large and weak country is in an era of progress; this is the source of the whole problem. It is in these circumstances that vast areas have come under enemy occupation and that the war has become a protracted one. The enemy is occupying vast areas of this large country of ours, but Japan is a small country, she does not have sufficient soldiers and has to leave many gaps in the occupied areas, so that our anti-Japanese guerrilla warfare consists primarily not in interior-line operations in support of the campaigns of the regular troops but in independent operations on exterior lines; furthermore, China is progressive, that is to say, she has a staunch army and broad masses of people, both led by the Communist Party, so that, far from being small-scale, our anti-Japanese guerrilla warfare is in fact large-scale warfare. Hence the emergence of a whole series of problems, such as the strategic defensive, the strategic offensive, etc. The protracted nature of the war and its attendant ruthlessness have made it imperative for guerrilla warfare to undertake many unusual tasks; hence such problems as those of the base areas, the development of guerrilla warfare into mobile warfare, and so on. For all these reasons, China's guerrilla warfare against Japan has broken out of the bounds of tactics to knock at the gates of strategy, and it demands examination from the viewpoint of strategy. The point that merits our particular attention is that such extensive as well as protracted guerrilla warfare is quite new in the entire history of war. This is bound up with the fact that we are now in the Nineteen Thirties and Nineteen Forties and that we now have the Communist Party and the Red Army. Herein lies the heart of the matter. Our enemy is probably still cherishing fond dreams of emulating the Mongol conquest of the Sung Dynasty, the Manchu conquest of the Ming Dynasty, the British occupation of North America and India, the Latin occupation of Central and South America, etc. But such dreams have no practical value in present-day China because there are certain factors present in the China of today which were absent in those historical instances, and one of them is guerrilla warfare, which is quite a new phenomenon. If our enemy overlooks this fact, he will certainly come to grief.

These are the reasons why our anti-Japanese guerrilla warfare, though occupying only a supplementary place in the War of Resistance as a whole, must nevertheless be examined from the viewpoint of strategy.

Why not, then, apply to guerrilla warfare the general strategic principles of the War of Resistance?

The question of strategy in our anti-Japanese guerrilla warfare is indeed closely linked with the question of strategy in the War of Resistance as a whole, because they have much in common. On the other hand, guerrilla warfare is different from regular warfare and has its own peculiarities, and consequently many peculiar elements are involved in the question of strategy in guerrilla warfare. Without modification it is impossible to apply the strategic principles of the War of Resistance in general to guerrilla warfare with its own peculiarities.

CHAPTER II
THE BASIC PRINCIPLE OF WAR IS TO PRESERVE ONESELF AND DESTROY THE ENEMY

Before discussing the question of strategy in guerrilla warfare in concrete terms, a few words are needed on the fundamental problem of war.

All the guiding principles of military operations grow out of the one basic principle: to strive to the utmost to preserve one's own strength and destroy that of the enemy. In a revolutionary war, this principle is directly linked with basic political principles. For instance, the basic political principle of China's War of Resistance Against Japan, i.e., its political aim, is to drive out Japanese imperialism and build an independent, free and happy new China. In terms of military action this principle means the use of armed force to defend our motherland and to drive out the Japanese invaders. To attain this end, the operations of the armed units take the form of doing their utmost to preserve their own strength on the one hand and destroy the enemies on the other. How then do we justify the encouragement of heroic sacrifice in war? Every war exacts a price, sometimes an extremely high one. Is this not in contradiction with "preserving oneself"? In fact, these is no contradiction at all; to put it more exactly; sacrifice and self-preservation are both opposite and complementary to each other. For such sacrifice is essential not only for destroying the enemy but also for preserving oneself--partial and temporary "non-preservation" (sacrifice, or paying the price) is necessary for the sake of general and permanent preservation. From this basic principle stems the series of principles guiding military operations, all of which--from the principles of shooting (taking cover to preserve oneself, and making full use of fire-power to destroy the enemy) to the principles of strategy--are permeated with the spirit of this basic principle. All technical, tactical and strategic principles represent applications of this basic principle. The principle of preserving oneself and destroying the enemy is the basis of all military principles.

CHAPTER III
SIX SPECIFIC PROBLEMS OF STRATEGY IN GUERRILLA WAR AGAINST JAPAN

Now let us see what policies or principles have to be adopted in guerrilla operations against Japan before we can attain the object of preserving ourselves and destroying the enemy. Since the guerrilla units in the War of Resistance (and in all other revolutionary wars) generally grow out of nothing and expand from a small to a large force, they must preserve themselves and, moreover, they must expand. Hence the question is, what policies or principles have to be adopted before we can attain the object of preserving and expanding ourselves and destroying the enemy?

Generally speaking, the main principles are as follows: (1) the use of initiative, flexibility and planning in conducting offensives within the defensive, battles of quick decision within protracted war, and exterior-line operations within interior-line operations; (2) co-ordination with regular warfare; (3) establishment of base areas; (4) the strategic defensive and the strategic offensive; (5) the development of guerrilla warfare into mobile warfare; and (6) correct relationship of command. These six items constitute the whole of the strategic programme for guerrilla war against Japan and are the means necessary for the preservation and expansion of our forces, for the destruction and expulsion of the enemy, for co-ordination with regular warfare and the winning of final victory.

CHAPTER IV
INITIATIVE, FLEXIBILITY AND PLANNING IN CONDUCTING OFFENSIVES WITHIN THE DEFENSIVE, BATTLES OF QUICK DECISION WITHIN PROTRACTED WAR, AND EXTERIOR-LINE OPERATIONS WITHIN INTERIOR-LINE OPERATIONS
Here the subject may be dealt with under four headings: (1) the relationship between the defensive and the offensive, between protractedness and quick decision, and between the interior and exterior lines; (2) the initiative in all operations; (3) flexible employment of forces; and (4) planning in all operations.

To start with the first.

If we take the War of Resistance as a whole, the fact that Japan is a strong country and is attacking while China is a weak country and is defending herself makes our war strategically a defensive and protracted war. As far as the operational lines are concerned, the Japanese are operating on exterior and we on interior lines. This is one aspect of the situation. But there is another aspect which is just the reverse. The enemy forces, though strong (in arms, in certain qualities of their men, and certain other factors), are numerically small, whereas our forces, though weak (likewise, in arms, in certain qualities of our men, and certain other factors), are numerically very large. Added to the fact that the enemy is an alien nation invading our country while we are resisting his invasion on our own soil, this determines the following strategy. It is possible and necessary to use tactical offensives within the strategic defensive, to fight campaigns and battles of quick decision within a strategically protracted war and to fight campaigns and battles on exterior lines within strategically interior lines. Such is the strategy to be adopted in the War of Resistance as a whole. It holds true both for regular and for guerrilla warfare. Guerrilla warfare is different only in degree and form. Offensives in guerrilla warfare generally take the form of surprise attacks. Although surprise attacks can and should be employed in regular warfare too, the degree of surprise is less. In guerrilla warfare, the need to bring operations to a quick decision is very great, and our exterior-line ring of encirclement of the enemy in campaigns and battles is very small. All these distinguish it from regular warfare.

Thus it can be seen that in their operations guerrilla units have to concentrate the maximum forces, act secretly and swiftly, attack the enemy by surprise and bring battles to a quick decision, and that they must strictly avoid passive defence, procrastination and the dispersal of forces before engagements. Of course, guerrilla warfare includes not only the strategic but also the tactical defensive. The latter embraces, among other things, containing and outpost actions during battles; the disposition of forces for resistance at narrow passes, strategic points, rivers or villages in order to deplete and exhaust the enemy; and action to cover withdrawal. But the basic principle of guerrilla warfare must be the offensive, and guerrilla warfare is more offensive in its character than regular warfare. The offensive, moreover, must take the form of surprise attacks, and to expose ourselves by ostentatiously parading our forces is even less permissible in guerrilla warfare than in regular warfare. From the fact that the enemy is strong and we are weak it necessarily follows that, in guerrilla operations in general even more than in regular warfare, battles must be decided quickly, though on some occasions guerrilla fighting may be kept up for several days, as in an assault on a small and isolated enemy force cut off from help. Because of its dispersed character, guerrilla warfare can spread everywhere, and in many of its tasks, as in harassing, containing and disrupting the enemy and in mass work, its principle is dispersal of forces; but a guerrilla unit, or a guerrilla formation, must concentrate its main forces when it is engaged in destroying the enemy, and especially when it is striving to smash an enemy attack. "Concentrate a big force to strike at a small section of the enemy force" remains a principle of field operations in guerrilla warfare.

Thus it can also be seen that, if we take the War of Resistance as a whole, we can attain the aim of our strategic defensive and finally defeat Japanese imperialism only through the cumulative effect of many offensive campaigns and battles in both regular and guerrilla warfare, namely, through the cumulative effect of many victories in offensive actions. Only through the cumulative effect of many campaigns and battles of quick decision, namely, the cumulative effect of many victories achieved through quick decision in offensive campaigns and battles, can we attain our goal of strategic protractedness, which means gaining time to increase our capacity to resist while hastening or awaiting changes in the international situation and the internal collapse of the enemy, in order to be able to launch a strategic counter-offensive and drive the Japanese invaders out of China. We must concentrate superior forces and fight exterior-line operations in every campaign or battle, whether in the stage of strategic defensive or in that of strategic counter-offensive, in order to encircle and destroy the enemy forces, encircling part if not all of them, destroying part if not all of the forces we have encircled, and inflicting heavy casualties on the encircled forces if we cannot capture them in large numbers. Only through the cumulative effect of many such battles of annihilation can we change the relative position as between the enemy and ourselves, thoroughly smash his strategic encirclement--that is, his scheme of exterior-line operations--and finally, in co-ordination, with international forces and the revolutionary struggles of the Japanese people, surround the Japanese imperialists and deal them the coup de grace. These results are to be achieved mainly through regular warfare, with guerrilla warfare making a secondary contribution. What is common to both, however, is the accumulation of many minor victories to make a major victory. Herein lies the great strategic role of guerrilla warfare in the War of Resistance.

Now let us discuss initiative, flexibility and planning in guerrilla warfare.

What is initiative in guerrilla warfare?

In any war, the opponents contend for the initiative, whether on a battlefield, in a battle area, in a war zone or in the whole war, for the initiative means freedom of action for an army. Any army which, losing the initiative, is forced into a passive position and ceases to have freedom of action, faces the danger of defeat or extermination. Naturally, gaining the initiative is harder in strategic defensive and interior-line operations and easier in offensive exterior-line operations. However, Japanese imperialism has two basic weaknesses, namely, its shortage of troops and the fact that it is fighting on foreign soil. Moreover, its underestimation of China's strength and the internal contradictions among the Japanese militarists have given rise to many mistakes in command, such as piecemeal reinforcement, lack of strategic coordination, occasional absence of a main direction for attack, failure to grasp opportunities in some operations and failure to wipe out encircled forces, all of which may be considered the third weakness of Japanese imperialism. Thus, despite the advantage of being on the offensive and operating on exterior lines, the Japanese militarists are gradually losing the initiative, because of their shortage of troops (their small territory, small population, inadequate resources, feudalistic imperialism, etc.), because of the fact that they are fighting on foreign soil (their war is imperialist and barbarous) and because of their stupidities in command. Japan is neither willing nor able to conclude the war at present, nor has her strategic offensive yet come to an end, but, as the general trend shows, her offensive is confined within certain limits, which is the inevitable consequence of her three weaknesses; she cannot go on indefinitely till she swallows the whole of China. Already there are signs that Japan will one day find herself in an utterly passive position. China, on the other hand, was in a rather passive position at the beginning of the war, but, having gained experience, she is now turning to the new policy of mobile warfare, the policy of taking the offensive, seeking quick decisions and operating on exterior lines in campaigns and battles, which, together with the policy of developing widespread guerrilla warfare, is helping China to build up a position of initiative day by day.

The question of the initiative is even more vital in guerrilla warfare. For most guerrilla units operate in very difficult circumstances, fighting without a rear, with their own weak forces facing the enemy's strong forces, lacking experience (when the units are newly organized), being separated, etc. Nevertheless, it is possible to build up the initiative in guerrilla warfare, the essential condition being to seize on the enemy's three weaknesses. Taking advantage of the enemy's shortage of troops (from the viewpoint of the war as a whole), the guerrilla units can boldly use vast areas as their fields of operation; taking advantage of the fact that the enemy is an alien invader and is pursuing a most barbarous policy, the guerrilla units can boldly enlist the support of millions upon millions of people; and taking advantage of the stupidities in the enemy's command, the guerrilla units can give full scope to their resourcefulness. While the regular army must seize on all these weaknesses of the enemy and turn them to good account in order to defeat him, it is even more important for the guerrilla units to do so. As for the guerrilla units' own weaknesses, they can be gradually reduced in the course of the struggle. Moreover, these weaknesses sometimes constitute the very condition for gaining the initiative. For example, it is precisely because the guerrilla units are small that they can mysteriously appear and disappear in their operations behind enemy lines, without the enemy's being able to do anything about them, and thus enjoy a freedom of action such as massive regular armies never can.

When the enemy is making a converging attack from several directions' a guerrilla unit can exercise initiative only with difficulty and can lose it all too easily. In such a case, if its appraisals and dispositions are wrong, it is liable to get into a passive position and consequently fail to smash the converging enemy attack. This may occur even when the enemy is on the defensive and we are on the offensive. For the initiative results from making a correct appraisal of the situation (both our own and that of the enemy) and from making the correct military and political dispositions. A pessimistic appraisal out of accord with the objective conditions and the passive dispositions ensuing from it will undoubtedly result in the loss of the initiative and throw one into a passive position. On the other hand, an over-optimistic appraisal out of accord with the objective conditions and the risky (unjustifiably risky) dispositions ensuing from it will also result in the loss of the initiative and eventually land one in a position similar to that of the pessimists. The initiative is not an innate attribute of genius, but is something an intelligent leader attains through open-minded study and correct appraisal of the objective conditions and through correct military and political dispositions. It follows that the initiative is not ready-made but is something that requires conscious effort.

When forced into a passive position through some incorrect appraisal and disposition or through overwhelming pressure, a guerrilla unit must strive to extricate itself. How this can be done depends on the circumstances. In many cases it is necessary to "move away". The ability to move is the distinctive feature of a guerrilla unit. To move away is the principal method for getting out of a passive position and regaining the initiative. But it is not the sole method. The moment when the enemy is most energetic and we are in the greatest difficulties is often the very moment when things begin to turn against him and in our favour. Frequently a favourable situation recurs and the initiative is regained as a result of "holding out a little longer".

Next, let us deal with flexibility.

Flexibility is a concrete expression of the initiative. The flexible employment of forces is more essential in guerrilla warfare than in regular warfare.

A guerrilla commander must understand that the flexible employment of his forces is the most important means of changing the situation as between the enemy and ourselves and of gaining the initiative. The nature of guerrilla warfare is such that guerrilla forces must be employed flexibly in accordance with the task in hand and with such circumstances as the

299

state of the enemy, the terrain and the local population, and the chief ways of employing the forces are dispersal, concentration and shifting of position. In employing his forces, a guerrilla commander is like a fisherman casting his net, which he should be able to spread wide as well as draw in tight. When casting his net, the fisherman has to ascertain the depth of the water, the speed of the current and the presence or absence of obstructions; similarly, when dispersing his units, a guerrilla commander must take care not to incur losses through ignorance of the situation or through miscalculated action. Just as the fisherman must keep a grip on the cord in order to draw his net in tight, so the guerrilla commander must maintain liaison and communication with all his forces and keep enough of his main forces at hand. Just as a frequent change of position is necessary in fishing, so a frequent shift of position is necessary for a guerrilla unit. Dispersal, concentration and shifting of position are the three ways of flexibly employing forces in guerrilla warfare.

Generally speaking, the dispersal of guerrilla units, or "breaking up the whole into parts", is employed chiefly: (1) when we want to threaten the enemy with a wide frontal attack because he is on the defensive, and there is temporarily no chance to mass our forces for action; (2) when we want to harass and disrupt the enemy throughout an area where his forces are weak; (3) when we are unable to break through the enemy's encirclement and try to slip away by making ourselves less conspicuous; (4) when we are restricted by terrain or supplies; or (5) when we are carrying on mass work over a wide area. But whatever the circumstances, when dispersing for action we should pay attention to the following: (1) we should never make an absolutely even dispersal of forces, but should keep a fairly large part in an area convenient for manoeuvre, so that any possible exigency can be met and there is a centre of gravity for the task being carried out in dispersion; and (2) we should assign to the dispersed units clearly defined tasks, fields of operation, time limits for actions, places for reassembly and ways and means of liaison.

Concentration of forces, or "assembling the parts into a whole", is the method usually applied to destroy an enemy when he is on the offensive and sometimes to destroy some of his stationary forces when he is on the defensive. Concentration of forces does not mean absolute concentration, but the massing of the main forces for use in one important direction while retaining or dispatching part of the forces for use in other directions to contain, harass or disrupt the enemy, or to carry on mass work.

Although the flexible dispersal or concentration of forces according to circumstances is the principal method in guerrilla warfare, we must also know how to shift (or transfer) our forces flexibly. When the enemy feels seriously threatened by guerrillas, he will send troops to attack or suppress them. Hence the guerrilla units will have to take stock of the situation. If advisable, they should fight where they are; if not, they should lose no time in shifting elsewhere. Sometimes, in order to crush the enemy units one by one, guerrilla units which have destroyed an enemy force in one place may immediately shift to another so as to wipe out a second enemy force; sometimes, finding it inadvisable to fight in one place, they may have to disengage quickly and fight the enemy elsewhere. If the enemy's forces in a certain place present a particularly serious threat, the guerrilla units should not linger, but should move off with lightning speed. In general, shifts of position should be made with secrecy and speed. In order to mislead, decoy and confuse the enemy, they should constantly use stratagems, such as making a feint to the east but attacking in the west, appearing now in the south and now in the north, hit-and-run attacks, and night actions.

Flexibility in dispersal, concentration and shifts of position is a concrete expression of the initiative in guerrilla warfare, whereas rigidity and inertia inevitably lead to passivity and cause unnecessary losses. But a commander proves himself wise not just by recognition of the importance of employing his forces flexibly but by skill in dispersing, concentrating or shifting them in good time according to the specific circumstances. This wisdom in sensing changes and choosing the right moment to act is not easily acquired; it can be gained only by those who study with a receptive mind and investigate and ponder diligently. Prudent consideration of the circumstances is essential to prevent flexibility from turning into impulsive action.

Lastly, we come to planning.

Without planning, victories in guerrilla warfare are impossible. Any idea that guerrilla warfare can be conducted in haphazard fashion indicates either a flippant attitude or ignorance of guerrilla warfare. The operations in a guerrilla zone as a whole, or those of a guerrilla unit or formation, must be preceded by as thorough planning as possible, by preparation in advance for every action. Grasping the situation, setting the tasks, disposing the forces, giving military and political training, securing supplies, putting the equipment in good order, making proper use of the people's help, etc.--all these are part of the work of the guerrilla commanders, which they must carefully consider and conscientiously perform and check up on. There can be no initiative, no flexibility, and no offensive unless they do so. True, guerrilla conditions do not allow as high a degree of planning as do those of regular warfare, and it would be a mistake to attempt very thorough planning in guerrilla warfare. But it is necessary to plan as thoroughly as the objective conditions permit, for it should be understood that fighting the enemy is no joke.

The above points serve to explain the first of the strategic principles of guerrilla warfare, the principle of using initiative, flexibility and planning in conducting offensives within the defensive, battles of quick decision within protracted war, and exterior-line operations within interior-line operations. It is the key problem in the strategy of guerrilla warfare. The solution of this problem provides the major guarantee of victory in guerrilla warfare so far as military command is concerned.

Although a variety of matters have been dealt with here, they all revolve around the offensive in campaigns and battles. The initiative can be decisively grasped only after victory in an offensive. Every offensive operation must be organized on our initiative and not launched under compulsion. Flexibility in the employment of forces revolves around the effort to take the offensive, and planning likewise is necessary chiefly in order to ensure success in offensive operations. Measures of tactical defence are meaningless if they are divorced from their role of giving either direct or indirect support to an offensive. Quick decision refers to the tempo of an offensive, and exterior lines refer to its scope. The offensive is the only means of destroying the enemy and is also the principal means of self-preservation, while pure defence and retreat can play only a temporary and partial role in self-preservation and are quite useless for destroying the enemy.

The principle stated above is basically the same for both regular and guerrilla war; it differs to some degree only in its form of expression. But in guerrilla war it is both important and necessary to note this difference. It is precisely this difference in form which distinguishes the operational methods of guerrilla war from those of regular war. If we confuse the two different forms in which the principle is expressed, victory in guerrilla war will be impossible.

CHAPTER V
CO-ORDINATION WITH REGULAR WARFARE
The second problem of strategy in guerrilla warfare is its coordination with regular warfare. It is a matter of clarifying the relation between guerrilla and regular warfare on the operational level, in the light of the nature of actual guerrilla operations. An understanding of this relation is very important for effectiveness in defeating the enemy.

There are three kinds of co-ordination between guerrilla and regular warfare, co-ordination in strategy, in campaigns and in battles.

Taken as a whole, guerrilla warfare behind the enemy lines, which cripples the enemy, pins him down, disrupts his supply lines and inspires the regular forces and the people throughout the country, is co-ordinated with regular warfare in strategy. Take the case of the guerrilla warfare in the three northeastern provinces. Of course, the question of co-ordination did not arise before the nation-wide War of Resistance, but since the war began the significance of such coordination has become obvious. Every enemy soldier the guerrillas kill there, every bullet they make the enemy expend, every enemy soldier they stop from advancing south of the Great Wall, can be reckoned a contribution to the total strength of the resistance. It is, moreover, clear that they are having a demoralizing effect on the whole enemy army and all Japan and a heartening effect on our whole army and people. Still clearer is the role in strategic co-ordination played by the guerrilla warfare along the Peiping-Suiyuan, Peiping-Hankow, Tientsin-Pukow, Tatung-Puchow, Chengting-Taiyuan and Shanghai-Hangchow Railways. Not only are the guerrilla units performing the function of co-ordination with the regular forces in our present strategic defensive, when the enemy is on the strategic offensive; not only will they co-ordinate with the regular forces in disrupting the enemy's hold on the occupied territory, after he concludes his strategic offensive and switches to the safeguarding of his gains; they will also co-ordinate with the regular forces in driving out the enemy forces and recovering all the lost territories, when the regular forces launch the strategic counter-offensive. The great role of guerrilla warfare in strategic coordination must not be overlooked. The commanders both of the guerrilla units and of the regular forces must clearly understand this role.

In addition, guerrilla warfare performs the function of coordination with regular warfare in campaigns. For instance, in the campaign at Hsinkou, north of Taiyuan, the guerrillas played a remarkable role in co-ordination both north and south of Yenmenkuan by wrecking the Tatung-Puchow Railway and the motor roads running through Pinghsingkuan and Yangfangkou. Or take another instance. After the enemy occupied Fenglingtu, guerrilla warfare, which was already widespread throughout Shansi Province and was conducted mainly by the regular forces, played an even greater role through co-ordination with the defensive campaigns west of the Yellow River in Shensi Province and south of the Yellow River in Honan Province. Again, when the enemy attacked southern Shantung, the guerrilla warfare in the five provinces of northern China contributed a great deal through co-ordination with the campaigns of our army. In performing a task of this sort, the leaders of each guerrilla base behind the enemy lines, or the commanders of a guerrilla formation temporarily dispatched there, must dispose their forces well and, by adopting different tactics suited to the time and place, move energetically against the enemy's most vital and vulnerable spots in order to cripple him, pin him down, disrupt his supply lines, inspire our armies campaigning on the interior lines, and so fulfil their duty of co-ordinating with the campaign. If each guerrilla zone or unit goes it alone without giving any attention to co-ordinating with the campaigns of the regular forces, its role in strategic co-ordination will lose a great deal of its significance, although it will still play some such role in the general strategy. All guerrilla commanders should give this point serious attention. To achieve co-ordination in campaigns, it is absolutely necessary for all larger guerrilla units and guerrilla formations to have radio equipment.

Finally, co-ordination with the regular forces in battles, in actual fighting on the battlefield, is the task of all guerrilla units in the vicinity of an interior-line battlefield. Of course, this applies only to guerrilla units operating close to the regular forces or to units of regulars dispatched on temporary guerrilla missions. In such cases, a guerrilla unit has to perform whatever task it is assigned by the commander of the regular forces, which is usually to pin down some of the enemy's forces, disrupt his supply lines, conduct reconnaissance, or act as guides for the regular forces. Even without such an assignment the guerrilla unit should carry out these tasks on its own initiative. To sit by idly, neither moving nor fighting, or to move about without fighting, would be an intolerable attitude for a guerrilla unit.

CHAPTER VI
THE ESTABLISHMENT OF BASE AREAS
The third problem of strategy in anti-Japanese guerrilla warfare is the establishment of base areas, which is important and essential because of the protracted nature and ruthlessness of the war. The recovery of our lost territories will have to await the nation-wide strategic counter-offensive; by then the enemy's front will have extended deep into central China and cut it in two from north to south, and a part or even a greater part of our territory will have fallen into the hands of the enemy and become his rear. We shall have to extend guerrilla warfare all over this vast enemy-occupied area, make a front out of the enemy's rear, and force him to fight ceaselessly throughout the territory he occupies. Until such time as our strategic counteroffensive is launched and so long as our lost territories are not recovered, it will be necessary to persist in guerrilla warfare in the enemy's rear, certainly for a fairly long time, though one cannot say

definitely for how long. This is why the war will be a protracted one. And in order to safeguard his gains in the occupied areas, the enemy is bound to step up his anti-guerrilla measures and, especially after the halting of his strategic offensive, to embark on relentless suppression of the guerrillas. With ruthlessness thus added to protractedness, it will be impossible to sustain guerrilla warfare behind the enemy lines without base areas.

What, then, are these base areas? They are the strategic bases on which the guerrilla forces rely in performing their strategic tasks and achieving the object of preserving and expanding themselves and destroying and driving out the enemy. Without such strategic bases, there will be nothing to depend on in carrying out any of our strategic tasks or achieving the aim of the war. It is a characteristic of guerrilla warfare behind the enemy lines that it is fought without a rear, for the guerrilla forces are severed from the country's general rear. But guerrilla warfare could not last long or grow without base areas. The base areas, indeed, are its rear.

History knows many peasant wars of the "roving rebel" type, but none of them ever succeeded. In the present age of advanced communications and technology, it would be all the more groundless to imagine that one can win victory by fighting in the manner of roving rebels. However, this roving-rebel idea still exists among impoverished peasants, and in the minds of guerrilla commanders it becomes the view that base areas are neither necessary nor important. Therefore ridding the minds of guerrilla commanders of this idea is a prerequisite for deciding on a policy of establishing base areas. The question of whether or not to have base areas and of whether or not to regard them as important, in other words, the conflict between the idea of establishing base areas and that of fighting like roving rebels, arises in all guerrilla warfare, and, to a certain extent, our anti-Japanese guerrilla warfare is no exception. Therefore the struggle against the roving-rebel ideology is an inevitable process. Only when this ideology is thoroughly overcome and the policy of establishing base areas is mutated and applied will there be conditions favourable for the maintenance of guerrilla warfare over a long period.

Now that the necessity and importance of base areas have been made clear, let us pass on to the following problems which must be understood and solved when it comes to establishing the base areas. These problems are the types of base areas, the guerrilla zones and the base areas, the conditions for establishing base areas, their consolidation and expansion, and the forms in which we and the enemy encircle one another.

1. THE TYPES OF BASE AREAS

Base areas in anti-Japanese guerrilla warfare are mainly of three types, those in the mountains, those on the plains and those in the river-lake-estuary regions.

The advantage of setting up base areas in mountainous regions is obvious, and those which have been, are being or will be established in the Changpai, [1] Wutai, [2] Taihang, [3] Taishan, [4] Yenshan [5] and Maoshan [6] Mountains all belong to this type. They are all places where anti-Japanese guerrilla warfare can be maintained for the longest time and are important strongholds for the War of Resistance. We must develop guerrilla warfare and set up base areas in all the mountainous regions behind the enemy lines.

Of course, the plains are less suitable than the mountains, but it is by no means impossible to develop guerrilla warfare or establish any base areas there. Indeed, the widespread guerrilla warfare in the plains of Hopei and of northern and northwestern Shantung proves that it is possible to develop guerrilla warfare in the plains. While there is as yet no evidence on the possibility of setting up base areas there and maintaining them for long, it has been proved that the setting up of temporary base areas is possible, and it should be possible to set up base areas for small units or for seasonal use. On the one hand, the enemy does not have enough troops at his disposal and is pursuing a policy of unparalleled brutality, and on the other hand, China has a vast territory and vast numbers of people who are resisting Japan; the objective conditions for spreading guerrilla warfare and setting up temporary base areas in the plains are therefore fulfilled. Given competent military command, it should of course be possible to establish bases for small guerrilla units there, bases which are long-term but not fixed.[7] Broadly speaking, when the strategic offensive of the enemy is brought to a halt and he enters the stage of safeguarding his occupied areas, he will undoubtedly launch savage attacks on all the guerrilla base areas, and those in the plains will naturally be the first to bear the brunt. The large guerrilla formations operating on the plains will be unable to keep on fighting there for long and will gradually have to move up into the mountains as the circumstances require, as for instance, from the Hopei Plain to the Wutai and Taihang Mountains, or from the Shantung Plain to Taishan Mountain and the Shantung Peninsula in the east. But in the circumstances of our national war it is not impossible for numerous small guerrilla units to keep going in various counties over the vast plains and adopt a fluid way of fighting, i.e., by shifting their bases from place to place. It is definitely possible to conduct seasonal guerrilla warfare by taking advantage of the "green curtain" of tall crops in summer and of the frozen rivers in winter. As the enemy has no strength to spare now and will never be able to attend to everything even when he has the strength to spare, it is absolutely necessary for us to decide on the policy, for the present, of spreading guerrilla warfare far and wide and setting up temporary base areas in the plains and, for the future, of preparing to keep up guerrilla warfare by small units, if only seasonally, and of creating base areas which are not fixed.

Objectively speaking, the possibilities of developing guerrilla warfare and establishing base areas are greater in the river-lake-estuary regions than in the plains, though less than in the mountains. The dramatic battles fought by "pirates" and "water-bandits", of which our history is full, and the guerrilla warfare round the Hunghu Lake kept up for several years in the Red Army period, both testify to the possibility of developing guerrilla warfare and of establishing base areas in the river-lake-estuary regions. So far, however, the political parties and the masses who are resisting Japan have given this possibility little attention. Though the subjective conditions are as yet lacking, we should undoubtedly turn our attention to this possibility and start working on it. As one aspect in the development of our nation-wide guerrilla warfare, we should effectively organize guerrilla warfare in the Hungtse Lake region north of the Yangtse River, in the Taihu Lake region south of the Yangtse, and in all river-lake-estuary regions in the enemy-occupied areas along the rivers and on the seacoast, and we should create permanent base areas in and near such places. By overlooking this aspect we are virtually providing the enemy with water transport facilities; this is a gap in our strategic plan for the War of Resistance which must be filled in good time.

2. GUERRILLA ZONES AND BASE AREAS

In guerrilla warfare behind the enemy lines, there is a difference between guerrilla zones and base areas. Areas which are surrounded by the enemy but whose central parts are not occupied or have been recovered, like some counties in the Wutai mountain region (i.e., the Shansi-Chahar-Hopei border area) and also some places in the Taihang and Taishan mountain regions, are ready-made bases for the convenient use of guerrilla units in developing guerrilla warfare. But elsewhere in these areas the situation is different, as for instance in the eastern and northern sections of the Wutai mountain region, which include parts of western Hopei and southern Chahar, and in many places east of Paoting and west of Tsangchow. When guerrilla warfare began, the guerrillas could not completely occupy these places but could only make frequent raids; they are areas which are held by the guerrillas when they are there and by the puppet regime when they are gone, and are therefore not yet guerrilla bases but only what may be called guerrilla zones. Such guerrilla zones will be transformed into base areas when they have gone through the necessary processes of guerrilla warfare, that is, when large numbers of enemy troops have been annihilated or defeated there, the puppet regime has been destroyed, the masses have been roused to activity, anti-Japanese mass organizations have been formed, people's local armed forces have been developed, and anti-Japanese political power has been established. By the expansion of our base areas we mean the addition of areas such as these to the bases already established.

In some places, for example, eastern Hopei, the whole area of guerrilla operations has been a guerrilla zone from the very beginning. The puppet regime is of long standing there, and from the beginning the whole area of operations has been a guerrilla zone both for the people's armed forces that have grown out of local uprisings and for the guerrilla detachments dispatched from the Wutai Mountains. At the outset of their activities, all they could do was to choose some fairly good spots there as temporary rear or base areas. Such places will not be transformed from guerrilla zones into relatively stable base areas until the enemy forces are destroyed and the work of arousing the people is in full swing.

Thus the transformation of a guerrilla zone into a base area is an arduous creative process, and its accomplishment depends on the extent to which the enemy is destroyed and the masses are aroused.

Many regions will remain guerrilla zones for a long time. In these regions the enemy will not be able to set up stable puppet regimes, however much he tries to maintain control, while we, on our part, will not be able to achieve the aim of establishing anti-Japanese political power, however much we develop guerrilla warfare. Examples of this kind are to be found in the enemy-occupied regions along the railway lines, in the neighbourhood of big cities and in certain areas in the plains.

As for the big cities, the railway stops and the areas in the plains which are strongly garrisoned by the enemy, guerrilla warfare can only extend to the fringes and not right into these places which have relatively stable puppet regimes. This is another kind of situation.

Mistakes in our leadership or strong enemy pressure may cause a reversal of the state of affairs described above, i.e., a guerrilla base may turn into a guerrilla zone, and a guerrilla zone may turn into an area under relatively stable enemy occupation. Such changes are possible, and they deserve special vigilance on the part of guerrilla commanders.

Therefore, as a result of guerrilla warfare and the struggle between us and the enemy, the entire enemy-occupied territory will fall into the following three categories: first, anti-Japanese bases held by our guerrilla units and our organs of political power; second, areas held by Japanese imperialism and its puppet regimes; and third, intermediate zones contested by both sides, namely, guerrilla zones. Guerrilla commanders have the duty to expand the first and third categories to the maximum and to reduce the second category to the minimum. This is the strategic task of guerrilla warfare.

3. CONDITIONS FOR ESTABLISHING BASE AREAS

The fundamental conditions for establishing a base area are that there should be anti-Japanese armed forces, that these armed forces should be employed to inflict defeats on the enemy and that they should arouse the people to action. Thus the establishment of a base area is first and foremost a matter of building an armed force. Leaders in guerrilla war must devote their energy to building one or more guerrilla units, and must gradually develop them in the course of struggle into guerrilla formations or even into units and formations of regular troops. The building up of an armed force is the key to establishing a base area; if there is no armed force or if the armed force is weak, nothing can be done. This constitutes the first condition.

The second indispensable condition for establishing a base area is that the armed forces should be used in co-ordination with the people to defeat the enemy. All places under enemy control are enemy, and not guerrilla, base areas, and obviously cannot be transformed into guerrilla base areas unless the enemy is defeated. Unless we repulse the enemy's attacks and defeat him, even places held by the guerrillas will come under enemy control, and then it will be impossible to establish base areas.

The third indispensable condition for establishing a base area is the use of all our strength, including our armed forces, to arouse the masses for struggle against Japan. In the course of this struggle we must arm the people, i.e., organize self-defence corps and guerrilla units. In the course of this struggle, we must form mass organizations, we must organize the workers, peasants, youth, women, children, merchants and professional people--according to the degree of their political consciousness and fighting enthusiasm--into the various mass organizations necessary for the struggle against Japanese aggression, and we must gradually expand them. Without organization, the people cannot give effect to their anti-Japanese strength. In the course of this struggle, we must weed out the open and the hidden traitors, a task which can be accomplished only by relying on the strength of the people. In this struggle, it is particularly important to arouse the people to establish, or to consolidate, their local organs of anti-Japanese political power. Where the original Chinese organs of political power have not been destroyed by the enemy, we must reorganize and strengthen them with the support of the broad masses, and where they have been destroyed by the enemy, we should rebuild them by the efforts of the masses. They are organs of political power for carrying out the policy of the Anti-Japanese National United Front and should unite all the forces of the people to fight against our sole enemy, Japanese imperialism, and its jackals, the traitors and reactionaries.

A base area for guerrilla war can be truly established only with the gradual fulfillment of the three basic conditions, i.e., only after the anti-Japanese armed forces are built up, the enemy has suffered defeats and the people are aroused.

Mention must also be made of geographical and economic conditions. As for the former, we have already discussed three different categories in the earlier section on the types of base areas, and here we need only mention one major requirement, namely, that the area must be extensive. In places surrounded by the enemy on all sides, or on three sides, the mountainous regions naturally offer the best conditions for setting up base areas which can hold out for a long time, but the main thing is that there must be enough room for the guerrillas to maneuver, namely, the areas have to be extensive. Given an extensive area, guerrilla warfare can be developed and sustained even in the plains, not to mention the river-lake-estuary regions. By and large, the vastness of China's territory and the enemy's shortage of troops provide guerrilla warfare in China with this condition. This is an important, even a primary condition, as far as the possibility of waging guerrilla warfare is concerned, and small countries like Belgium which lack this condition have few or no such possibilities.[8] In China, this condition is not something which has to be striven for, nor does it present a problem; it is there physically, waiting only to be exploited.

So far as their physical setting is concerned, the economic conditions resemble the geographical conditions. For now we are discussing the establishment of base areas not in a desert, where no enemy is to be found, but behind the enemy lines; every place the enemy can penetrate already has its Chinese inhabitants and an economic basis for subsistence, so that the question of choice of economic conditions in establishing base areas simply does not arise. Irrespective of the economic conditions, we should do our utmost to develop guerrilla warfare and set up permanent or temporary base areas in all places where Chinese inhabitants and enemy forces are to be found. In a political sense, however, the economic conditions do present a problem, a problem of economic policy which is of immense importance to the establishment of base areas. The economic policy of the guerrilla base areas must follow the principles of the Anti-Japanese National United Front by equitably distributing the financial burden and protecting commerce. Neither the local organs of political power nor the guerrilla units must violate these principles, or otherwise the establishment of base areas and the maintenance of guerrilla warfare would be adversely affected. The equitable distribution of the financial burden means that "those with money should contribute money", while the peasants should supply the guerrilla units with grain within certain limits. The protection of commerce means that the guerrilla units should be highly disciplined and that the confiscation of shops, except those owned by proved traitors, should be strictly prohibited. This is no easy matter, but the policy is set and must be put into effect.

4. THE CONSOLIDATION AND EXPANSION OF BASE AREAS
In order to confine the enemy invaders to a few strongholds, that is, to the big cities and along the main communication lines, the guerrillas must do all they can to extend guerrilla warfare from their base areas as widely as possible and hem in all the enemy's strongholds, thus threatening his existence and shaking his morale while expanding the base areas. This is essential. In this context, we must oppose conservatism in guerrilla warfare. Whether originating in the desire for an easy life or in overestimation of the enemy's strength, conservatism can only bring losses in the War of Resistance and is harmful to guerrilla warfare and to the base areas themselves. At the same time, we must not forget the consolidation of the base areas, the chief task being to arouse and organize the masses and to train guerrilla units and local armed forces. Such consolidation is needed for maintaining protracted warfare and also for expansion, and in its absence energetic expansion is impossible. If we attend only to expansion and forget about consolidation in our guerrilla warfare, we shall be unable to withstand the enemy's attacks, and consequently not only forfeit the possibility of expansion but also endanger the very existence of the base areas. The correct principle is expansion with consolidation, which is a good method and allows us to take the offensive or the defensive as we choose. Given a protracted war, the problem of consolidating and expanding base areas constantly arises for every guerrilla unit. The concrete solution depends, of course, on the circumstances. At one time, the emphasis may be on expansion, i.e., on expanding the guerrilla zones and increasing the number of guerrillas. At another, the emphasis may be on consolidation, i.e., on organizing the masses and training the troops. As expansion and consolidation differ in

nature, and as the military dispositions and other tasks will differ accordingly, an effective solution of the problem is possible only if we alternate the emphasis according to time and circumstances.

5. FORMS IN WHICH WE AND THE ENEMY ENCIRCLE ONE ANOTHER

Taking the War of Resistance as a whole, there is no doubt that we are strategically encircled by the enemy, because he is on the strategic offensive and is operating on exterior lines while we are on the strategic defensive and are operating on interior lines. This is the first form of enemy encirclement. We on our part encircle each of the enemy columns advancing on us along separate routes, because we apply the policy of the offensive and of exterior-line operations in campaigns and battles by using numerically preponderant forces against these enemy columns advancing on us from exterior lines. This is the first form of our encirclement of the enemy. Next, if we consider the guerrilla base areas in the enemy's rear, each area taken singly is surrounded by the enemy on all sides, like the Wutai mountain region, or on three sides, like the northwestern Shansi area. This is the second form of enemy encirclement. However, if one considers all the guerrilla base areas together and in their relation to the battle fronts of the regular forces, one can see that we in turn surround a great many enemy forces. In Shansi Province, for instance, we have surrounded the Tatung-Puchow Railway on three sides (the east and west flanks and the southern end) and the city of Taiyuan on all sides; and there are many similar instances in Hopei and Shantung Provinces. This is the second form of our encirclement of the enemy. Thus there are two forms of encirclement by the enemy forces and two forms of encirclement by our own--rather like a game of weichi.[9] Campaigns and battles fought by the two sides resemble the capturing of each other's pieces, and the establishment of strongholds by the enemy and of guerrilla base areas by us resembles moves to dominate spaces on the board. It is in the matter of "dominating the spaces" that the great strategic role of guerrilla base areas in the rear of the enemy is revealed. We are raising this question in the War of Resistance in order that the nation's military authorities and the guerrilla commanders in all areas should place on the agenda the development of guerrilla warfare behind the enemy lines and the establishment of base areas wherever possible, and carry this out as a strategic task. If on the international plane we can create an anti-Japanese front in the Pacific region, with China as one strategic unit, and the Soviet Union and other countries which may join it as other strategic units, we shall then have one more form of encirclement against the enemy than he has against us and bring about exterior-line operations in the Pacific region by which to encircle and destroy fascist Japan. To be sure, this is of little practical significance at present, but such a prospect is not impossible.

CHAPTER VII

THE STRATEGIC DEFENSIVE AND THE STRATEGIC OFFENSIVE IN GUERRILLA WAR

The fourth problem of strategy in guerrilla war concerns the strategic defensive and the strategic offensive. This is the problem of how the policy of offensive warfare, which we mentioned in our discussion of the first problem, is to be carried out in practice, when we are on the defensive and when we are on the offensive in our guerrilla warfare against Japan.

Within the nation-wide strategic defensive or strategic offensive (to be more exact, the strategic counter-offensive), small-scale strategic defensives and offensives take place in and around each guerrilla base area. By strategic defensive we mean our strategic situation and policy when the enemy is on the offensive and we are on the defensive; by strategic offensive we mean our strategic situation and policy when the enemy is on the defensive and we are on the offensive.

1. THE STRATEGIC DEFENSIVE IN GUERRILLA WAR

After guerrilla warfare has broken out and grown to a considerable extent, the enemy will inevitably attack the guerrilla base areas, especially in the period when his strategic offensive against the country as a whole is brought to an end and he adopts the policy of safeguarding his occupied areas. It is essential to recognize the inevitability of such attacks, for otherwise the guerrilla commanders will be caught wholly unprepared, and in the face of heavy enemy attacks they will undoubtedly become alarmed and confused and their forces will be routed.

To wipe out the guerrillas and their base areas, the enemy frequently resorts to converging attacks. For instance, in each of the four or five "punitive expeditions" directed against the Wutai mountain region, the enemy made a planned advance in three, four or even six or seven columns simultaneously. The larger the scale of the guerrilla fighting, the more important the position of the base areas, and the greater the threat to the enemy's strategic centres and vital communication lines, the fiercer will be the enemy's attacks. Therefore, the fiercer the enemy's attacks on a guerrilla area, the greater the indication that the guerrilla warfare there is successful and is being effectively coordinated with the regular fighting.

When the enemy launches a converging attack in several columns, the guerrilla policy should be to smash it by counter-attack. It can be easily smashed if each advancing enemy column consists of only one unit, whether big or small, has no follow-up units and is unable to station troops

313

along the route of advance, construct blockhouses or build motor roads. When the enemy launches a converging attack, he is on the offensive and operating on exterior lines, while we are on the defensive and operating on interior lines. As for our dispositions, we should use our secondary forces to pin down several enemy columns, while our main force should launch surprise attacks (chiefly in the form of ambushes) in a campaign or battle against a single enemy column, striking it when it is on the move. The enemy, though strong, will be weakened by repeated surprise attacks and will often withdraw when he is halfway; the guerrilla units can then make more surprise attacks during the pursuit and weaken him still further. The enemy generally occupies the county towns or other towns in our base areas before he stops his offensive or begins to withdraw, and we should encircle these towns, cutting off his grain supply and severing his communications, so that when he cannot hold out and begins to retreat, we can seize the opportunity to pursue and attack him. After smashing one column, we should shift our forces to smash another, and, by smashing them one by one, shatter the converging attack.

A big base area like the Wutai mountain region forms a military area, which is divided into four or five, or even more, military subareas, each with its own armed forces operating independently. By employing the tactics described above, these forces have often smashed the enemy's attacks simultaneously or successively.

In our plan of operations against a converging attack by the enemy, we generally place our main force on interior lines. But when we have the strength to spare, we should use our secondary forces (such as the county or the district guerrilla units, or even detachments of the main force) on exterior lines to disrupt the enemy's communications and pin down his reinforcements. Should the enemy stay put in our base area, we may reverse the tactics, namely, leave some of our forces in the base area to invest the enemy while employing the main force to attack the region whence he has come and to step up our activities there, in order to induce him to withdraw and attack our main force; this is the tactic of "relieving the state of Chao by besieging the state of Wei".[10]

In the course of operations against a converging attack, the local anti-Japanese self-defence corps and all the mass organizations should mobilize for action and in every way help our troops to fight the enemy. In fighting the enemy, it is important both to enforce local martial law and, as far as possible, to "strengthen our defence works and clear the fields". The purpose of the former is to suppress traitors and prevent the enemy from getting information, and of the latter to assist our own operations (by strengthening our defence works) and prevent the enemy from getting food (by clearing the herds). "Clearing the fields" means harvesting the crops as soon as they are ripe.

When the enemy retreats, he often burns down the houses in the cities and towns he has occupied and razes the villages along his route, with the purpose of destroying the guerrilla base areas; but in so doing he deprives himself of shelter and food in his next offensive, and the damage recoils upon his own head. This is a concrete illustration of what we mean by one and the same thing having two contradictory aspects.

A guerrilla commander should not think of abandoning his base area and shifting to another, unless it proves impossible, after repeated operations to smash the enemy's heavy converging attacks. In these circumstances he must guard against pessimism. So long as the leaders do not blunder in matters of principle, it is generally possible to smash the converging attacks and hold on to the base areas in the mountainous regions. It is only in the plains that, when confronted by a heavy converging attack, the guerrilla commander should consider other measures in the light of the specific circumstances, namely, leaving many small units for scattered operations, while temporarily shifting large guerrilla formations to some mountainous region, so that they can return and resume their activities in the plains once the main forces of the enemy move away.

Generally speaking, the Japanese cannot adopt the principle of blockhouse warfare, which the Kuomintang employed in the days of the civil war, because their forces are inadequate in relation to China's vast territory. However, we should reckon with the possibility that they may use it to some extent against those guerrilla base areas which pose a particular threat to their vital positions, but even in such circumstances we should be prepared to keep up guerrilla warfare in those areas. Since we have had the experience of being able to maintain guerrilla warfare during the civil war, there is not the slightest doubt of our greater capacity to do so in a national war. Though, in point of relative military strength, the enemy can throw forces that are vastly superior in quantity as well as in quality against some of our base areas, there remain the insoluble national contradiction between us and the enemy and the unavoidable weaknesses of his command. Our victories are based on thorough work among the masses and flexible tactics in our operations.

2. THE STRATEGIC OFFENSIVE IN GUERRILLA WAR

After we have smashed an enemy offensive and before the enemy starts a new offensive, he is on the strategic defensive and we are on the strategic offensive.

At such times our operational policy is not to attack enemy forces which are entrenched in defensive positions and which we are not sure of defeating, but systematically to destroy or drive out the small enemy units and puppet forces in certain areas, which our guerrilla units are strong enough to deal with, and to expand our areas, arouse the masses for struggle against Japan, replenish and train our troops and organize new guerrilla units. If the enemy still remains on the defensive when these tasks are under way, we can expand our new areas still further and attack weakly garrisoned cities and communication lines and hold them for as long as circumstances permit. These are all tasks of the strategic offensive, and the purpose is to take advantage of the fact that the enemy is on the defensive so that we may effectively build up our own military and mass strength, effectively reduce the enemy's strength and prepare to smash the enemy methodically and vigorously when he mounts an offensive again.

It is essential to rest and train our troops, and the best time for doing so is when the enemy is on the defensive. It is not a question of shutting ourselves off from everything else for rest and training, but of funding time for rest and training while expanding our areas, mopping up small enemy units and arousing the people. This is usually also the time for tackling the difficult problem of getting food supplies, bedding, clothing, etc.

It is also the time for destroying the enemy's communication lines on a large scale, hampering his transport and giving direct support to the regular forces in their campaigns.

At such times the guerrilla base areas, guerrilla zones and guerrilla units are in high spirits, and the areas devastated by the enemy are gradually rehabilitated and revived. The people in the enemy-occupied territories are also delighted, and the fame of the guerrillas resounds everywhere. On the other hand, in the camp of the enemy and his running dogs, the traitors, panic and disintegration are mounting, while there is growing hatred of the guerrillas and their base areas and preparations to deal with them are intensified. During the strategic offensive, therefore, it is impermissible for the guerrilla commanders to become so elated as to underrate the enemy and forget to strengthen unity in their own ranks and to consolidate their base areas and their forces. At such times, they must skilfully watch the enemy's every move for signs of any new offensive against us, so that the moment it comes they can wind up their strategic offensive in good order, turn to the strategic defensive and thereby smash

CHAPTER VIII

DEVELOPMENT OF GUERRILLA WAR INTO MOBILE WAR

The fifth problem of strategy in guerrilla war against Japan is its development into mobile war, a development which is necessary and possible because the war is protracted and ruthless. If China could speedily defeat the Japanese invaders and recover her lost territories, and if the war were neither protracted nor ruthless, this would not be necessary. But as, on the contrary, the war is protracted and ruthless, guerrilla warfare cannot adapt itself to such a war except by developing into mobile warfare. Since the war is protracted and ruthless, it is possible for the guerrilla units to undergo the necessary steeling and gradually to transform themselves into regular forces, so that their mode of operations is gradually regularized and guerrilla warfare develops into mobile warfare. The necessity and possibility of this development must be clearly recognized by the guerrilla commanders if they are to persist in, and systematically carry out, the policy of turning guerrilla warfare into mobile warfare.

In many places, such as the Wutai mountain region, the present guerrilla warfare owes its growth to the strong detachments sent there by the regular forces. The operations there, though generally of a guerrilla character, have contained an element of mobile warfare from the very beginning. This element will gradually increase as the war goes on. Herein lies the advantage which makes possible the swift expansion of the present anti-Japanese guerrilla warfare and its rapid development to a higher level; thus the conditions for guerrilla warfare are far superior to what they were in the three northeastern provinces.

To transform guerrilla units waging guerrilla warfare into regular forces waging mobile warfare, two conditions are necessary--an increase in numbers, and an improvement in quality. Apart from directly mobilizing the people to join the forces, increased numbers can be attained by amalgamating small units, while better quality depends on steeling the fighters and improving their weapons in the course of the war.

In amalgamating small units, we must, on the one hand, guard against localism, whereby attention is concentrated exclusively on local interests and centralization is impeded, and, on the other, guard against the purely military approach, whereby local interests are brushed aside.

Localism exists among the local guerrilla units and local governments,

317

which are frequently preoccupied with local considerations to the neglect of the general interest, or which prefer to act each on its own because they are unaccustomed to acting in larger groups. The commanders of the main guerrilla units or of the guerrilla formations must take this into account and adopt the method of gradual amalgamation of part of the local units, allowing the localities to keep some of their forces and expand their guerrilla warfare; the commanders should draw these units into joint operations and then bring about their amalgamation without breaking up their original organization or reshuffling their cadres, so that the small groups may integrate smoothly into the larger group.

As against localism, the purely military approach represents the wrong viewpoint held in the main forces by those who are bent on expanding their own strength and who neglect to assist the local armed units. They do not realize that the development of guerrilla warfare into mobile warfare means not the abandonment of guerrilla warfare but the gradual formation, in the midst of widespread guerrilla warfare, of a main force capable of conducting mobile warfare, a force around which there must still be numerous guerrilla units carrying on extensive guerrilla operations. These guerrilla units are powerful auxiliaries to the main force and serve as inexhaustible reserves for its continuous growth. Therefore, if a commander of a main force has made the mistake of neglecting the interests of the local population and the local government as a result of a purely military approach, he must correct it in order that the expansion of the main force and the multiplication of the local armed units may both receive due attention.

To raise the quality of the guerrilla units it is imperative to raise their political and organizational level and improve their equipment, military technique, tactics and discipline, so that they gradually pattern themselves on the regular forces and shed their guerrilla ways. Politically, it is imperative to get both the commanders and the fighters to realize the necessity of raising the guerrilla units to the level of the regular forces, to encourage them to strive towards this end, and to guarantee its attainment by means of political work. Organizationally, it is imperative gradually to fulfil all the requirements of a regular formation in the following respects--military and political organs, staff and working methods, a regular supply system, a medical service, etc. In the matter of equipment, it is imperative to acquire better and more varied weapons and increase the supply of the necessary communications equipment. In the matter of military technique and tactics, it is imperative to raise the guerrilla units to the level required of a regular formation. In the matter of discipline, it is imperative to raise the level so that uniform standards are observed, every order is executed without fail and all slackness is eliminated. To accomplish all these tasks requires a prolonged effort, and it cannot be done overnight; but that is the direction in which we must develop. Only thus can a main force be built up in each guerrilla base area and mobile warfare emerge for more effective attacks on the enemy. Where detachments or cadres have been sent in by the regular forces, the goal can be achieved more easily. Hence all the regular forces have the responsibility of helping the guerrilla units to develop into regular units.

CHAPTER IX
THE RELATIONSHIP OF COMMAND
The last problem of strategy in guerrilla war against Japan concerns the relationship of command. A correct solution of this problem is one of the prerequisites for the unhampered development of guerrilla warfare.

Since guerrilla units are a lower level of armed organization characterized by dispersed operations, the methods of command in guerrilla warfare do not allow as high a degree of centralization as in regular warfare. If any attempt is made to apply the methods of command in regular warfare to guerrilla warfare, its great flexibility will inevitably be restricted and its vitality sapped. A highly centralized command is in direct contradiction to the great flexibility of guerrilla warfare and must not and cannot be applied to it.

However, guerrilla warfare cannot be successfully developed without some centralized command. When extensive regular warfare and extensive guerrilla warfare are going on at the same time, their operations must be properly co-ordinated; hence the need for a command co-ordinating the two, i.e., for a unified strategic command by the national general staff and the war-zone commanders. In a guerrilla zone or guerrilla base area with many guerrilla units, there are usually one or more guerrilla formations (sometimes together with regular formations) which constitute the main force, a number of other guerrilla units, big and small, which represent the supplementary force, and many armed units composed of people not withdrawn from production; the enemy forces there usually form a unified complex to concert their operations against the guerrillas. Consequently, the problem arises of setting up a unified or centralized command in such guerrilla zones or base areas.

Hence, as opposed both to absolute centralization and to absolute decentralization, the principle of command in guerrilla war should be centralized strategic command and decentralized command in campaigns and battles.

Centralized strategic command includes the planning and direction of guerrilla warfare as a whole by the state, the co-ordination of guerrilla warfare with regular warfare in each war zone, and the unified direction of all the anti-Japanese armed forces in each guerrilla zone or base area. Here lack of harmony, unity and centralization is harmful, and every effort must be made to ensure all three. In general matters, that is, matters of strategy, the lower levels should report to the i higher and follow their instructions so as to ensure concerted action. Centralization, however, stops at this point, and it would likewise be harmful to go beyond it and interfere with the lower levels in matters of detail like the specific dispositions for a campaign or battle. For such details must be settled in the light of specific conditions, which change from time to time and from place to place and are quite beyond the knowledge of the distant higher levels of command. This is what is meant by the principle of decentralized command in campaigns and battles. The same principle generally applies in regular operations, especially when communications are inadequate. In a word, it means guerrilla warfare waged independently and with the initiative in our hands within the framework of a unified strategy.

Where a guerrilla base area constitutes a military area divided into sub-areas, each comprising several counties, each of which is again divided into districts, the relationship between the various levels, from the headquarters of the military area and sub-areas down to the county and district governments, is one of consecutive subordination, and every armed force must, according to its nature, be under the direct command of one of these. On the principle that has been enunciated, in the relationship of command at these levels matters of general policy should be centralized in the higher levels, while actual operations should be carried out in the light of the specific circumstances by the lower levels, which should have the right of independent action. If a higher level has something to say about the actual operations undertaken at a lower level, it can and should advance its views as "instructions" but must not issue hard and fast "commands". The more extensive the area, the more complex the situation and the greater the distance between the higher and the lower levels, the more advisable it becomes to allow greater independence to the lower levels in their actual operations and thus give those operations a character conforming more closely to the local requirements, so that the lower levels and the local personnel may develop the ability to work independently, cope with complicated situations, and successfully expand guerrilla warfare. For an armed unit or bigger formation which is engaged in a concentrated operation, the principle to be applied is one of centralization in its internal relationship of command, since the situation is clear to the higher command; but the moment this unit or formation breaks up for dispersed action, the principle of centralization in general matters and of decentralization in details should be applied, for then the specific situation cannot be clear to the higher command.

Absence of centralization where it is needed means negligence by the higher levels or usurpation of authority by the lower levels, neither of which can be tolerated in the relationship between higher and lower levels, especially in the military sphere. If decentralization is not effected where it should be, that means monopolization of power by the higher levels and lack of initiative on the part of the lower levels, neither of which can be tolerated in the relationship between higher and lower levels, especially in the command of guerrilla warfare. The above principles constitute the only correct policy for solving the problem of the relationship of command.

NOTES

1. The Changpai mountain range is situated on the northeastern border of China. After the Japanese invasion on September 18, 1931, the region became a base area for the anti-Japanese guerrillas led by the Chinese Communist Party.

2. The Wutai mountain range is situated on the borders between Shansi, Hopei and what was then Chahar Province. In October 1937 the Eighth Route Army led by the Chinese Communist Party started building the Shansi-Chahar-Hopei anti-Japanese base area with the Wutai mountain region as its centre.

3. The Taihang mountain range is situated on the borders between Shansi, Hopei and Honan Provinces. In November 1937 the Eighth Route Army started building the southeastern Shansi anti-Japanese base area with the Taihang mountain region as its centre.

4. The Taishan Mountain is one of the chief peaks of the Tai-Yi mountain range in central Shantung. In the winter of 1937 the guerrilla forces led by the Communist Party started building the central Shantung anti-Japanese base area with the Tai-Yi mountain region as its centre.

5. The Yenshan mountain range is situated on the border of Hopei and what was then Jehol Province. In the summer of 1938 the Eighth Route Army started building the eastern Hopei anti-Japanese base area with the Yenshan mountain region as its centre.

6. The Maoshan Mountains are in southern Kiangsu. In June 1938 the New Fourth Army led by the Communist Party started building the southern Kiangsu anti-Japanese base area with the Maoshan mountain region as its centre.

7. Experience gained in the War of Resistance proved that it was possible to establish long-term and, in many places, stable base areas in the plains. This was due to their vastness and big populations, the correctness of the Communist Party's policies, the extensive mobilization of the people and the enemy's shortage of troops. Comrade Mao Tse-tung affirmed this possibility more definitely in later directives.

8. Ever since the end of World War II, the national and democratic revolutionary movement has been surging forward in Asia, Africa and Latin America. In many countries the people, led by their own revolutionary and progressive forces, have carried on sustained armed struggles to overthrow the dark rule of imperialism and reaction. This demonstrates that in the new historical circumstances--when the socialist camp, the revolutionary forces of the people in the colonial countries and the forces of the people striving for democracy and progress in all countries are taking giant strides forward, when the world capitalist system is weakening still further, and when the colonial rule of imperialism is heading for disintegration--the conditions under which the people of various countries conduct guerrilla warfare today need not be quite the same as those which were necessary in the days of the guerrilla warfare waged by the Chinese people against Japan. In other words, guerrilla war can be victoriously waged in a county which is not large in territory, as for instance, in Cuba, Algeria, Laos and southern Viet Nam.

9. Weichi is an old Chinese game, in which the two players try to encircle each ocher's pieces on the board. When a player's pieces are encircled, they are counted as "dead" (captured). But if there is a sufficient number of blank spaces among the encircled pieces, then the latter are still "alive" (not captured).

10. In 353 BC the state of Wei laid siege to Hantan, capital of the state of Chao. The king of the state of Chi, an ally of Chao, ordered his generals Tien Chi and Sun Pin to aid Chao with their troops. Knowing that the crack forces of Wei had entered Chao and left their own territory weakly garrisoned, General Sun Pin attacked the state of Wei whose troops withdrew to defend their own country. Taking advantage of their exhaustion, the troops of Chi engaged and routed them at Kueiling (northeast of the present Horse County in Shantung). The siege of Hanean,

capital of Chao, was thus lifted. Since then Chinese strategists have referred to similar tactics as "relieving the state of Chao by besieging the state of Wei".

Mao Zedong Volume 2
Iconoclast Publishing
Transcription By Maoist Documentation Project
Documents Sourced From Marxists.org (Marxist Internet Archive)
Compiled and Formatted by Astrid Ronaldson

Printed in Great Britain
by Amazon

17936320R00190